Without Hesitation

Without
Hesitation

Without Hesitation

**An Account of an Iraqi
Prisoner of Conscience**

Anisa Abdul-Razzaq Abbas

Translated by Alhan Irwin

ONE VOICE
PRESS

WILMETTE, ILLINOIS

One Voice Press
401 Greenleaf Avenue, Wilmette, Illinois 60091

ISBN: 978-1-61851-190-4

Cover design by Carlos Esparza
Book design by Patrick Falso

The author, Anisa, in her thirties

This memoir is dedicated to my mother, Zakiyyeh Jameel, a patient and steadfast Bahá'í whom I called "the mother of prisoners." We, four of her children, were incarcerated in the "Abu Ghraib" prison in Baghdad, Iraq. From her, I learned patience and contentment with whatever God ordains for us. These and other virtues she cultivated in me without lecturing or dictating, but rather through her calm demeanor and loving attitude toward everyone. The virtues I cherish and appreciate I learned from her, and I credit her for instilling them in me. Whenever I confided to her my pain and distress, her comforting words and her peaceful lovely countenance were like a beam of light penetrating my being and filling me with ease and calm. Dear Mother, I pray to gain your good pleasure, after God's, in the Kingdom of Abhá!

This memoir is also a gift to the dearest people to my heart—my three children Abir, Alhan, and Ruwa—who were the source of my strength and who pushed me forward on the path of steadfastness.

The difficult equation—the decisive experience in my life—was when human vulnerability and weakness wrestled with the majesty of God and His will. The loud cry of motherhood nearly deafened my ears and created a haze that would have veiled His splendor from my eyes had it not been for His providence that came to my rescue. His words shone brightly in the core of my soul, and they poured down like pure drops of water that silenced that call and cleared my vision so I could take my path and make my choice without hesitation. As Bahá'u'lláh has revealed, "Wouldst thou have Me, seek none other than Me; and wouldst thou gaze upon My beauty, close thine eyes to the world and all that is therein."*

—Anisa Abdul-Razzaq Abbas

---

* Bahá'u'lláh, The Hidden Words, Persian no. 31.

Zakiyyeh Jameel

Contents

Acknowledgments

I owe an enormous gratitude to those who gave me the motivation and the courage to translate my mother's book, *Without Hesitation,* from Arabic to English. I want to thank my beloved daughter Zina and her husband Eamon, my son Mcnar and his wife Amanda, my niece Mona and her husband Dan, my nephew Zane, my nephew Remz and his wife Norah, and my dear cousins and their families! For a long time, I had wanted for you to know the courage of my beloved mother and all who accompanied her in that journey of honorable sacrifice. Now, at last, her story is being made available for all to read. May her spirit of courage and steadfastness inspire you and everyone who reads this book.

I am also immensely grateful to my husband Robert, who pushed me to keep going when I was discouraged and doubting my capabilities, and my brother Abir and sister Ruwa for their loving assistance whenever I came to a roadblock in my translation.

This book would not have been possible without my dear friend Linda Roche and son-in-law Eamon and their wonderful editorial support and guidance. Thank you!

Finally, I would like to extend my ceaseless gratitude to Mr. Christopher Martin at the Bahá'í Publishing Trust for his tremendous job editing the book and making it ready for completion.

Thank you, and may you all be blessed.

Translator's Note

My mother, Anisa Abbas, was born on May 16, 1925 in Baghdad, Iraq. She was the daughter and oldest child of Abdul-Razzaq Abbas and Zakiya Jameel.

As a young woman, she was independent-minded and fearless, especially for a woman of her time. In the 1940s, she went to Alexandria, Egypt, where she obtained a Bachelor of Arts in Philosophy and Psychology. She also pursued a Master's degree in Egypt and completed all of the program's requirements except a dissertation.

While in Egypt, she was involved in numerous Bahá'í activities and was elected to the Local Spiritual Assembly of the Bahá'ís of Alexandria on April 21, 1951. She was among the first group of women to be elected to various Local Spiritual Assemblies in Egypt. While there, she met her future husband, Siddiq 'Abdu'l-Majid Sulaiman, also of Iraq, whom she married after her return to Baghdad in 1952. They had three children: Abir, Alhan, and Ruwa.

My mother worked as a high school teacher for most of her professional life. In that role, she was highly regarded and admired by colleagues and her superiors, and she was loved by her students.

Her Bahá'í activities in Iraq included service on the Local Spiritual Assembly of the Bahá'ís of Baghdad. She also taught children's classes and composed Bahá'í songs for children.

As a prominent Bahá'í in Iraq, she was one of a large group sent to prison in the 1970s, where she was incarcerated for nearly six years. She and her husband Siddiq were sentenced to life in prison, and theirs was the only Bahá'í family in which both parents were incarcerated. Her time in prison was, for her, a badge of glory. Among her requests was that she be buried in her prison uniform.

My mother is remembered by her friends and family as one of the wisest and most humble individuals they ever encountered. She was sought by everyone that loved her for sage counsel and advice. This was also true in prison, where she acted as the beloved mother and wise older sister to the other young Bahá'í women prisoners in her ward. Anisa possessed such empathy toward several of the other inmates, who were incarcerated for different reasons, that she assisted them to petition the authorities with eloquent and compassionate pleas that ultimately resulted in their gaining release from prison. She accepted her suffering in prison with resignation and contentment out of her deep belief in her Faith.

She was a published poet—although, out of humility, she sent much of her work to magazines anonymously.

With the help of her children, she was able to come to the United States in 1990 and ultimately settled in New Hampshire. There she lived out the remainder of her life by becoming an American citizen and enjoying the love of her children and grandchildren, whom she loved especially.

She departed this earthly life on July 13, 2011.

Just a few days after my mother's passing, I had an overwhelming urge to connect with her again in whatever way I could. I picked up the memoirs she had written many years earlier, in which she described her time as a Bahá'í prisoner of conscience in Baathist-ruled Iraq in the 1970s. I read the weighty volume, written in her unmistakably impeccable Arabic, in two days. I knew right then that her inspirational story needed to be shared, especially with my immediate family members here in the United States.

My first inclination was to search for Arabic-to-English translators. A few promised to give the text the care it deserved, but all eventually changed their minds. One told me that he found my mother's writing style—she was a teacher and a published poet, and unusually well-educated for her generation—too intimidating for his ability.

One day, at the peak of my frustration and fully aware of my very humble and limited capacity, I resolved to attempt the absolutely absurd task of translating the book myself. With God's gracious help, and perhaps my mother's as well, I was finally able to finish the translation two years later.

In truth, the path toward a fitting translation had been many years in the making. My mother finished writing the memoir soon after she and my father immigrated to the United States in early 1990. Their arrival marked the first time I had seen either of them in more than a decade, as my sister and I had escaped Iraq during my parents' years behind bars. When my mother finally finished her manuscript, she proudly gave bound copies of her handwritten testament to each of her children. I knew she was eager for me to read it.

I tried and failed.

The still-raw emotions of my youth that stemmed from watching my parents dragged to prison, and the years of pain and anguish from the separation that followed, overwhelmed me while I was reading her words. Simply recounting that period of my life left my body quivering with sadness.

Years later, translating the memoir turned out to be the healer of my soul's old wounds and filled me with abundant gratitude for the outstanding example of faith and steadfastness provided by my parents. For me, the book serves as more than just a way to remember my mother and her extraordinary life. It is also a beloved symbol of the honor that she and my father bestowed upon our family through their extraordinary sacrifice for their religious faith.

There is no way that my humble translation can do justice to the beauty and eloquence of my mother's writing. I hope it at least helps tell her story.

—Alhan Irwin

"Beyond the prison wall," an illustrated tribute by my daughter Alhan

1 / My Childhood and General Thoughts on Imprisonment

I grew up in the old part of the city of Baghdad, which consisted of a cluster of narrow alleys connected to a main street crossing the city. These were curvy, depressing alleys with brick houses built in the old style. They had a central, open courtyard surrounded by a few rooms including a kitchen, basement, and a second floor where the bedrooms were connected to a wood-covered porch that sat above an open view of the courtyard. I remember that our home lacked the luxuries of modern homes. It was just like all the other old homes, including the blessed house of Bahá'u'lláh, which was in an alley on the other side of the Tigris River in the heart of Baghdad.

The courtyard in our house had a myrtle tree (or sometimes called "True Myrtle"), known for its fragrant white flowers. It was left to grow tall enough to reach the second floor and, later, the flat roof of the house where the family (like all others in Iraq) used to sleep under the open sky that was decorated by the moon and the stars during the summer and sometimes part of the late spring and early fall. That myrtle tree always reminded me of my love of nature. It had delicate, little white flowers whose penetrating fragrance I used to love. Sometimes I would pick them and place them in my dad's collection of copper vases. Playtime with my friends involved imaginary characters such as a tall and terrifying genie from old tales told by our parents. The genie would appear in the next alley when the sun set every evening. Sometimes after our play in the late afternoon, we would run home screaming out of fear of the genie and the ghosts chasing us. The old, crowded markets in the city were covered by a roof and had little natural light. Despite this, I enjoyed accompanying my father while he was shopping there, and I always felt a sense of freedom.

Just a short distance beyond the heart of the city, my family and I could see gardens and orchards surrounding Baghdad on nearly every side. To the North, toward Al-Athamiyyeh, there were orchards of citrus trees of all kinds, and to the south, towards the Al-Karradeh suburb, lay orchards of other types of fruits and palm trees. The soul-refreshing fragrance of the citrus tree blossoms constantly filled the air during the spring and summer. There was a garden across from the blessed Garden of Riḍván (where Bahá'u'lláh and His followers pitched their tents and collected piles of fragrant roses, and where the light of the Ancient Beauty shone, carrying a message of unity and love to all mankind). This other garden was designated for children and had a playground. When my family and I used to visit the Garden of Riḍván, I wanted to stay in that garden all day, as it gave me feelings of calmness, inner joy, and comfort. It meant running happily and freely and laughing far away from the depressing old alleys. However, my memories of our visits to the Garden of Riḍván also held different, conflicting emotions. Despite the beauty of the garden with all its citrus and palm trees, and the fragrance of the flowers and the refreshing breeze coming from the adjacent Tigris River, my state of mind was that of a little girl, who had been told by her father on cold nights plentiful stories about the martyrs who preceded the declaration of Bahá'u'lláh, about their suffering, their sacrifice, and the injustices inflicted on them and their families. Following those stories, my father would also tell us about the majestic spirt of those blessed days when the beloved followers were granted the bounty and experienced the ecstasy of His (Bahá'u'lláh's) declaration in the Garden of Riḍván. My father described how their lengthy yearning was quenched by this joy, a joy that kept them awake all night along with the nightingales. We heard these and other stories about the suffering of Bahá'u'lláh and His blessed family and the ordeals that forced Him to leave society and travel to a secluded cave in Kurdistan, north of Iraq.

Najibiyyeh-Riḍván Garden

In addition to those memories, every time our family visited the Garden of Riḍván, we had to pass through the section where a hospital (Al-Majeediyyeh Hospital at that time) had been built. It occupied the main part of the garden. This was the hospital where my dad used to take me every time I was sick, and I continued to visit doctors there when I was in my youth. In that blessed spot (the Garden of Riḍván), I experienced a diverse array of emotions, including a proud faith that evoked a desire to cry and also excitement as I sensed the glory and blessedness of that spot. These sentiments continued even later on, after I left prison and visited that blessed place. I would imagine the procession of the Blessed Beauty arriving at the garden, then Him inside the

3

tent surrounded by the reverent believers, and the piles of roses around His blessed tent. At times, these images would blend with others of the doctors and nurses in their white coats moving around the Majeediyyeh Hospital, tending patients in wards by the tens or even hundreds sometimes. And the fragrance of the citrus blossoms in the garden of Riḍván would fuse with the smell of medications and sanitizers used at that hospital, bringing conflicting emotions of happiness and repulsion.

These feelings remained with me even when I gave birth to my firstborn son Abir at that same hospital, in that same blessed place of Bahá'u'lláh's declaration as told to me by my father. The greatest happiness, my son's birth, was mixed with those old emotions that I had carried with me since my childhood. The images of the procession of the Blessed Beauty leaving the garden—beginning His journey to exile in Turkey, with all the people mourning His departure, and some holding on to His horse's reins and saying their farewell while He started that long and difficult journey—were on my mind.

Despite moving out of the old city area during my elementary school period, my fear of dark, narrow, and enclosed places continued. We had moved to a house on the Tigris River that had plenty of trees and birds that would not stop chirping and singing until the evening unless we banged on trays so they would calm down and rest. I fell in love with freedom; I adored nature in every meaning of the word. The trees were my loved ones and the river my best friend, just as later on I adored the sea in Alexandria, Egypt (where I continued my education). The sea was my lover, whom I cherished and feared. As time passed during my youth, I came to realize that freedom is part of this wonderful nature and that God created man free so he would enjoy all the blessings bestowed upon him.

After I finished my studies in Egypt and went back home to Baghdad, we built a new house surrounded by a beautiful garden that my husband lovingly cared for. We enjoyed its beautiful flowers and the shade of its trees where we often had our dinner and tea. I wish to share with you in this chapter what

4

will hopefully help you imagine how difficult and oppressive the later imprisonment was for someone like me. I had to suppress my yearning for freedom, my love for nature, and the infinite love I had for my children—all of which penetrated every vein and cell in my body—and instead accept and submit to a bitter fate, deprived of all happiness and comforts. In addition, I had to exhibit utter bravery and strength and nurture a new attitude of sacrifice, contentment, and self-denial—all for a divine belief, the seeds of which had been planted in the very core of my being since childhood but which needed the right environment to grow and prosper.

While I was in prison, I had to resist emotionally breaking down and had to battle anxiety, depression, and even feelings of resentment for my captors. I had to fight every hostile thought that human dignity produces against abasement and humiliation, as my sister prisoners and I were living in a place governed by harsh rules and severe punishment. The guards and prison employees, who were nearly illiterate and who followed regulations to the letter, without any flexibility, even when the regulations were unreasonable, watched every move we made. Once I told one of the guards, who was about to lock the gate of our ward, to wait, as one of the prisoners assigned to bring food to the ward was about to return with lunch. I even pointed to that prisoner as she was approaching the gate.

The guard ignored my request and locked the gate anyway, laughing and saying that the motto here was "execute the task first, then question it." The guards implemented the rules without exceptions, and we prisoners had to obey without question, even if the guard was ignorant and uneducated.

My aim is to gradually take you to the horrifying atmosphere of a prison. Perhaps most of you have seen pictures or movies about prisons with cells that have metal bars, whether on one side or more, and those narrow hallways that divide the facing cells. Our prison—with its bars, narrow windows, and reinforced cement walls—was not much different from what you have seen.

Once, after our release from prison, I went to the zoo with my nephew. I had not recognized prior to my release from prison the close resemblance between the cages of the lions and tigers and my cell in the Abu Ghraib prison. I turned to my nephew and jokingly said, "You didn't have the opportunity to visit us in prison; these cages that you see very much resemble our cells, except these lions and tigers have the luxury of enjoying an air-conditioner during this sizzling summer of temperatures above 50 degrees Celsius (120+ Fahrenheit). Perhaps it was the same architect who designed them both!" I intended to say it to make him laugh, but my nephew's eyes flooded with tears.

Still, if we were to compare our modern prison to the old prisons of the past, we would find a huge difference with many improvements. Those old prisons were places for total isolation from society, much like facilities where one would treat a patient infected with a dangerous and contagious disease. They were places for severe punishment. But over time, after the population had been given greater education and awareness, prisons were transformed to some extent into correctional facilities, where a prisoner could become a reformed citizen and return to society to function in a new life, away from crime. He could remember and learn from his years in prison, contemplate what he had done wrong, and try to avoid his old mistakes. Some crimes are committed without premeditation but are rather a result of rage and impulsive reactions to the stresses of past events, which are related to the offender and are not in direct association with his crime. For this reason, and with the development of the science of criminal justice, psychologists started to focus on finding the cause behind a person's criminal act, and the prison system began to look at a criminal as a human being who had committed a mistake but who could be rehabilitated.

Some prisoners are fortunate to find people in psychology, law, and other fields who sympathize with them. For other prisoners, prisons remain a place of self-reflection, as feelings of guilt and remorse can at times be harsher than material punishment. However, a prisoner who is innocent and is being victimized for a crime he/she has not committed—in fact, if the person is a well-wisher of others and an honest and outstanding citizen participating in building his society—such a prisoner will certainly feel injustice, degradation, and repression. His sense of justice will leave him utterly defiant against those in charge of his fate, because those who are innocent will refuse to submit to anyone save their Creator. Even if these prisons are luxurious in appearance, containing all the comforts for the prisoners, even if they look like royal palaces, they will still be places of repression and degradation.

Anisa and her father

The Old Prisons in Iraq

We had a visit from the prison's chief administrator a few months after our sentencing. She was a decent, well-dressed, and dignified lady, who spoke to us in a kind and respectful manner. She gave us the adequate respect that we deserved, and I remember well her words as we sat near the outdoor fenced courtyard. We were sitting on homemade seats that we had made from stacked leftover egg cartons available in the prison and that we had covered with fabric. When we offered her one of those seats, she said, "Be thankful to God that you have been imprisoned in such a modern facility that has all the means of comfort. The prison I worked at before I came here was horrible, unbearable, and not to be compared with this one."

All the inmates nodded in agreement.

I added a few words by saying, "You are right, Mrs. Selma (that was her name) because I remember the old prison to which you are referring. I visited there during my childhood where, during the thirties, my aunt Bedriyyah Abbas was one of the first women to become a director of a women's prison in Iraq." I continued, "A prison is a prison, madam. For the captured bird, there is no difference between a cage made of gold or of wood. What is most important is to be free."

She agreed and went on re-explaining her point about the improvements of the current prison. In regard to my visit to the old prison (where my aunt Bedriyyah was a director—later on she left with her husband to become the first Bahá'í pioneers to Sulaimaniyyeh, where they spent the remaining days of their lives)—it was an experience I would never forget. It was a true prison and a place of harsh punishment.

At the time of our arrest in the police facility of Zafaraniyyeh, during the period before our trial, we Bahá'í prisoners dismissed any thoughts of possibly receiving a prison sentence. I remember once I was lying down on the floor at night, and beside me lay a woman talking to another about her fears of being sent again to prison. I gathered my courage and asked her, "Were you imprisoned before?"

She replied, "Yes, in Abu Ghraib prison."

I gathered more courage and asked her more about it (because I had not known of that prison before, and that was the truth. This might surprise you, but I had never even seen a picture of it on TV or anywhere else, not even a mention of it!).

I said to her, "Is that prison dark and constricted?"

She said, "On the contrary, it is large with open areas, with sewing workshops and more."

I continued to ask as my heartbeat started to slow down a little: "Would a prisoner be left there free, or handcuffed or chained?"

She said, "No, only when an inmate is transported to an outside hospital will she be handcuffed or legcuffed to the bed she is lying on, and if she is really dangerous, then both sets of cuffs will be used."

After this conversation, I prayed to God to spare us the misery of imprisonment if His will allowed, and to save us from the humiliation of the shackles, because they would be unbearable in case any one of us were ill! This is how I continued to think while I was in prison. I tried my hardest to shun the thought of ever needing to go to a hospital outside the prison, and I tried at times to remind myself of the suffering of Bahá'u'lláh in the dark and horrible prison of the Síyáh-Chál and the marks the heavy shackles and chains left on His blessed body until the end of His life. I wished sometimes I could receive the same honor of being bound in chains for my faith, but then I would retreat and beg God to spare me that test because I am a human who is weak, lowly, unworthy, helpless, and without courage. I needed to take care of my children until they reached a stage of independence and were able to face life's struggles on their own. This is how my motherly emotions would, every time, let me down and take me to a place of helplessness, despite my continuous efforts in supplication to God to empower me to rely on Him alone. Then, I would gather myself together and show courage and strength in front of the young Bahá'í prisoners accompanying us in those very difficult circumstances. Those young ladies were a symbol of bravery, heroism, and blazing faith to the extent of being overzealous and enthusiastic while facing difficulties in that polluted place, the hall of the Al-Zafaraniyyeh police station (where they were arrested and waiting for a trial).

I was not fully conscious of the hidden power and strength with which God has endowed man for times of trial and adversity. This power can make a frail and weak person a hero and can assist him with weapons of strength, patience, and endurance. This is what I witnessed on several occasions during those long and harsh days of confinement. I cannot say that there is a human being who can easily accept the humiliation of captivity right from the start; rather, I believe one has to train oneself to do that. Man is not a restraint-accepting animal but rather a noble being that God has created with a free will. If you see a cat that is gentle and tamed, you cannot say this is in its nature but rather that it has been trained to see man as a provider of food, love, comfort, and protection. But if, from the beginning of its life, it had been given the choice between being free and being confined indoors, it would have definitely chosen to be free. Only after being forcibly domesticated would it have chosen submission and become accustomed to confinement.

If we put aside the negative aspects of prisons in Iraq and look at the positive ones, we will see that prisons are not such bad places for a temporary stay. One of the guards once asked me to do a research paper that she could submit to her college about the Al-Rashaad prison (to which the female Bahá'í prisoners were moved in later years). I wrote for her several pages on the positive aspects of the prison—the points that benefit the prison administration—and I gave a general outlook on the way the prison operated. I wrote about the medical care the inmates received and the prison's clinic, the light diet that suited the inactive life of the prisoners, the cleanliness and providing of hot water once a week for all to bathe, the prison's library, the outdoor court for exercise, and other aspects that would give a positive impression to those who have no knowledge of prisons and have never experienced the bitter taste of being in one even for a day. Indeed, everything has two sides, even the moon!

If we were to describe a person (or an object), the way to praise him would be to mention his good traits, and the way to degrade him would be to present his negative qualities. This is also the case in describing a prison. While prisons are large places that offer their inhabitants a place to sleep and eat, they also produce agony and suffering. They can gradually take away the humanity from prisoners and, with enough time, can paralyze even their senses and their ability to think on their own. Then others may begin to regard those prisoners as inept and incompetent. A prisoner is deprived of all civil rights, such as buying and selling, writing a will, and signing an official document—all privileges a competent citizen enjoys. The sad fact is that some of the prisoners become accustomed to that slow and repetitive style of living and slowly become similar to emotionless robots. Even the excitement of seeing their loved ones during visits becomes less intense. Life for them is stagnant, while it passes with great speed for their families. Their children grow older, get married, and have a different outlook on life. A prisoner, however, remains an invariable number. With the passing of time and the long depressing nights, the ray of hope that once seemed bright and warm starts to lose its brilliance and becomes like a distant star that cannot be reached.

My memoir of the imprisonment of the Bahá'ís of Iraq, which lasted over six years, includes four periods. The first period covers my sister prisoners and I being under arrest for eight days at the General Security Directorate (called Al-Amn) in Baghdad. This confinement began a few days before Christmas, 1973 and ended on January 1, 1974. I consider this period the most difficult. The second period includes our incarceration for two months at Al-Zafarani-yyeh Police Headquarters. The third period comprises our imprisonment in the well-known Abu Ghraib prison, northeast of Baghdad, and this imprisonment lasted three years. The fourth and final period includes our imprisonment for three years in Al-Rashaad prison. I have written my memories about each of these periods separately.

2 / Interrogation and Detention Period at the Iraqi General Security Directorate (Al-Amn)

On the sixteenth of December 1973, one of the Bahá'í brothers, Mr. Nimat Sabour, and his daughters Nida, Rafa, Ala, and Huda were arrested. On the same day, my brother-in-law Saiid Majid and his two daughters, May and Shetha, were also arrested. We heard the news the next day and assumed the arrest was just an inquiry that would end with their release. That day I had returned home before sunset, and while we were discussing the news of the arrests, my older daughter Alhan (who was sixteen years old at the time) asked me to do a thorough search inside our home for any remaining Bahá'í books, handwritten documents, and literature that we had not included with the large suitcase of books we had sent to the government upon their previous order to collect such materials from all Bahá'ís. All Bahá'ís had complied with this order.

I told my daughter that I was very tired and that it was late in the day, and that therefore I would do it the next day. But she firmly insisted that I do the search right then. We started to comb the house for any additional items, and we were able to collect a large bag of some Bahá'í books that had been missed, some precious photo albums containing pictures of believers and Hands of the Cause (Bahá'ís appointed to serve and protect the Bahá'í Faith), photos of the Bahá'í holy shrines, and some poems. It was decided that I should take the bag of collected items in my car to my father (may God send blessings

13

upon his soul), who at the time was living by himself in his old home in the Al-Aathamiyyeh (a suburb of Baghdad). I drove to my father's, handed the books to him, and drove the long distance back home to find my daughters Alhan and Ruwa all alone. They were in a state of gloom and suspense. At the time, their brother Abir was a student in Sulaimaniyyeh University and was therefore away from home. I asked where their father was, and I was told that men from the Iraqi Al-Amn had taken him away for interrogation—after searching our home! The men had promised my daughters to bring my husband back in a short while. We had no idea that the "short while" would come to mean six years!

On the next day, I took some of my husband's clothes and a few necessary items with me to Nimat Sabour's home to ask if anyone knew the location of the detention center. The weather was extremely cold, and I was concerned. Mrs. Sabour comforted me by saying she had been assured by the Al-Amn men that the detention center her husband and daughters would be taken to would have all the necessities for comfort, such as heat, blankets, and clothing! My answer was, "God willing, let what they said be the truth." I returned home in a state of turmoil between doubt and trust. I tried to comfort my daughters and assure them that their father was OK, not knowing that he and the others were lying on cold floors without covers, receiving beatings and humiliation, and that it was only the beginning of the events that later resulted in my own arrest at the Al-Amn headquarters.

The night my husband was taken, with the promise he would be returned in a short while, I waited up for him until 3 a.m. I believe that this was the night that my insomnia, which afterward I became accustomed to, began. When my children were little, I would stay up all night if any of them were ill, but it was not insomnia, because as soon as my child became better, I would be comforted, and sleep would return.

I woke up very early the next morning and said to myself that surely they would return my husband home that day. When I went to my daughters' bedroom, I was surprised not to find them in bed. I saw the front door open, so I hurried out to the front garden, where each was busy planting new flowers. It was the first time I had ever seen them do that, as my husband was usually the one who tenderly and carefully planted the new flowers, despite the fact that we had a gardener. My husband had just bought new pots of various flowers that week. Usually it was a tiring task that took long hours—sorting, distributing, and planting new flowers in our beautiful garden. My daughters told me that they wanted to make their father happy when he returned home so that he could see that the planting had been done.

That day became so very long—so long that the plants eventually flowered until the end of their season. Then they died. Our home was locked, the garden was left untended for the next six years, and when we left prison and returned home, my husband had become entirely blind. Nothing remained in his memory except ghosts of where the trees were. He felt their branches with his fingers and smelled their leaves in an attempt to bring back memories of a garden whose beauty we were deprived of enjoying for long years. Oh, how I longed to care for my true flowers, my children. I so wished time had given me that chance.

Our Detention at the Al-Amn Agency

On December 5, I had planned to visit my beloved son Abir, a student at the college of science in Sulaimaniyyeh University, north of Iraq. It was a week after his father's arrest, and I wanted to let him know what was going on. I took my daughters to my mother's home so they could stay with her while I was away. I remember my mom had prepared lunch for us: okra stew with rice on the side, which is a favorite Iraqi meal. I had barely taken my first bite when I heard a knock on the door. There were two Al-Amn men asking me to accompany them for questioning at their center. My mother and daughters hurried to find out what was going on, and they became noticeably disturbed. Despite their concern, each tried to comfort me by saying that God was with me and that I was going to be OK. Their optimism about my quick return gave me assurance that my questioning would not be prolonged.

Siddiq Sulaiman, Anisa's husband

I was certain I had done nothing to worry about. Besides, I had not been involved in any activity or served on a committee or a Spiritual Assembly for many years.

I quickly said good-bye to my mother and daughters, walked with the two men, and headed toward their car. Inside that car was my brother-in-law Saiid, who had brought them to find me at my mother's house. At first, I wasn't sure it was him at all. His face was pale, and he looked very tired. His white beard had grown long, and his head was down. I was used to seeing him with a shaved beard. We did not exchange any greetings, as the circumstance did not allow for that. I was then taken to my home to get some blankets, since it was very cold. The men asked if I had any money hidden in the house—so they could steal it—but I had only a few dinars left.

The men then drove us to the Al-Amn Directorate. I was taken to a room where several of their men were, but no one spoke to me at all. The atmosphere was one of fear and suspense. The men were talking among themselves about crimes, arrests, weapons, and other matters that were of concern to them only. In between, there were periods of terrifying silence. Four hours passed and maybe more, while I sat there without moving, until someone came and ordered me in a rough manner and a stern voice to stand up, so I did. He had a long wool winter scarf in his hand, the kind men wear around their necks, and he started to twist it very hard until it became like a thick rope. I was watching him with no idea of what he was about to do with it. He ordered me to turn around and quickly blindfolded me with the twisted scarf. The tightness around my head was unbearable, and I asked him politely whether that was necessary, as I was ready to honestly and truthfully answer any of their questions. But he did not respond. The pressure of the blindfold was so severe that I felt my eyes being pushed out of their sockets. Darkness was consuming me in a terrifying way, for a reason I will explain later on.

The man took me by the hand and walked while I was stumbling. Every minute he asked me to lower my head, then raise it up, lower it again, and raise it up. We walked a long distance until we reached a stairway. He took me down into the darkness—many steps down, until we reached a very damp and unbearably cold cellar. I was seated on a small wooden bench, low to the ground. He began tightening my blindfold again, this time even harder. I felt his breath penetrating my neck while he said, "Empty your purse of all sharp items." I told him I did not have anything sharp and that he could check my purse if he wished to do so. He then ordered me not to try lifting the blindfold from my eyes, and he left the place.

When I knew I was alone, I found a minute amount of courage to feel my surroundings. I lifted my hand slightly and discovered that the ceiling was barely above my head. I then extended my arm to the left and to the right and found that I could touch the walls. The fear of the unknown began to slowly take over and paralyze my thinking. I started to imagine myself being in a small grave—perhaps my space was even smaller than a grave. I turned in supplication and prayer to the Greatest Holy Leaf (daughter of Bahá'u'lláh), and beseeched her, by her purity, to protect me and the other detained Bahá'í ladies, so our honor would not be soiled and violated. The source of my fear was all the stories and rumors we had heard of the Baath party members and their despicable abuse of women who were considered to be opposed to their party.

After I had said my prayers, my mind became empty of everything, and I found myself in total surrender to peacefully face my death. Even prayers had become hard to recite. I could no longer remember their words.

I have no idea how long I was in that state of total silence and absolute detachment from all worldly matters before I heard something waking me from my bewilderment. It was a moaning in a familiar voice—that of Bahiyyeh Mesjoon, one of the Bahá'í ladies. I gathered courage and said, "Be enduring and put your reliance on the Blessed Beauty (Bahá'u'lláh)." I was comforted to know that we were together.

She replied, "Have they arrested you too, Um Abir?" ("Abir's mother." It is a tradition in the Arab world to call someone after their eldest son's name.)

We became silent after that. The unbearable cold could have almost killed us in that deep, underground cellar. A long while later, we heard a third lady being brought in and being forced to sit on the cold floor. She was pleading with them to bring her a blanket to sit on, but she was laughed at. Before the men left, they reminded us not to dare remove our blindfolds. Every now and then, one of them would come down and threaten us with his southern accent: "Do not remove your blindfolds. You are being watched!"

From her groaning, we came to recognize that the third lady was Bedriyyeh Ghulam Husain, another one of our Bahá'í sisters. She kept on calling, "Oh you who have honor and mercy, I am an elderly lady and it is very cold in here."

But no one seemed to care. There was nothing we could do to help her except offer words of encouragement to be patient and bear the situation. Gradually, I came to realize that there must have been one common accusation that brought us all there. I said it must be about the money that belonged to the former National Spiritual Assembly, which was placed in the bank under our names. I never thought at the time that our cruel punishment for that would be ten years of imprisonment! What did come to my mind, though, at that critical moment, was to remind my friends to keep our answers truthful and honest so there would not be any differences in our answers that could bring conflict, although I had no idea of the exact amount of money each one had in her name.

Every time I heard one of them moan because of that deadly cold, I reminded them that God wants us to be patient, steadfast, and truthful. I was fearful that one of them would alter her answer by saying the money was theirs, as a way of protecting what belonged to the Bahá'í Faith.

It would have been natural to assume that each one of us would have a small sum of money in the bank, since I was a high school teacher, Bahiyyeh was a nurse, and Bedriyyeh came from a well-off family. Many thanks be to God, each of us had agreed on her own to speak the truth: that the money belonged to the Bahá'í community in Iraq. In regard to the sum in my account, my brother-in-law Saiid had come one day to ask me to put two thousand dinars (about $6,600) in the bank in my name, since the National Spiritual Assembly of the Bahá'ís of Iraq had to be dissolved (by an order from the government). The community's money was in my sister Afaf's name, but she had left the country.

I asked Saiid, "What if the government asks me to hand them the money, just as we had to give them all our books?" His answer was, "We will worry about that when that time comes." He continued on to say, "The government is not in a hurry. When we delivered our Bahá'í books to them, their answer was, 'What's the hurry? Who's running after you?'"

I agreed to take the responsibility of placing the two thousand dinars in my account. A while later, I thought of withdrawing the money and giving it back to Saiid, because I had a mysterious, uneasy feeling about it. But it was God's will that I deterred that thought and said to myself, "If I don't sacrifice, then who will?" A while later, a Bahá'í property in Sulaimaniyyeh—a piece of land designated for building a Bahá'í center (called Ḥaẓíratu'l-Quds)—was sold. Saiid came again and asked me to add a thousand more dinars to my account, which made a total of three thousand dinars (about $10,000—one dinar was equivalent to 3 1/3 dollars).

I later found out that this amount was the reason for my arrest. The law had prohibited Bahá'í activities and indicated that Bahá'í properties were to be handed over to the Ministry of Internal Affairs. During the confiscation of the Bahá'í center in Baghdad and all its furniture and assets, the government created an inventory for all the seized items but never included any funds. The National Spiritual Assembly was never asked about funds belonging to the community and therefore did not know how to handle that matter. It was not at fault. If the government had asked, they would have received all the information. The first time the subject was brought up was during our interrogations, when the inventory had been completed.

Back to the condition of the three of us in that dark and horrifying cellar at the Al-Amn Directorate—our concern started to rise as the time went by. We did not know if it was the beginning or the middle of the night. The startling periodic loud threats from one of the men brought to my attention that there was still an open area behind me and that the space was not a closed grave. At 8 p.m. (as I had heard one of the men tell the time), I was called for questioning. In the same way I was brought down, I was taken up the stairs—still blindfolded—to appear in front of the interrogators.

From their voices, I came to realize there were more than three interrogators. I was in a very difficult condition of fatigue and exhaustion. The room was filled with cigarette smoke, and the temperature was suffocatingly hot in comparison to the frigid cellar. I started to feel lightheaded, so I respectfully asked if I could please sit down, but they refused to allow it. The exhaustion caused my body to swing back and forth, and the blindfold was causing me a lot of pain, but God gives us strength in such situations. Soon, my fear left me, and I put my trust in God and His Blessed Beauty to inspire me. The interrogation started with questions about Bahá'í leaders, and who they were. My answer was that Bahá'ís do not have leaders but that we did in the past have elected individuals, equal in rank to any other member of the community but who had specific assigned services to the community. However, my answer was rejected.

Each interrogator sternly repeated the same question, and I replied with the same answer. I said that our National Spiritual Assembly and the local assemblies were all dissolved after their prohibition by the law, and that we had never elected any replacements since then. They asked me to give the names of the members of the last National Assembly, which had been dissolved seven or eight years earlier. I tried hard to remember all the names, but my exhausted mind was unable to do so. I told them that the names were written in large letters on a board at the confiscated Bahá'í center, and there was no reason for me to hide any information.

Their next question was about the number of properties around the holy house of Bahá'u'lláh in Baghdad purchased by the Bahá'ís in the past. I told them I only knew of two, but they were insistent that I give them more information. They said other detained Bahá'ís had confessed that all the houses in that alley were purchased.

Their third question was about Bahá'í gatherings and activities, such as the nineteen-day Feasts. I told them there were no real Bahá'í activities (which were against the law), but only small gatherings among relatives, during which prayers for the sick and such were read, and that these gatherings were not prohibited by the law. In any case, Bahá'ís are obedient and would never violate the law.

That first interrogation was prolonged and grueling. When it ended, I was taken to a roofless passageway. It was raining and very cold, and my blindfold was still on. They stood me there facing a wall, so I leaned on it with both hands, since I was in an extreme state of fatigue. The guards were ridiculing and mocking me because, to them, anyone who is brought to Al-Amn is a criminal. An hour later, still standing in the rain, I was taken for another interrogation.

Their new questions were about the number of Bahá'ís in Iraq, which Bahá'ís were at the base of the pyramid, and which Bahá'ís were at the top. In truth, that analogy was new to me, so my answer was that we are all equal and that any individual is eligible to vote or be voted for if he or she has met the requirements of the Bahá'í standards of honesty, integrity, and age.

Another question was about how a circumambulation around the house of Bahá'u'lláh is done. My answer was that we do not observe such a specific ceremony at this time. The house is sacred to us, but we do not visit it specifically, nor do we go inside. Sometimes it just happens that we are in the area.

Then they asked about the purpose of buying the houses close to the house of Bahá'u'lláh. My answer was that just as with all sacred places in the world, visitors long to be and stay close to the house of Baháu'lláh. This house is sacred to us, and so is the area in which it is located. In fact, for Bahá'ís, the whole city of Baghdad is a blessed spot. Apparently, this question was presented to each

one of us detainees, and each gave a personal answer applicable to herself, such
as a suggestion that gardens and orchards will be placed around the house, etc.

One of the interrogators asked me, "How do you like the fact that the Shiite Muslims were the ones who took your holy house from you, and turned
it into a Husayniyyeh?" (A Husayniyyeh is a house for Shiite commemoration
ceremonies, especially during the anniversary of the martyrdom of Imám
Husayn in the Islamic month of Muharram.)

I said, "It is now a place of worship where God's name is mentioned."

He then asked, "What do you consider this 'Bahá' (he meant Bahá'u'lláh)?"

I said, "He is the Messenger of God for this age and the return of the
Imám Husayn." (Imám Al-Husayn was Prophet Muhammad's grandson, and
there are prophecies in Islam that He would return, similar to prophecies of
the return of Jesus Christ).

They laughed at and mocked my answer, and then asked, "And how does
the Husayn return?" I briefly explained the meaning of "return," which has
a spiritual connotation and not physical. It is the renewal of God's message.

When their questions ended, so did my answers, and I stood in silence.
The interrogator became agitated, and asked me in a rough manner to keep
talking.

"What would you like me to talk about?" I asked.

"Everything you know."

I said, "Kindly specify your question, so I can answer."

He became even more agitated and said, "We are here to question you,
and not for you to question us!" The other interrogator then added, "Most of
your answers were absolute lies. Your score was only 1/10."

His remark was very hurtful and a great insult, worse than any insult I
have ever encountered in my life. I felt as if my head was going to explode. I
swore to them, with tears pouring under my blindfold, that I had said nothing but the truth. But they did not believe me and did not care.

I was called again for yet another questioning. This time I felt I was being
recorded (I could hear the sound of a tape recorder near me). Therefore, I

made sure I was talking with a very clear voice, being brief, and using the modern standard Arabic (Al-fuṣḥá).

The first question was, "Who is in charge of your community now, since you no longer have a spiritual assembly?"

"We have a liaison, who looks after the community." I felt extremely guilty that I mentioned the liaison's name, but I found out later that they already knew about him from interrogating the younger ladies earlier, as well as from the detained men, from whom they had extracted all kinds of information, sometimes through beatings and torture.

Next question: "Who is your husband?"

"Siddiq Sulaiman."

"Tell us about the land you had in Sulaimaniyyeh. How was it sold, what was the reason, and how much was it sold for?" (The land in Sulaimaniyyeh was purchased in the 1940s for the purpose of building a House of Worship someday in the future.)

"The land was neglected and had become a place where trash was disposed. Therefore, the decision was made to sell it. The price was, as far as I know, three thousand dinars. I don't know anything else."

"Who is this new believer by the name of Kawakib Husain?"*

"I don't really know her well, and I only met her once for a few minutes."

"She is a student with your son Abir in Sulaimaniyyeh University."

"Yes, I am aware of that."

"How did you know of it?"

---

* She was a new believer in the Bahá'í Faith, who came from a Shí'í family. Soon after, five of her sisters and her young brother all followed her footsteps and became unwavering Bahá'ís. They were subjected to persecution. After the period of our interrogation and our temporary release, I advised my son Abir in those hard circumstances to cut his contact with Kawakib, for later on she became the center of all investigations.

"She came once to our house one evening and stayed in the front yard, while it was dark. She had come to pick up my son's military service booklet" (this is a permit of deferred military service for students, or others in certain circumstances).

He asked, "How does your son know Kawakib?"

"Perhaps she had heard of his being in the same university, and had gone to meet him."

My interrogators continued to focus on Kawakib.

I was then asked about a party at the home of Nimat Sabour. The investigator said, "It was a welcoming party for Kawakib!"

I replied, "It was simply a birthday party for one of the Sabour daughters, to which school friends and neighbors were invited. Bahá'ís don't hold parties and rituals for those who join the Faith, because that is a personal choice. Some might join out of curiosity, and some might leave."

Another interrogator then asked, "Kawakib abandoned the Muslim Faith and has embraced the Bahá'í Faith!"

My reply, "Perhaps she admired the Bahá'í teachings, and youth get enthusiastic."

He angrily replied, "We know how to deal with Kawakib. Her punishment will certainly be imprisonment."

At that moment I thought of calming him down, so I said, "Perhaps the prison will cause her to become more heroic and firmer in her belief. I had no idea at that moment that prison was awaiting most of us."

He returned to questioning me about Kawakib.

"What do you know about her?"

"I barely know her. It was a very short encounter, as I had mentioned."

"Who brought her to your home?"

"Nida Sabour."

"What was your conversation with her about?"

"I only asked how she knew my son, and she told me they are students at the same university."

"Did she meet your daughters, Alhan and Ruwa?"

"No, she did not. They were inside the house, and our conversation was by the gate of our front yard."

Then the questions turned to the sum of money I had in my name.

"What is the cash amount you have in the bank?"

"What I have is not my money, but the possession of the community."

"How much money of your own do you have in the bank?"

"I have no savings at the bank."

"Why didn't you claim the money as yours, since it is in your name?"

"How can I make such a claim when it is a trust, left with me for safekeeping?"

"Does the community have other accounts in other banks?"

"No, sir."

"What are the amounts left in Bedriyyeh and Bahiyyeh's names?"

"I don't know."

"Where is your bank book?"

"At my home."

"Bahá'ís permit usury (interest), yet it is forbidden in Islam. Correct?"

"Investments deal with interest, in the same way the banks operate."

"What is the amount of interest in your faith?"

"It is not set yet, but it cannot exceed reason and fairness."

"Who will decide that amount?"

"The Universal House of Justice (the Bahá'í-elected governing body at the Bahá'í World Center in Haifa, Israel). That will be in the future."

There were other questions asked, but I can't recall them now.

It was nearly midnight. I was still tightly blindfolded and in utter exhaustion when armed Al-Amn men decided to drive me in a small car to my home in Al-Dawoodi, a suburb of Baghdad. The purpose was to get my bank book. When we reached my home, I was concerned and embarrassed to be seen by my neighbors with the Al-Amn men, especially because our house was dark and empty. I was too nervous to ask the men if I could use the bathroom or even get a few drops of water. The atmosphere was terrifying. I opened my closet drawer, got the bank book, and handed it to them.

They continued to search my closet and found a small notebook that I had missed seeing earlier when I searched the house. It was handwritten by my husband and contained some Bahá'í tablets and prayers. They brought a chair and climbed on it to search above the closet. I watched and did not dare to sit down in my own home. One of them found a copper plate with engraved writing that read "Ya-Bahá'ul-Abhá" (God is most glorious) hanging on the wall. For them, it was an "evidence of guilt" and a violation. I watched and pitied them, for their hearts were stripped of all compassion and left in that miserable state.

The whole time those men were inside our home, our pet dog was barking in a very agonized manner. The harsh circumstances forced a gentle creature like her to share our suffering. We had raised her up since she was a little pup. She was a beautiful dog of pure breed (a Jack Russell Terrier) that we loved and cared for and that our children had played with and become very attached to. She was very intelligent and knew those who loved her and those who did not.

It was not customary in Iraqi culture for families to have dogs as pets. Some people believed they were not clean. Most of the dogs were stray dogs, and when their population became large and a threat to health, the government would collect and exterminate them.

When the Al-Amn men brought me home at midnight, the dog began to bark ferociously at them, and she came to me and rubbed her head on my leg in a very affectionate way. She tried hard to stay close to me, as if she were aware of my dire and awkward position. She barked so hard that one of them tried to kick her with his leg. I pleaded with him not to do that and said that I would take her out. I let her out to the fenced area we had for her in the back of our house, but her barking grew louder.

One of the men said, "Ha ha, look at that! She's trying to frighten us! Does she know that I have a bullet ready for her head? This is what I have done to all other dogs like her encountered during our search."

His words made my body shiver, especially since I was very exhausted after that long day of interrogation. I feared for her life. She finally changed her bark to a doleful cry, a sad howling that she rarely did, except when she needed attention. For example, she would do this when my son Abir came to visit and would be busy greeting us first, and not paying her any attention.

As the dog continued to howl, one of the men gave a signal to another to do something about her. My heart filled with pure terror that they might shoot her, so I pleaded with them to give me a chance to quiet her down. I extended my leg outside the door so she could rub her head and be comforted. I couldn't give her anything to eat nor to drink, as I was afraid to ask for water, even though I was dying of thirst myself. But, at least, I was able to save her life that night.

As we were leaving the house, her barking became very loud, as if she knew that was our last good-bye. My daughters were unable to take her with them to their grandparents' home and, eventually, had to give her away to another family. We heard the news later on that she had escaped and had been hit by a car and died. She suffered the same pain that we did when fate decided to disperse our family.

We left the house and headed back to the Al-Amn detention center with a driver who was speeding like a lunatic. My blindfold had been removed earlier, after we had driven far from the directorate and come closer to my house. But now it had to be put on again as we approached the central area. We finally arrived, and I had to wait for a while, fearing the unknown, until I was taken to another room. They took off my blindfold, and I saw that Bahiyyeh and Bedriyyeh were both in the room.

One of the men said to the other, "Take them to the machine room!"

I remembered hearing horror stories of torture machines that the Baathis used during their interrogations. An instant response came without my volition, and I said, "What is this for, and what fault have we committed to deserve this?"

The man laughed and told me he was just joking. The truth be told, he was much kinder than all the rest of the men. I gathered some courage and asked, "Why is there such harshness in your interrogation while we have hidden nothing from you?"

He answered, "This is a method that saves us a lot of time, and extracts all information from those we've arrested."

I hurried and asked again, "Why do you (meaning the party) criticize your former opponents while you use their same inhumane methods with such a peaceful group of people who never harmed anyone?"

He said, "How would you have liked it if we had brought you a box full of scorpions and other insects, as we have done with other people while they're blindfolded, and they have to try to kill them with their shoes?"

I said, "May God forbid!"

After that, we were taken to the upper level, to a room that had bookshelves. They laid a rug so the three of us could sleep on it. For the first time, I was able to sit on a chair. There was a large photo of President Ahmed Hasan Al-Bakr right in front of me, which added to my feelings of uneasiness. The door was locked, and we were left there alone to embrace each other. We feared we were being monitored with hidden microphones. Each whispered to the others about the exact amount of money she had in her name (three thousand dinars), which was the reason for our arrest.

The effect of the horrible events of that day, and worrying about my son and daughters, kept me awake all night. My tongue felt as if it were glued to the top of my mouth, due to extreme thirst and anger. I was afraid to drink from the glass jug of water they had left for us on the table, because it looked foggy and unclean. Early the next morning, two Al-Amn men armed with machine guns came to take us to use the bathroom, which was in a roofless area of the building. As I was washing my face and getting my first drink of cold water from a faucet attached to the old stone sink, I heard from the upper level a beautiful voice chanting prayers. I lifted my head and saw the young ladies—Nida, Ala, Kawakib—calling me: "Auntie Anisa, Auntie Anisa!" I saw their beloved faces through a small glass window, and tears started to pour from my eyes while I was washing my face. I felt peace as I directed my inner gaze toward the Blessed Beauty (Bahá'u'lláh), and I asked Him to protect our young ladies. Their courage filled me with pride.

We were conducted to the second floor, where they brought me the blankets I had taken from my home. I put one under me, covered myself with another, and gave a third blanket to Bahiyyeh, who was very cold. In that room, there was a small window facing the roof of one of the areas of the Al-Amn center. The guard brought us pieces of bread and some butter. He threw them through the door, and they landed on the blanket. Then he locked the door again.

We whispered to each other the details of our interrogation the day before, and when it was midday, lunch was brought to us in dirty plastic plates. Each plate had a few white beans (five in mine and seven in Bedriyyeh's) in a watery tomato sauce (called "marga"), with a small piece of bread. Thankfully, I had absolutely no appetite to eat anything that day. Everyone was in a state of worry, anticipating the unknown. The door would be locked until the evening, when we would be allowed to use the bathroom again. Then, we were locked in until the next morning. The guards would keep startling us with their sudden banging on the door locks or, at night, with dragging the furniture across the room above our heads, for the purpose of terrifying us and disturbing our sleep.

One afternoon, I was leaning against the wall, and I noticed some small handwriting on it. It read: "And if thou art overtaken by affliction in My path, or degradation for My sake, be not thou troubled thereby. Rely upon God, thy God and the Lord of thy fathers." (This quotation is from a Bahá'í prayer by Bahá'u'lláh.) It made me smile, for I knew it must have been written by one of our young ladies. I still felt it would be safer to erase it before it was found by the Al-Amn men, so I took a paper napkin from my purse, folded it several times, and wiped the wall until it was clean.

On the evening of the following day, I was called again for questioning. As usual, I was blindfolded before being taken down the stairs to the interrogation room. Some of the same old questions from my previous interrogation were asked, but in further detail, such as why I had agreed to save money in my name, and why it was I who had been chosen for that job.

My answer was, "It was a matter of trust."

"What were the funds going to be used for?"

"Expenses such as taxes the Bahá'ís still had to pay for the Bahá'í center confiscated by the government, for the Bahá'í cemetery, its maintenance, water, electricity and caretaker, etc."

"Do you receive funds from outside the country?"

"No."

"How were you able to build your Bahá'í center? With foreign money or from local Bahá'ís?"

"Local Bahá'ís contribute what they can afford, and no money was received from any foreign country."

"Have you personally received any money from outside the country?"

"Yes. Twenty dinars sent from my brother to my father."

"Did you give the twenty dinars to the Bahá'ís?"

"No. The community is not in need of twenty dinars."

"Have you contributed money to this family (he then gave me the name of a family from Baquba)?"

"Yes. A very small amount to help a family with children who had lost their father."

The purpose of those questions was to hold evidence against me. I was asked also about who my friends were and whom I visited—all so they could be called in for questioning. I told the interrogator I was a very busy mother and did not have time to socialize much outside my home, except for visiting

31

family members. I was asked about the names of all my family members. My sisters Warqa and Fatima and my father were already detained as well, but I was not able to see them. Many other Bahá'ís were arrested for questioning. We were blindfolded as we were moved around and taken to different rooms at different times; therefore, we did not see each other. Our rooms were often changed, as if we were being played like chess pieces.

One day, some of our young ladies were brought to stay with us in our small room. The space became too crowded. The man who brought them in nailed a piece of cardboard onto the small window to block it completely. The room became dark and the air suffocating, despite the cold December weather. One of the young ladies lifted the corner of the cardboard to let some air in. When the man saw what had happened, he became extremely upset, yelling and cursing. He threatened us all and nailed the cardboard back in place. There was nothing we could do.

The young ladies—with their youthful, cheerful spirit—sang spiritual songs and chanted prayers with loud voices. The guards would hush them and sometimes mock them by saying, "What are you singing? Are these Kindergarten songs?" We heard after our release that all the rooms were wired with hidden microphones and cameras.

In the following days, each one of us was called for questioning at night. We would then face more questions.

"What is the Universal House of Justice? What does it do, and who are its members?"

My reply was, "With all due respect, I do not know their names."

"How do you communicate with them?"

"We don't. "

"They are in Israel, and Bahá'ís do communicate with them."

"Since 1948 (the establishment of the state of Israel), Bahá'ís in Arab countries have cut communication with the Bahá'í World Center." I then briefly explained the history of the Bahá'í Faith and the exile of Bahá'u'lláh by the Ottoman Empire to 'Akká, Palestine, before Israel had ever existed, and our holy places there.

The Ruler from Mosul

On the seventh day, our last day at the Al-Amn center, I was taken to meet a new interrogator, a man from Mosul, who was sitting alone in his room. He asked me about the one hundred dinars (about $330.00) that were in my account before we deposited the money that belonged to the community, and if it belonged to the Bahá'ís as well.

I had forgotten about that amount, so I asked him to please allow me to look at my bank book; perhaps I would remember the details.

He ordered the guard to take off my blindfold and give me the bank book.

I took a look and told him that the one hundred dinars were mine and that I had withdrawn that money before depositing the community's money. When my blindfold was taken off, and although there was a distance between us, I could clearly see what this man (whom I thought was an interrogator) was writing in his notes. Every time he asked me a question and received an answer, he would put down a reworded version of my answer, a version that would incriminate me. Sometimes he would even repeat with his own voice my answer in his demented interpretation!

I was overpowered and defenseless and could not argue with him, fearing a hostile reaction. Therefore, I had no choice but to leave my situation in God's hands. Behind that man there was a big banner hanging on the wall. On it was beautiful large calligraphy that read, "If you have the power to oppress others, know that God's power is greater than yours." At that instant, I supplicated with my whole being to the Blessed Beauty (Bahá'u'lláh) to shield His servants from the injustice of such oppression.

Afterward, I answered all his questions with my eyes fixed on the words of that banner, while he was watching me.

The barrage of questions continued.

"Do you teach your children about the Bahá'í Faith?"

"My children are learning about Islam at school; when they get older, they can choose their preferred religion after investigating the truth."

"What if they asked you about your prayers while you are praying?"

"Then I would give them an honest answer."

He then wrote in his notes, "She teaches her children about the Bahá'í teachings and rituals."

"Do you hold Bahá'í ceremonies in your home, and do you receive visits from Bahá'ís?"

"We don't have ceremonies in our Faith, and only family members visit us."

He wrote, "She hosts Bahá'í ceremonials in her home."

"Have you visited your holy shrines in Israel? If not, why not?"

"I have not. It was not in my good fortune to do that."

"What is your word of greeting?" (His manner was one of mocking and disrespect.)

"We use all greeting words such as good morning, good evening and such, and sometimes we say 'Allah'u'Abhá'" ("God is the most Glorious").

He mocked me again and again, repeating "Allah'u'Abhá." He continued to speak with incivility about my son's admirers among his college girls, which was nonsense. He continually repeated questions I had been asked before and falsified my answers as he wished. He also told me that they had "shaken" my brother-in-law Saiid (as in shaking a tree so the fruits would fall, meaning they gave him a good beating), and that "he confessed everything about the money you have; therefore, don't try to hide anything from us."

I was also asked about the Bahá'ís who were from a Jewish background (he referred to them as Jews), who had left Iraq, and what country they had moved to.

I told him they were Bahá'ís, not Jews, and that I did not know of their location.

He then asked about my personal old car, and if the community had bought it for me.

I said, "No. My car is an inexpensive Russian-made car that I purchased for one thousand dinars ($3,300). I was a teacher for twenty-two years. I took a bank loan to purchase it. Is it too much for someone like me to have such a car?"

I was then asked about the Bahá'í who acted as our liaison and why he in particular had been chosen as a liaison.

My answer was that he was a respectable older man, who gave sound advice to others.

He then asked, "Your husband is older, so why was he not elected to be the liaison instead of this other Bahá'í?"

I said, "It was because my husband had lost his eyesight and became unable to perform certain duties, such as keeping his teaching job at school, or serving the community.* In the past, therefore, he had to resign from his Bahá'í administrative duty."

A year after our imprisonment, we heard the news that this official had died in Europe after a failed surgical procedure. Thus, God's wrath had fallen very fast on that cruel and unjust man.

A new agent looked at my statement—the statement the previous person had written—and signed it with ultimate trust that everything in it was accurate and in my own words!

---

* My husband had suffered two retinal detachments years before imprisonment. His two surgeries abroad (in Europe) were unsuccessful and left him legally blind. His very poor eyesight forced him to resign from his duties as a member of the former National Spiritual Assembly of Iraq.

3 / Temporary Release and the Al-Zafaraniyyeh Detention Center

On New Year's Day, 1974, we were told that we were going to be released on bail, and that our families had been notified. A photographer was brought in, and mug shots of each one of us were taken (front and side shots). In another room, we had to fill out bail forms and other personal information. It was the first time for us to be without blindfolds; therefore, we were able to see the faces of our interrogators and those we were in direct communication with. After that, I was invited to go to another room for tea! It was my first cup of tea in eight days.

One of the Al-Amn men said, "Your arrest should be a lesson for you not to perform any Bahá'í activity in the future."

I replied, "We are peaceful and obedient people, and if we had had clear instructions from the government, we would have gladly complied." I went on to say that we were honest well-wishers of all humanity.

Another Al-Amn man heard me say that while he was passing by. He sarcastically said, "What you said will be of no use to save you!" (He meant that it wouldn't be of any use in our defense).

Since he was a person in charge, his words had a weighty effect on me, and I realized then that our case was not about to end anytime soon, and we had nothing left to do but to be patient and accept the will of God.

Two days before we were discharged, one of our young ladies, our dear Raja Husain (Kawakib's sister), fell ill, and she was brought to our room with a high fever. Our captors never thought of taking her to a doctor or calling a doctor to come and see her. The paperwork for her release was not completed on the day of our discharge, and we were very concerned about her staying there alone. The Islamic festival (Eid) had coincided with the New Year festivities, and all businesses were closed. It just happened by coincidence that the procedure for Bedriyyeh's bail was delayed as well. I was comforted to know that Bedriyyeh would be taking good care of Raja until the period of Eid was over.

The horrible and agonizing period of interrogation had ended with indefinite results. We spent the following days in apprehension of what might come next and fear of the unknown. Were they finished questioning us? Would there be a court appearance to follow? Would we be set free, since we were totally innocent of any crime? Naturally every one of us hoped we would not have to face a trial, but as we were told later on by a lawyer, our release on bail meant there would definitely be a trial to follow.

Back to the day of our discharge: My father and my brother Suhail were waiting for me with a taxi outside the Al-Amn headquarters. The terrifying atmosphere of our cruel circumstances caused our exchange of greetings to be emotionless. I was walking like a zombie who had just come out of the grave from a mythical story.

The taxi took us away, and we reached one of the famous landmarks in Baghdad, called Sahatul-Tahreer. That is where my father shocked me with something far worse than what I had gone through. He told me that my son Abir had been arrested and taken to the Al-Amn headquarters.

I felt as if my heart had been ripped out of my chest, and my anxiety increased more than could ever be described or measured by anything I had experienced. I had hoped my son would have been spared arrest to take care of his sisters if imprisonment was awaiting my husband and me. My daughters were still so young—one was sixteen and the other thirteen, and their father's fate was unknown. My father and sisters, however, had all been arrested and had been released on bail.

Summary of Our Treatment at the Al-Amn Directorate

This is how the period of our arrest and interrogation at the Intelligence Service center ended. It was the first chapter of the series of continuous sufferings that lasted over six years. This first period was the harshest of what followed in the succeeding years of imprisonment, and its main characteristics were the terror and the fear of the unknown.

In truth and for historical documentation, I need to mention that none of the ladies who were detained and questioned at the Al-Amn Directorate were beaten or physically tortured. We had heard stories of captured Communists and other groups and how female prisoners were subjected to physical torture of various methods, including torture equipment and rape.

However, we only received fear-inducing threats—many thanks be to God and His great mercy. The focus of our captors was mainly on the new believer, Kawakib, and her sister Raja. At one point, Kawakib was threatened with being hung, and a rope was placed around her neck so she would stop asserting her faith. In another instance, her sister Raja was taken to a cellar while blindfolded. The men pretended they were going to throw her down a water well (there was no well in that cellar). They added to her terror by telling her that her friends had been killed and that their corpses had been put into sacks close to her. Raja started to scream so loudly that the men had to stop their tactics.

Those methods were used to terrify the captive and easily extract all information. When blindfolded, one's fears can intensify, and self-confidence can weaken. We heard a story from a lady in her fifties about how vicious, barking dogs were brought close to her while she was blindfolded. One of the interrogators would tell the other to take the black dog away before it shredded her body into pieces, and bring a gentler dog instead, so she would confess all information. She would scream and plead with them, but the barking grew louder, until she came to find out that there were no actual dogs, but only a recorded sound coming from a cassette player.

At Al-Amn, our young ladies' hands had been tied behind their backs with thin ropes, and they had been blindfolded very tightly. This hurt my sister Fatimah's eyes more than the others, and she felt the effects for a long time afterward.

However, most of our men received a significantly harsh beating during their stay at Al-Amn, and among them—as I found out much later—was my son Abir. The severe foot whipping (bastinado) made it difficult for him to walk for quite a while (this fact was kept a secret from me until after our release from prison). My elderly and frail father was humiliated and kicked down a whole flight of stairs, all the way to the basement. And my husband, who was nearly blind, was severely beaten with a water hose on his back, and left very thirsty for two days. When his thirst became unbearable, they brought him a can containing urine to drink.

Another memory of the Al-Amn experience is that one night while I was lying on the floor, I heard loud screaming and wailing coming from the lower floor right below our room. When I put my ear closer to the floor, it became clear to me that it was from Ihsan 'Abdu'l-Wahid, one of our Bahá'í men. I could hear the Al-Amn men beating him, and he was screaming. I became very sad and began to sob. Bedriyyeh came quickly and covered my mouth, pleading that I stop crying before someone heard me and a bad situation arose. I stopped crying, but could still hear Ihsan plead with them to stop their torture. They continued questioning him about funds, not believing any of his answers, then hitting him more.

On another night, I heard the voice of another one of our men, Nimat Sabour. The interrogators told him to go join his daughters in the cellar, then shoved him down the stairs. I could hear him scream in pain. Another time they took him up the stairs blindfolded, stumbling with every step, while they laughed and forced him to say: "Oh Blessed Beauty" (one of Bahá'u'lláh's titles) over and over, which he did. I watched him from the keyhole in the door and cried.

My dad recounted to me that he was very thirsty one day and had health issues with his urinary tract. He asked for a drink, and the guard sarcastically said, "What type of drink would you like?" My dad said, "Pepsi." They laughed at him very hard and kicked him down those stairs that I mentioned earlier.

I hope that you will be able to read what my son Abir has written about his own harsh experience, his arrest from Sulaimaniyyeh (north of Iraq), and his very difficult transport in an open vehicle in the middle of a cold winter all the way to the General Security Directorate in Baghdad. I also hope that others will share their experiences and suffering as well.

While we had been detained at Al-Amn, I had wondered about my sisters and the other young ladies, and if they were all right. On my mind were questions such as, had they been beaten or—God forbid—abused, as in the stories we had heard about others? Had some of them been released, or was everyone still here?

One day, I remember the rain was falling heavily outside, and I wondered about my daughters. What were they doing now, and who was taking them to school, especially on a rainy day like today, while I could hear the downpour outside our window? It was only the afternoon, but it was totally dark outside, and it was time for my daughters to get out of school. What should I do, my Lord? Who is going to take them home?

My daughters were not accustomed to taking a bus or traveling home alone, and I kept on blaming myself for not giving them the opportunity to learn independence. When I was their age and even younger, I used to roam freely the streets of Baghdad on foot, sometimes miles from Al-Athamiyyeh, north of Baghdad. I would go to school or gatherings at the Bahá'í center, all the way south of Baghdad, yet I still felt very safe.

These thoughts would come into my mind, but I would try to forgive myself and say, "Perhaps it was only the time back then that gave me the impression of being safe, especially since I came from a large family and since our parents were too busy to worry about our going and coming." This is how I continued to converse with myself and tried to calm down in that small room at the Al-Amn Directorate.

If I say that I was able to rise from that emotional state of anxiety, the agony of my physical state was no less challenging. Our cell was small and tight, with cardboard covering the tiny window; a cold, damp tile floor that we sat and slept on with one blanket only; and an equally cold brick wall we leaned against when we became tired and had to sit. We could only warm up this wall with the heat of our body.

During this time, my blood never had a chance to renew itself during the entire period of our arrest, as I had no appetite. As a result, my stomach was continually empty, except for a few bites of bread in the morning and evening, and perhaps a few pieces of white beans in a watery sauce. One of the hardest things to do was use the bathroom. I have to mention this, despite the fact that it is a very upsetting matter in my memory, but we are all human and have the same need. I suffered from calcification in my left knee, which made it very hard for me to use the Eastern-style toilet (a squatting toilet). My difficulty was unbearable, as the door would be open in the morning with a commotion of shouting and screaming that followed the violent rattling of the door locks by the heavily armed men—all for the purpose of terrorizing everyone. Then each one of us would be blindfolded and taken down the stairs through a hallway to the uncovered outdoor courtyard. We were then allowed to enter the bathroom after our blindfolds were taken off. The bathroom was very small—about one square meter in space—and was extremely dirty. It was more like a small canal filled with filth, and, of course, it had no seat. It would be more appropriate to call it a torture room than a restroom. I could barely bend to empty my bladder, and the guard standing outside the door would be hurrying me to finish. We were allowed to use the restroom twice a day only, once in the morning and once in the evening. We were allowed then to wash our hands and faces with the ice-cold faucet water, scoop some of it to drink, and then we were taken back. We had to control any urge for hours until we were allowed to go again.

One of my Bahá'í friends, Bahiyyeh (may God bless her soul), had health difficulties with her urinary tract. She had saved a small, square-shaped plastic yogurt container that she had to use at night for emptying her bladder. She would then discard the contents by lifting the corner of the cardboard covering the window, then carefully return the nail back to the cardboard. One night, I was unable to hold myself any longer, so I pleaded with her to let me borrow her container. After I used it, I tried to empty it like Bahiyyeh did, but the container got caught, slipped from my hand, and fell onto the roof, right below the window.

Bahiyyeh became very upset and harshly reprimanded me because she relied on that container to such a large extent. I was very understanding of her feelings, so I apologized. I said perhaps they will be kind to us the next day and bring another container if we ask, but Bahiyyeh refused the idea and tried to reach the container, relying on the street light for visibility. But she was unable to reach it. I tried to help, but neither of us had any success, as the container was beyond our reach. We had to be very cautious not to make any noise.

Bahiyyeh got a pencil from her purse, but it wasn't long enough. Then I got another pencil from my purse, took off my stockings' elastic, and tied the two pencils together so that we had the length needed to reach the container, which we could barely see in the dark! Believe me, this operation required a lengthy amount of time. Every time one of us got tired, the other would take over. We kept trying until we succeeded in grabbing it! We then laughed and embraced, and I gave my apologies again. I never dared to ask for that container again after that, even in my most desperate times.

Another incident that I recall occurred on the morning after that horrific first night. I remembered that it was time for my monthly period to arrive. I became very distressed and did not know what to do, as these matters are very private in our culture and very embarrassing for women to talk about, especially with the Al-Amn men. I wished then that I had thought more clearly the previous night when I was taken to my home and had had the opportunity to bring with me some necessities. I could have done so, since I was not under suspicion and had not done anything wrong. One of the men had hinted to me to take the box of tissues that was on the table, but I had told him I had enough in my purse.

I said a short prayer: "Please God, what should I do now, and what if I am called for interrogation and I am unprotected with what I need?" All I could think of was to take my heavier stocking off—the one I had put on in preparation for travel the previous day—and use it. I calmed down for a while, but my anxiety returned. I did not want to be the subject of humiliation by those men. I did not think of tearing the lining of my coat to use, which was what the young ladies had to do. This was what I heard later on.

My anxious thoughts about the subject passed away, as nothing happened. I came to realize that the mind has great control over the biological functions of the body, just as athletes performing sports that require incredible physical and emotional strain can have the ability to regulate bodily functions. These God-given capabilities of man are worthy of astonishment. What happened to me, though nothing extraordinary, enabled me to avoid an embarrassing situation during those eight days.

Our Temporary Discharge after the End of the Interrogation Period

On New Year's Day, I returned to my family's home with my brother Suhail. My sisters had been released earlier. I met my beloved daughters Alhan and Ruwa there. Anxiety was evident on their faces. Each had been extremely worried about their brother, Abir, since they heard the news of his arrest from Sulaimaniyyeh and his transfer to the Directorate of General Security (Al-Amn headquarters). What added to their anguish was the distress that was deeply etched on my face since my hearing the news. As for my beloved mother, she was the symbol of unshakable faith and patience. She welcomed me back with a warm embrace while praying to God to increase my steadfastness. She thought our test was over and that there was nothing left but to endure it all and be thankful to God. The whole family (my parents, sisters, brothers, and daughters) sat together, with our thoughts fixed on Abir. We wondered if there was a way to be sure of his whereabouts and if there was a way to see him.

I spent the night in a state of prayer and meditation, asking God to protect my son. The next day, my father and my brother Suhail accompanied me to the Al-Amn headquarters, which consisted of many buildings. We asked about Abir but received no answer. It was rainy and cold while we moved from one building to another, standing for hours and pleading with the guards to at least tell us if Abir was among the detainees in their buildings. I had taken some clothes and necessities for him in the hope he would receive them and in that way his location would be confirmed. I asked God not to test me with an unbearable hardship, for we had heard that many families search for their loved ones in Al-Amn centers all around the country, sometimes for months without knowing where they are!

I begged God to ordain imprisonment for me instead of my son. That was what I constantly prayed for during our detention period. And later on, during our years of imprisonment, my friend Bedriyyeh reminded me of it every time I was in a state of downheartedness. She would say, "Remember, you prayed to be imprisoned instead of your son. What would your condition have been if you were free and your son was in prison?" Then I would thank her and say, "Thank God for this, because I don't think I would have been able to endure such a hard test." I thank God I was spared that trial.

After I had been standing in the rain near a tree for a while, a guard came with a small piece of paper that had the word "Abir" handwritten on it. I was so nervous then that I could not be sure if it was my son's handwriting or not. I remained in that state of doubt and uncertainty when we got home.

My son remained in custody for twenty-five days. As I mentioned, later on, he wrote in English about his experiences during that period. I hope I can improve my English so I will be able to read it and have an exchange of thoughts regarding that time.

Abir was released on bail with his dear friend Rithwan, a fine young Bahá'í man. I remember waiting for him that day outside the Al-Amn center. He was shocked to see the signs of tiredness and anguish painted on my face. I, however, was very thankful to God to see him healthy and in high spirits.

We gave Rithwan a ride to a part of the city where his father was waiting for him. Abir was able to return to his university for a short while but was called again to appear in front of the Revolutionary Court. He was detained again with his father and the other men for more than two months in the Al-Fthailiyyeh detention center, located outside Baghdad, and he eventually received a fine after the last court trial.

In the period following the interrogations, a bit longer than a month, I was under constant watch in my neighborhood by the Al-Amn men. Their surveillance was very noticeable during my coming and going anytime and anywhere. One of the men would be at the top of the street, while another would be at the nearby corner or by my parents' house. I became skilled at recognizing them in the midst of other men, and I could read in their faces clear and distinct signs. If I drove my car to go to the doctor or the market, there was always a car following me.

During those days, we were able to visit the men two times at the Al-Fthailiyyeh detention center, south of Baghdad. In our first visit, the excitement and exhilaration of all the Bahá'ís was at its highest. When we were allowed to enter the open court at that detention center, we saw that all the detained men were gathered together.

The old building used to be a military stable for horses. The metal trough (where the horses used to eat) was still in the center. After the conversion of the building to a detention center, the police installed faucets and converted the trough to a large public basin for washing.

The first meeting with our men was truly a historic event. Each family member embraced the other, holding hands tightly in an affectionate manner. The greeting *Allah'u'Abhá* (God is the most glorious) came from every mouth. We thanked God that everyone was safe. The exception was one of our men, who was still in solitary confinement at the Al-Amn center because they thought he was the leader of the Bahá'í community. We were very concerned about his safety. I gave my husband some fruit, clothing, and money that we had brought for them. We took their dirty clothes, which we found out were filled with fleas roaming everywhere. We even found fleas tucked inside the folds of their underwear! During that visit, my husband handed me a power of attorney, which authorized me to receive his monthly retirement paycheck.

We were also able to have a second visit with the men. We all encouraged each other, and we were all very optimistic that a positive outcome and a declaration of innocence would be made by the court. On our return home from that second visit, I prayed that none of the men would be subjected to any torture. Before we were allowed to enter the detention center, I had heard loud screams coming from a man who was being severely beaten for refusing to eat. I thanked God that he wasn't one of our men.

My daughters and I returned to our home, and we tried to think it was a good sign that some of the men had been released on bail. Perhaps the others would shortly follow and be able to go home. My son Abir had left us to go back to his college in Sulaimaniyyeh. We were optimistic for a good outcome, and I was busy providing an appropriate environment for my daughters, who were working hard to prepare for their midterm exams. However, the ghost of the court and the possibility of being called to another unjust hearing were hanging over my head and my sisters', but we tried to push it away by thinking that if the intent were to imprison us again, we would not have been released in the first place. We would then calm down and hope our troubles would soon come to an end and that all the men would be free.

There was an uneasy, dreary feeling in our house. We enjoyed being with my family during that time; therefore, we packed our belongings and returned to their home. We hoped we would be comforted by my mother's chanting of prayers and her words of consolation. My father's words lifted our spirits as well. He told us that these trials were just tests of patience and endurance. We were comforted to be together, and we exchanged thoughts and talked about our experiences in detention.

One day, just as I was returning from the market close to my family's home, I saw one of the Al-Amn men knocking on our door, with a car parked close to him. I was at a distance, but I could still see him clearly.

I was overcome by a sense of gloom when I saw my father and siblings signing some small papers the man had given them. When the car left, my father came out to show me a summons to appear on an appointed date at the Iraqi Revolutionary Court. The language of the content was stern enough to rip my heart out of its cage. The Revolutionary Court! That horrifying name came as a bolt of lightning that terrified every Iraqi citizen, even the bravest. The Iraqi TV broadcasted trials from that court of all kinds of people whom the government considered opponents of the governing political party. Even in the time of the former President 'Abdu'l-Karím Qásim, those trials were characterized by extreme sternness, harsh interrogations, and cruel sentencing—often executions or life sentences with hard labor. These trials left penetrating terror in the hearts of every civilian who only heard the name of that court, let alone had to appear in front of it!

I hurried and drove to my house to check whether I had received a summons as well, because the Al-Amn man had asked my family about me. Only minutes after my arrival at my home, I heard the dreadful doorbell ring. It was a man sent by the Al-Amn. I collected myself, walked with calm, and, relying on God, opened the door. He handed me the court's summons to sign to indicate that it had been received. I will not hide the fact that my body was trembling as his car left our house. I went inside again. I was all alone. I prostrated myself with my forehead on the floor in total reverence to the Almighty God, asking for His aid, for courage, and for steadfastness in His Cause. Deep inside myself I felt confirmation: that this was the path of sacrifice, that we were Bahá'u'lláh's soldiers, and that we must walk with our heads high.

I went back to my family's home. My daughters, Alhan and Ruwa, were there. The paper in my hand told the story better than any words I could utter. Everyone said, "You too?"

I nodded in agreement and took my place by my daughters. Everyone was in a high state of worry, but we were trying our best to conceal it. Later on in the afternoon, we collected ourselves and sat together to consult about the matter. A mutual decision was made to hire a lawyer for our defense. We felt similar to a drowning man, reaching out to a straw of hay in hopes of being saved. My father reminded us that the Revolutionary Court would not allow any lawyers except the ones it hired for a masquerade of defense, a show of deception. But the need to ease and comfort our minds was so strong that we insisted on going ahead with our decision to seek a lawyer.

I went to the home of one of the Bahá'í friends and presented the idea. He immediately put his shoes on and accompanied me to the offices of several lawyers. Every one of them refused to take our case after examining it and finding that we were summoned to appear at the Revolutionary Court. Despair started to take hold of us as we traveled for hours that night and the doors of the lawyers' offices started to close.

Finally, we knocked on the door of another lawyer by the name of Husain Bedri. He was a man of magnanimity, courage, and boldness in defending the truth! We were able to give him a brief summary of our situation, and he immediately accepted the case. He put us at ease by saying, "There is nothing in your case that is a cause for harsh punishment. You have not committed any serious crime or a clear violation of the law, and, most importantly, you are not against the governing party (Al-Baath), nor do you oppose the government." He also told us that he was able to ask the court to delay the date so he could further study our case. He asked for a down payment of five hundred dinars (equivalent to about $1800 at the time), and he would receive the rest of his fee after the trial. We left his office and went to several Bahá'í households to ask their help for the needed amount, and someone volunteered to collect the money and take it to Mr. Bedri.

The Al-Zafaraniyyeh Detention Center

Despite that spark of hope, I could not sleep. I worried about my daughters and wondered who would care for them if anything happened to my husband and me, especially because my son Abir had been arrested earlier with my husband and was also asked to appear in front of the same court. This matter was of great concern to me. None of the relatives had the space or the means to care for them while the fate of their parents was unknown and surveillance at its highest. My brother Sati's home was crowded with our parents and my brothers and sisters. There was no room for them there. Where would my daughters sleep, and how would they live? My parents were two elderly people who at that time were exhausted with rearing a large family of their own. They did not have the financial means for one more human being. These thoughts devoured my sense of peace and comfort and deprived me of sleep, even in times of absolute submission to the will of God.

I would picture the petrifying look of cruelty of the commanders and judges of the Baath party who used to appear on television, and the way they would horrify those they questioned. Their interrogation methods included harsh smacks on the face that left the accused unfocused, thunderstruck, paralyzed, shivering like someone who has lost all hope, and unable to speak.

I cannot be anything but honest when I say my concern about my daughters was at its maximum. At the same time, I must add how proud I was of each of my daughters, who, despite their young age, had observed my anxiety and tried to comfort me. They encouraged me to go on and reminded me of the importance of sacrificing for the noble principles of this mighty Cause. Their words brought consolation to my soul and made me realize that they had truly grasped the importance of steadfastness. I could see how proud they were of us, their parents, and how ready they were to be independent.

The only choice we had was to leave them in the care of my elderly parents, at my brother Sati's home, despite there being insufficient funds and other problems. That decision was extremely hard to make and caused that night to be unbearably difficult.

The next morning—gloomy and rainy—was miserable. Even the sky seemed to be full of sorrow and shared our tears. My mother stood at the door with my daughters, Alhan and Ruwa, to say good-bye to us before we headed to the Revolutionary Court. We had rented a taxi to take us there. My father and my two sisters, Warqa and Fatima, sat in the back seat; my son Abir and I sat in front. My mother looked at us with compassionate eyes and a facial expression that was inspiring, and she encouraged us to rely on God and put our trust in Him. She hugged and kissed each one of us and mumbled hopeful prayers. The beloved of my heart—my daughters Alhan and Ruwa—had a ghost of a smile on their beautiful faces. They struggled to wear these smiles, but they were clothed in worry and fear that could not be concealed. None of us thought at that moment that this documented day would be the last page of our "family diary." On that memorable day, the destiny of our life as a family was determined. It was a day that folded up a chapter of our life, and opened another, whose secret only God could disclose.

I hugged each one of them close to my heart, with my tears mixing with the raindrops. When my father entered the taxi, he kissed each one of us and loudly called upon the name God. Then we all followed with our prayers. My brother Suhail, who lived next door with his family, was standing to say good-bye with worry and sadness on his face. The taxi driver became disturbed when we mentioned the name of our destination: "the Revolutionary Court." He was a kind old man who went quiet for a moment but then said, "Rely on God, for He is the Most Merciful." When he started his engine and the taxi began to move, I felt as if I were harshly pulled away from my roots like a helpless shade tree. I did not know at that time what destiny God had ordained for us in His Book.

In the horrifying basement of the court, all the accused Bahá'ís (women and men) were assembled. Our feelings were a mix of pride and honor at the oppression and injustice we were facing. We were innocent people being tried in a military revolutionary court that dealt with top criminals who opposed the government and were enemies of the State. Each one of us greeted the other by saying "Allah'u'Abha" and invoking God to bring whatever would promote the loftiness of His Cause and keep His servants safe. We encouraged each other with loving words of steadfastness and strength. The longer the time that passed, the stronger grew our concern about what would happen in that court.

That afternoon, we were notified that our court date had been postponed. We breathed a sigh of relief after a long morning of extreme anxiety, and we hoped perhaps that the delay meant something good. Outside the court there were police cars waiting for us, with armed guards carrying automatic weapons. We entered the police vehicles, calling upon His all-glorious Name in our hearts. It was late in the afternoon, and we had yet to have a drop of water. The Bahá'í men were driven back to the Al-Fthailiyyeh police headquarters. The Bahá'í ladies were taken to the Al-Zafaraniyyeh police headquarters, located outside the suburbs of the city.

Arriving at Al-Zafaraniyyeh

Exactly at sunset, we arrived at the Al-Zafaraniyyeh jail under maximum security by armed guards. The Al-Zafaraniyyeh jail had two halls—one for women on the left side of the main building, and one for men to the right. We entered a hallway that had metal bars on both sides and that led to a large hall. There were big locks on the entry door, and the hall was crowded with detainees accused of various crimes—some of which were of a violent nature, but the majority of which were prostitution. All were sitting on the floor on worn-out blankets.

We (the Bahá'í ladies) chose an area near a wall, close to each other and away from the crowd. A hostile inmate came and poured water on the spot we had chosen, but we could not complain. After that, all of the detainees gathered around us to investigate the reason we were there. They could sense we were different, a breed unaffiliated with crime. They calmly pulled away after that and allowed us a bit of rest after a long and difficult day. The other beloved Bahá'í friends and families had also arrived at that jail with blankets, pillows, and some food. We sat on the floor to say prayers in soft voices, invoking the Almighty to grant us steadfastness, to keep us faithful to His Covenant, and to lead us to accept His will. Surprisingly, the pervading tone of that crowded hall and the armed guard did not frighten us, for we were receiving a fairly respectful treatment by the head of police and the guards. It was not as horrifying as the previous experience we had had at the Al-Amn headquarters and the Revolutionary Court.

We spent the night talking about that day's events at the court. The young Bahá'í ladies among us (between the ages of fifteen and twenty years old) were trying to adjust to this unfamiliar place. The light was very dim in that large, square-shaped hall (around one hundred square meters or a little larger in size; I measured it later on by counting the tiles while walking). The hall had only a few small, high windows that prevented us from seeing the outside courtyard. The general atmosphere was depressing, and the air was full of smoke (most of the detainees were heavy smokers) despite the small, open windows and the metal barred gate. At times, the smoke would be so thick it felt like a cloud. Until then, none of us had had any idea about that strange world we found ourselves in. When I was young, I thought the books I read and the movies I watched (especially Egyptian movies) had imaginary stories of prisons that were simply made up. Even when I lived in Egypt for six years, I still thought of these movies as farfetched and detached from reality. But being in that hall allowed me to see and hear what exceeded all imagination. Together in that one space, we could not help but witness events, hear conversations, and react emotionally.

I will document some of the events we witnessed at that time, which lasted two full months.

Our Daily Life at that Hall

The area we occupied by the wall was narrow and cold. We slept on the floor. Four of the ladies stayed by the wall; the younger ladies and I were squeezed next to their feet, forming a very tight block. In the morning, we folded our blankets to sit on them. The guards would come and conduct a search, then give orders to some of the detainees to clean and mop the place with a disinfectant in order to prevent the spread of germs and lice. Despite the cleaning, the hall was still infested with insects. Soon after cleaning, it would become dirty again with cigarette butts and trash. There were about one hundred detainees in that hall, with only one bathroom for the whole crowd. The filthy bathroom was the old style with a hole in the middle of the floor and no seat (a squat toilet). We were forced to clean that disgusting place before using it. All day long the inmates did not stop talking and fighting about insignificant matters. Their filthy and obscene vocabulary was from a dictionary that only that rank of people is familiar with. These events would continue until the guards came and beat or kicked them so the battle would end, and peace would be restored.

Our sleep at night would often be disturbed by the noise of newcomers being shoved into the room, accompanied by yells and curses from the guards, followed by crying and howling from the newcomer. Everyone would wake up and try to find out who the new guest was. Strangely, and in most cases, some of the older detainees would have met the newcomer on a previous occasion.

The detainee (who was a prostitute) who welcomed us the first night by pouring water on our spot had visible authority and was feared by the others. We were told that at one time she was favored by a high official in the government who was executed for not conforming with the government. She was in constant communication with the police, which made us suspicious and fearful of her. Around midnight, she would start a party right after everyone had retired to sleep. She would turn her music on and start to dance, or talk to other prostitute friends until dawn. This behavior kept me deprived of sleep.

Eventually, we were allowed to have a very small gas stove (a small gas tank with a burner on top) that we had requested. We used it to warm our food or make some tea. We were allowed to have the abundance of food our Bahá'í friends outside the prison would lovingly bring to us. We would divide it for lunch and dinner, and we often shared our portions—especially the sweets—with other inmates who were accompanied by their young children, to lift up their spirits and ease their suffering. Prison food was mostly soup, described by the inmates as being completely tasteless and repulsive.

For me personally, there were other difficult issues to deal with, such as not having anything to lean back on when sitting far from the wall. That caused me severe knee and lower back pain. The pain would at times be unbearable, but I had no choice except to endure all of it for two months. The dampness of the tile-covered hall would increase after the daily mopping, which did not dry fast (it was winter). Our legs and feet constantly felt that bitter cold, and the disinfectant did not succeed in preventing lice from spreading and reaching some of us.

The Deterioration of our Health

The dampness of the place, the heavy smoke, the cold February draft coming through the iron gate and windows, and the lack of sufficient bedding caused the cold to penetrate into our bones and to have a significant effect on our health, especially for the older ladies. We had colds—from the flu to chronic coughs—which were impossible to avoid as they spread in that crowded space. The nearby clinic was unavailable and could only be used for urgent cases. Once I had heavy bleeding that forced me to plead with the facility's administrator so I could seek specialized medical help. I was afraid to go to that clinic because this kind of rural facility was usually run by newly-graduated medical students with little experience. The police officer looked at me and said, "This is the first time I take such a chance in this prison and allow someone to seek an outside doctor." He sent me with an armed guard to the doctor, but the biggest favor of all was that he allowed me to go with my hands uncuffed. To send me off to a large hospital full of hallways that would tempt anyone to escape was the highest form of trust from the administrator, and I will always be greatly appreciative of that trust.

Upon our arrival, I asked the nurse to inform the doctor about my situation as a prisoner. The doctor had me seen first, and I was able to describe my condition. He was aware of my beliefs and he said, "Even you?" (meaning "you Bahá'ís"). "You are known for your good conduct and fine reputation." He expressed his sympathy and tried to comfort me by saying that we were innocent and that we would definitely be released. I received my prescription and took it with the armed guard (who turned out to be a very kind man) to the pharmacy to fill. He walked with me a good distance in the streets of Baghdad carrying his rifle, but I was not in a condition to feel any embarrassment, even though a situation like that would normally humiliate any human being, especially a respectable lady. My having a guard with me made the pharmacist nervous and brought the attention of all the customers.

We went back to prison in a taxi. The doctor's prescription helped restore my strength, especially my emotional strength so I would appear strong and courageous in front my daughters and the rest of the family. They were accustomed to seeing strength in me, and I will be forever grateful to the kind administrator who helped me in a way I will never forget.

Planting Trees in the Garden

On the side of the prison hall, there was a neglected garden full of dry grass. The young Bahá'í detainees wanted to plant some trees in memory of our incarceration. It was a beautiful idea that we presented to the office. We explained that it would beautify the building and provide shade, which would reduce the heat from the sun. The proposal seemed very odd to them, but it was eventually accepted. There were seventeen of us Bahá'í ladies: Bedriyyeh Husain, Fakhriyyeh Mirza, Hajir Al-Wakeel, Bahiyyeh Mesjoon, Anisa Abdul-Razzaq, Warqa Abdul-Razzaq, Fatima Abdul-Razzaq, May Saiid, Shetha Saiid, Iqbal Al-Wakeel, Nida Sabour, Rafa Sabour, Aala Sabour, Huda Sabour, Kawakib Husain, Raja Husain, and Ahlaam Husain. We asked for additional help from younger detainees, and they liked the idea. A few days later, a pickup truck full of cypress trees arrived. With the help of a few guards, our young ladies were able to plant the seventeen trees dedicated to each one of us. I had yearned to see trees all those weeks, and I begged the guards at the end of that day to allow us a few moments to look at the trees that bore our names. We let the young ladies pick their trees first and leave the others for the "aunties," as they called us older ladies. We felt the happiness of witnessing the transformation of that space, and we gained hope and steadfastness from those evergreens. They were like friends who came to share our suffering in that crowded place. Years after our release from prison, I passed through that area and saw that the trees had grown and prospered. They remained a witness to the difficult ordeal we managed to pass through with an endurance and steadfastness we could not have had without heavenly assistance.

Time Eked Out for Leisure

There is no doubt that the time we spent in Al-Zafaraniyyeh, among all kinds of criminals, was vastly different from our normal, everyday lives before prison. We were among women accused of murder, espionage, drug trafficking, prostitution, robbery, and infidelity. I had always wondered why a woman would be accused and punished for the crime of infidelity, while a man who commits the same crime goes unpunished! We were in a loud and crowded world, and we were unable to separate ourselves from those around us. We had nothing to occupy us in that strange place, except watching those around us and listening to their shallow conversations repeat like a broken record. Their foul language was not only abrasive to our hearing, but pounded on it like hammers. We sat close to each other in a circle and talked with each other. When the noise around us became overwhelmingly loud, we turned to prayers and reciting poems, unnoticed by the busy crowd. It was a true blessing that we were accompanied by the young Bahá'í ladies, despite our concerns about their missing out on school. The presence of their youthful spirits, enthusiasm, and deep faith brought us joy, humor, hope, and courage. They sang uplifting Bahá'í songs, in which I joined sometimes. At other times, they would invent fun games. For example, one of them would wear a traditional body cover called an *abaya,* while another hid behind her, under the cover, with her arms out, and acted in an exaggerated, humorous way that made us laugh. These games, though simple, were very much needed to reduce our stress. They were something we were in desperate need of. It is human nature and a method of survival to seek what uplifts the spirit in times of anxiety and despair. We used humor to keep our emotional state in balance and prevent the situation from bringing us down to the point of collapse.

Among the detainees there was a Kurdish lady who wore a *sherwal* (Kurdish wide pants). Every time she washed them, she would insert a blade of a ceiling fan into each leg using a pole. When the fan was turned on, the inflated legs of her pants and the noise they made were extremely funny. We called it the parachute. The girls would laugh. There was no place to dry our clothes except for a short rope that the detainees used for their underclothes. We did not want to use it out of fear of contracting transmitted diseases common among such society (prostitutes). It was hard for us to change often into a clean set of clothes, and we had to wait for family members to bring them to us. I hesitated to ask my daughters to bring me more clothes because our house was locked. It was difficult for them to go there while living with my family and enduring difficult ordeals and struggles they were never accustomed to. I would keep my shirt and skirts on for a long time.

Nearly two months passed, and we were in desperate need of bathing. The filthy living situation became unbearable. Dirty bodies and unwashed hair had caused lice to invade the hair of some of us. We gathered some courage and asked the officers if we could heat water so each of us could bathe before Naw-Rúz (Bahá'í New Year). After long deliberations, we were granted approval. It was the first (and last) time they agreed to such a request, as their policy prevented the detainees from bathing while incarcerated in that place! There was no bathing area, only a filthy toilet area and a cold water faucet where we also brushed our teeth and used a washcloth to wipe our bodies. We had to do that at great speed because of the waiting crowd. There was, however, an unfinished area in the corner of that hall that we chose to use to bathe. It was dark and very cold, with no access for water to drain. Each had to sweep the water out through a hole in the wall so the next person could bathe after warming up some more water in a pot on that miniature gas stove. We were worried that the guards would be looking at us through a hole in that wall, so we had to hurry while bathing. That was the first and last time we were allowed to bathe until we were sentenced later on to serve time in the Abu Ghraib prison, close to the festival of Riḍván, and that is another story.

Family Visits

We were allowed a very short visitation time with family in the small hallway by the gate. The high-spirited and greatly excited Bahá'í youth who were not incarcerated were very eager to see us, and they did not mind being in such a heavily guarded place. In fact, some of them wished to be with us and share the honor of sacrifice for their Faith. The visits increased the spiritual enthusiasm of both the incarcerated and the free. The guards seemed uncomfortable to see that very noticeable excitement. At the time, I wished for fewer visits so we would not attract such attention. Our formal visiting time with family members was scheduled every other week, and our families were eagerly awaiting our court sentencing date so we would be freed from any charges, since we were all innocent. We tried to comfort our families by telling them we were OK, but our pale faces told a different story.

My main concern was for my daughters. I tried to assure them that this ordeal would end, and that I would be going home to take care of them soon. I asked them about their life with my parents, and if they were OK. I also asked them about my beloved son Abir, who was detained with the other Bahá'í men. They would tell me he was OK and that he was with my husband. This was basically how our visits would go, and they would always end with embraces and kisses and the hope we would be leaving that place someday soon.

The Nomadic Group

The number of the inmates waiting for trial was always changing. There were those who waited for days only, and others who waited for months. The hall was very full most of the time.

One day, a large nomadic group of people was brought in. They had entered Iraq illegally and had had no access to bathing water during their entire journey. They were hungry, miserable, and exhausted.

When we heard the news, we hurried to take a look at them from the gate, but we were astonished to see a huge swarm of flies circling above their heads. You can believe me when I say the flies looked like a moving black cloud above them. The dirty, oily clothes they wore looked like leather. The foul odor that came from them was unbearable, and this odor is what attracted the flies.

Soon after this group entered the hall, the area they occupied became filled with the lice that were living in every fold of their clothing and every strand of their hair. We had just finished having our lunch on a piece of cloth that we had spread on the floor, and we had not yet had the chance to clear the area of the leftover bread and dates we were eating. All of a sudden, this new group attacked our leftovers and started to fight and shove each other for what was left. The guards had to come in, and they easily broke up the fight.

The flies, on the other hand, were hard to control. Each of us had to constantly shoo them away. The flies were not even the biggest problem—the lice were. They started to move into our area because this group occupied an area fairly close to ours. The odor that came from the group, combined with the odor coming from the toilet area, became intolerable. Being in close proximity to this group was something we could not avoid, and we were fortunate that their stay lasted only two weeks. They were deported and sent back across the border to find their fate there again.

We were relieved. We could finally breathe again after the extermination, with the help of antiseptics, of the last louse.

Visits from Our Lawyer

During our incarceration, we received visits from our lawyer, Mr. Husain Bedri (may God bless his soul). His visits were a source of comfort, for he always seemed optimistic about the eventual outcome of our sentencing. With a smile on his face, through the iron bars of the gate, he told me once, "Your wish has been granted."

"What do you mean?" I replied.

He said, "You (the Bahá'ís) have won the sympathy of all, and everyone is unhappy about your confinement. Everyone you know has been telling others about your innocence and fine reputation."

I was very thankful to God to hear this. He continued to say, "Such a reaction will definitely be of a benefit to your case."

Hearing him say this was a cause for hope and optimism. We didn't know then that a conspiracy to soil our reputation was in the works, with results that would last for years, even after our release.

With time, the leading prostitute informant, who went back and forth to the office spying on us, and who was hostile toward us at the beginning, eventually changed her attitude and became very sympathetic, respectful, and kind to us. We heard later that after our sentencing, she was extremely saddened. She sobbed and screamed, "How can that happen to those innocent ladies?" She and others among the detainees had been our cellmates day and night. Therefore, we treated them all with love and kindness.

Being in a high spiritual state of excitement and love for the principles of the Faith, the young Bahá'í ladies tried to morally educate the young detainees who, as I have mentioned, were mostly prostitutes. The older ladies (me included) hesitated to associate too closely with them since we were living in a culture that did not accept that lifestyle and, in fact, firmly condemned it. We tried to protect our young ladies and their reputations during our stay. I confess that perhaps, at times, I was overprotective of them. There is a wise proverb that says, "The immoral is like coal; even if it doesn't burn, it can still soil you," and it was considered best to avoid too many interactions with the prostitutes at the time.

My constant concern and prayers were for our girls to go home soon, to get back to school, and to get away from that polluted place. It was still very strange to think that despite our being out of place there, we shared the imposed reality that we were all "inmates" with accusations and that we were all awaiting a trial. During times of bad conduct by some of the detainees, the guards would yell at them by saying, "Learn good behavior from these colleagues" (meaning us). We would smile, though we were uncertain whether we were happy with this "colleagueship" that fate had forced upon us, as if we were all colleagues in one university!

A week after we arrived at Al-Zafaraniyyeh, we were asked to appear again at the Revolutionary Court. Our hearts started to flutter all over again, and we gathered to pray. We each took a turn reciting the prayer "The Remover of Difficulties" several times. Each one encouraged the others to stay as steadfast and as firm as a mountain that no force could cause to tremble.

Early the next morning, we started with prayers and then changed our clothes. I had asked my daughters to bring me my best two-piece winter suit (a skirt and a jacket), which I continued to wear day and night for a whole month in the Abu Ghraib prison. That morning, we tried to have a light breakfast, but most of us could not take more than a cup of tea and a forced little piece of bread. The mere thought of the ghost of the Revolutionary Court was enough to kill any appetite.

The police truck with armed guards arrived, and we got in, putting our trust in God. As the vehicle started to speed away, our hearts started to beat faster. As usual, we tried to ease our anxiety by making humorous comments to each other. When we entered through the court's door, I found myself facing the moment with certainty. My nervousness had mostly subsided, especially when I asked the Blessed Beauty (Bahá'u'lláh) to bless me with strength and courage. I felt like a courageous, well-armed soldier in a battle. We met with our brothers, the Bahá'í men, including my husband Siddiq and my beloved son Abir, and I was comforted to know they were OK. My husband stood tall, patient, in total reliance on God and optimistic that the outcome would be positive since we were all innocent, having never violated any law. He thought the sentence most likely would only be the prohibition of Bahá'í gatherings. We remained in the court until the afternoon (just like the first time) in that horrifying, dark basement hall. But this time, the men and the women were separated on each side.

After a long wait, an official came to inform us that the trial had been postponed once more to an undetermined date. We took a deep breath again, and hope returned to our hearts that our innocence would definitely be determined. It had been clear that we had been open and truthful about our Faith and that our beliefs in no way opposed the government nor harmed society. The same police truck returned us to the Al-Zafaraniyyeh detention center. We were then in much better spirits than we had been that morning. Despite the noise and annoyances, the prison hall felt safer and more comforting than the dark basement of the court.

We were called to appear at the court nine times during those two months at Al-Zafaraniyyeh! Sometimes the police truck would be an hour or two late, only for us to hear that the trial had been delayed once more. Each time, we would get ready and pray. We were overwhelmed by all kinds of emotions— of hope and of fear of that horrifying court that was known for such cruelty that it caused even the mightiest people in Iraq to break down.

Every time the trial was postponed, we breathed a sigh of relief that recharged our spirits with hope, and we relied more and more on God to assist us under all conditions. Before our sentencing at the last trial, we were asked again to appear at the court. Our Bahá'í brothers had arrived earlier, but we were not permitted to talk with them at all. A designated official stood by the court's door calling with a loud voice each one of us by name: the accused so and so, and then the next, and the next. At the time, we were close to fifty in number. Every one entered with total dignity and grace.

I remember hearing one of the officials telling another, "Look how the women are walking with their heads high!" I felt such pride and wished I could tell him, "This is the manner of the innocent." We were all dressed in dignified and elegant clothes. The men stood inside the defendant's cage, and the women stood outside the cage.

Please allow me to describe my feelings at those historic moments. One of the amazing things that happened, which I consider a miracle from the Almighty, was that I felt such unexpected peace and serenity. All the previous dread and anxiety that I had had in anticipating that day had subsided. I had absolutely no fear in my heart of that court, which could horrify even the bravest of men. I had no fear of those judges, the mere thought of whom used to make me tremble. I had no feelings in that moment except that God was on my side and very near. I felt overwhelming happiness, like a child, as if I were watching a humorous movie.

I remembered at that moment a film I had seen of the early Christians in Rome being offered to the hungry lions. While on their way to the arena of death, they would be joking with each other. The fat man would tell the thin one, "The lion will find nothing but bones in you," and the thin man would reply, "I will definitely be spared death, as the lion will be so full after eating you that it could not eat more." Yes, they joked on their way to death, for they were innocent and at the summit of their sacrifice. I wished at that moment for God to help me reach that station.

We had entered the court before the arrival of the judges. In soft voices and whispers, we exchanged with each other loving words of encouragement, beseeching God for His assistance. When the judges entered, we were standing in reverence and readiness. The three judges, all dressed in military clothing, sat down. In front of them was a stack of papers containing our "pre-decided sentencing," already ordained by the higher authorities. That fact was confirmed to us later on by certain officials.

A horrifying silence filled the court while the judges examined our faces. One of the older Bahá'í ladies was sitting on the floor, and one of her shoes had come off far from her foot. She asked permission from the court to remain seated, due to her inability to stand. Her position was rather humorous and made the judges smile. This put everyone at ease. Then four fine, accomplished lawyers took the stand in our defense, something unheard of for that court, which ordinarily assigns a lawyer for show in all their cases.

Mr. Husain Bedri (may God rest his soul), whom I mentioned earlier, showed once again that he was a fine man of high education and integrity. He had had the opportunity to carefully study the Bahá'í Faith and the details surrounding our case, and he demonstrated great competence, fine skill, and courage in defending us and proving our innocence of all charges that had been leveled against us.

Our second lawyer was Mr. Kahtaan (a son-in-law of a well-known Bahá'í), a very fair and knowledgeable person who knew a great deal about the Faith due to his marriage to a Bahá'í. His father-in-law and his wife's four sisters were all among the defendants. He stood up, and with all courage, sincerity, and grace gave proof of our innocence. A third lawyer by the name of Ibrahim did the same, as well as another lawyer—a lady, who had been assigned to defend two of the accused men only.

The last lawyer to take the stand was Mr. Muthhir Al-Azzawi, who was the head of the Bar Association at the time, and who had accepted our case. One of the judges then asked each one of us to say his or her name and age. He started by asking one of the young Bahá'í ladies. She said sixteen "and a half," which made him smile. He then proceeded to ask us if we were innocent. All replied with one voice: "Yes!" At first, the judges found that to be humorous, but then started to whisper to each other, which made us suspicious.

It was then the prosecutor's turn to read the harsh charges and unjust accusations against us, such as communication with the Universal House of

Justice in Israel, possession of large sums of money (Bahá'í contributions and properties), converting the daughters of a Muslim family to become Bahá'í, participating in prohibited Bahá'í activities, such as planning to build a house of worship (Mashriqu'l-Adhkár), buying the land for it, and actively participating in supporting the construction of other Bahá'í houses of worship in other countries. Also, the prosecutor accused us of being in possession of three banned Bahá'í books (which he brought with him to show the judges). One was a book written about the Faith by the author J. E. Esslemont, and the second was a story about the Queen of Romania, who embraced the Bahá'í Faith. I regret that I have forgotten the third book.

These accusations were the prosecutor's evidences of guilt and violation of the law. He mispronounced many Faith-related names in a way that almost made us laugh, despite his harsh and cruel speech aimed at soiling our reputations and making us appear to be criminals of unspeakable misconduct. These organized, incriminating charges were made to counter the sympathy that Bahá'ís had gained from the public. We had to be presented as disloyal followers of a criminal organization that spies for Israel and aims to destroy the country in order for the government to get away with the harsh sentencing that followed. Later, those unjust accusations had a great influence on the way we were treated in prison. Despite all the horrific accusations, the report was brief and did not include any allegations against our moral character as Bahá'ís. We were astonished and saddened later on to find out that a judgment of criminality was added to our verdict and sent to the prison for the purpose of harsher treatment.

After the prosecutor's punitive speech, the defense lawyers' turn came again. Their truly extraordinary defense exhibited an in-depth knowledge of the Bahá'í Faith. Each made their best defense against our incriminating charges and reminded the court that we were citizens of excellent repute. They also added a brief description of the Bahá'í Faith and its sacred places in the Holy Land, which had been there before Israel was born. One of the lawyers read short excerpts from the Bahá'í writings and prayers. Each of the lawyers spoke with such sincerity and fairness that reflected the essence of the Faith's lofty teachings. Their speech, which we would never forget, left a sense of deep gratitude and pride in our hearts.

The judges' attitudes, on the other hand, were of extreme unfairness. The prosecutor was given a lengthy amount of time, but when it was the turn of the president of the bar association to present his defense, he was asked to shorten his speech. Shocked by the judges' request, he asked if they would prefer him to leave his papers of his defense presentation with them and exit the court, but they ordered him to carry on. By the time he was done, it was late in the afternoon, and we were asked to leave the court. The lawyers' just defense, still echoing in my ears, with their words presenting us and the Faith in the most glorious way in a court known for inducing terror in the hearts of everyone who enters it, all the way from the north of the country to the south, left me with unimaginable gratitude.

Outside the court, family members and friends were waiting for us as usual. We were not allowed to get too close to them. In fact, we had only had seconds to exchange brief greetings from a distance and then to do so again while we were inside the police vehicle to be taken back again to Al-Zafaraniyyeh.

During the ride back to the prison, I turned to my sisters and with sincerity and pride told them, "After such an honorable and exalted defense of our Faith in the Revolutionary Court, I am ready to accept even a prison sentence." As God is my witness, I felt it would be an honor to be imprisoned in His name.

One very positive event that day in court was that the attorney general affirmed the innocence of one of the Bahá'í lady prisoners, Dr. Iqbal Wakeel, who was studying to be a surgeon. That meant her release would soon arrive. We took turns happily embracing and congratulating her. As we arrived back at Al-Zafaraniyyeh, we were all expecting to hear our sentencing results, which would either be a full affirmation of our innocence, or at the most a very light sentence of a few weeks' imprisonment, especially after the excellent defense by our lawyers. We started to dream and prepare to reunite with our families at home very soon.

That evening, we had two visitors: Iqbal's mother and her aunt, who were full of joy. We extended our congratulations to them, and sweets were offered to all for the anticipated happy occasion. Soon after their visit, we learned that the officials had changed their mind about declaring her innocent and had tried to tempt her to recant her faith in exchange for a full scholarship abroad to receive her PhD in medicine. This is how her story changed, and she remained a prisoner with the rest of us. Despite the changed outcome, Iqbal Wakeel was still able to receive her primary medical degree while in Al-Zafaraniyyeh, as I will explain in an interesting story.

During our incarceration, and amidst all the turmoil and disorder, Dr. Iqbal Wakeel was determined to apply for her primary medical qualification at Baghdad's College of Medicine, where she had earned her medical degree and had practiced surgery. The exam was to be supervised by attending doctors from Europe. Dr. Iqbal Wakeel was a brilliant honors student, who had always excelled in her class. Her father (who was a Knight of Bahá'u'lláh, one of the first pioneers to the Khuriya Muriya Islands in the Arabian Sea, and who introduced the inhabitants there to the Bahá'í Faith) had also encouraged her to take the exam.

Dr. Iqbal Wakeel courageously asked the authorities for permission to apply for the exam. Her request was accepted, and soon she was able to get the books she needed to study. The loud noise in that crowded hall made it almost impossible for anyone to study, but Dr. Iqbal put her trust in God and proceeded with determination. She had only two weeks to prepare for her exam, and her efforts were truly impressive and extraordinary.

The day of her exam arrived. It was to be held in the part of the medical university built on the grounds of what used to be the blessed Garden of Ridván. Members of the police accompanied her to the exam, and so did our prayers. A few hours later, she was brought back, with her face beaming with joy. She had passed the exam with great success and had astonished the foreign visiting doctors! She received her degree a few days later, and all rejoiced with sweets and a celebration. This time, the guards were present not to break up a fight but to join everyone celebrating her achievement Her exceptional and excellent accomplishment filled our hearts with pride.

4 / More Time at Al-Zafaraniyyeh and Our Transfer to the Abu Ghraib Prison

The Arrival of the Directorate of General Security (Al-Amn) Members to the Prison

A while after our incarceration, members of Al-Amn arrived to meet with us. We were notified by the police headquarters, and the news brought terror to our hearts. We had thought our initial dreadful meetings with that agency were over.

We were individually called in to a new interrogation and were asked all kinds of questions. I was again asked for my name, religion, names of my siblings, names of my relatives one by one, which family members were Bahá'ís, and which were not. When I told them the names of the non-Bahá'í family members, I was accused of not telling the truth.

I said, "You can ask them yourselves if they are Bahá'ís or not, because a Bahá'í will not hide his belief. For us, it is a source of honor and pride, and if someone says they have recanted, then it's the truth that he is not a Bahá'í."

The purpose behind their questioning was to see if we were still persistent in our belief or if, perhaps, the harsh incarceration period and the fear of the trial had shaken our commitment and determination. Many thanks be to God, all remained faithful and staunch. Every one of us tried to be very brief in our answers, as we had learned from the previous interrogation not to give more than needed and not allow ourselves to become trapped in a verbal maze that would worsen the situation. Briefness was the safest approach.

The Bahá'í Month of the Fast

The blessed month of fasting (in March) had arrived while we were still incarcerated. We requested the prison to delay our lunch meal until later in the afternoon and to allow us to heat the food at sunset (no dinner was served there) and to prepare a simple breakfast at dawn. The authorities agreed, and that kind initiative was a favor we would never forget. We very quietly gathered at each dawn so as not to disturb the still sleeping inmates. Then we would start a round of prayers, which increased our sense of spirituality and tranquility in a peaceful space, before the start of the morning's commotion. We prepared tea and either ate food saved from the previous day or prepared simple food such as boiled potatoes and eggs. Our prayers and meditation continued throughout the day, and we waited to eat until it was time at sunset. The fast continued until the blessed Festival of Naw-Rúz (the Bahá'í New Year) arrived. The days of the fast were memorable indeed, for we felt such peace and tranquility during our dawn prayers in that quiet hall, with the cool March breeze entering through the window. The breeze cleaned the air of the flies and smoke from the previous day, and the detainees' sleeping made it possible for the place to be peaceful and serene. The breeze was cold, so we stayed wrapped in our blankets and exchanged quiet conversations with each other. We experienced great happiness and gratitude that God had enabled us to fast with such high spirits and joy, despite the circumstances. We were ready to accept His will, whatever it would be—whether being freed or receiving the honor of imprisonment in His all-glorious name—and we were ready to endure hardships just as He (Bahá'u'lláh) had done during His long and agonizing years of imprisonment to deliver humanity to the shore of peace, unity, and true understanding.

The following are some of the events I witnessed while in Al-Zafaraniyyeh that brought me severe emotional distress.

The Fire

The prison was a strange and foreign environment compared to the society we knew. In the past, we had heard of crimes and prisons, but witnessing that kind of life in person was something beyond our belief. Some of the events were so distressing that they left a deep impression that remains in my memory to this day. This is one of those stories.

One night, the guards brought a beautiful young woman, seventeen years old, wearing an abaya (as I mentioned, this was a black traditional cloth to cover the head and body but leave the face exposed). The guards shoved her in, accompanied by their usual insults, with her crying. The poor young lady sat in a corner, not wanting to talk to anyone. The detainees were curious about her, but she had nothing to say. She only sobbed loudly. The prostitutes' leader (the lady who intimidated all) reprimanded her to stop crying. She did, then curled up on an old blanket.

The next morning, the curiosity of the detainees increased even more. The "leader," who as I mentioned had a close relationship with the officials because she was their informant, was finally able to find out more about the newcomer. The young lady seemed to have had an intimate relationship with her brother-in-law. The news spread like wildfire among the inmates, and they began their scolding and insults aimed at her. The young lady started to sob, and she swore she was innocent. She explained that her brother-in-law was the one who had fabricated that accusation, since she would not surrender to his sexual advances. She avoided him and was fearful to let her sister and parents know something that could bring shame to the family.

Deep inside, we were certain of her truthfulness, just from the way she sobbed, the sincerity in her voice, and the innocent expression on her face, but I think we were alone in that thought. It was natural for the other detainees to dismiss her claim because they came from a life of prostitution and deception. Things got worse when one of the guards came in and started to kick and slap her so she would stop crying, which she forced herself to do. We were heartbroken and felt helpless for not being able to intervene. She then sat quietly, like a lifeless statue.

Later that afternoon, she headed silently to the bathroom, and no one knew what she planned to do. She poured the gasoline—from a can used for the portable small stove we had—all over herself and set herself on fire. We were sitting and chatting with each other, and we had spread out our bedding and were ready for the evening.

All of a sudden, we saw a large, moving ball of fire coming toward us. Loud screams from everyone, especially the young children, filled the hall. The unfortunate soul was in flames, like the lit wick of a big candle moving around, and she was not even crying or screaming! The horrific pain caused her to move aimlessly around the hall. In every direction she turned, the women ran away and screamed in horror. Because we were trapped with no way out, the fear of the fire spreading throughout the hall was overwhelming.

In that critical moment, one of my Bahá'í sisters performed a heroic act— she ran toward the burning lady, threw a blanket over her, and held it there tightly to stop the flow of oxygen and put out the fire that had already started to spread to the surrounding blankets on the floor. The attempt to save her life was unsuccessful, as the fire had penetrated her flesh. She collapsed on the bedding of the Bahá'í lady who had tried to save her and had saved the lives of the others.

All this happened in minutes, but it seemed like years. Despite the loud screams, it took a long time for the guards to come in. They might not have expected something more serious than the usual quarreling between the detainees, which they always allowed a few moments to subside before responding. By the time they finally arrived, the young lady was already dying. An ambulance was called, but it was too late; she had taken her last breath.

That night, an investigation was made by an official, and all testified that the young lady had willingly taken her own life. This is how that young woman became a victim of her soiled honor and took her own life either to avoid disgracing her family or out of fear of their wrath. Many innocent girls in her situation become victims of society if accused of infidelity, even when they are victims of rape or incest. They are treated as criminals or damaged goods that need to be eradicated (killed) by the family. Society, in most cases, allows and covers crimes that have been committed against them, even in cases of rape.

That painfully unforgettable night was very hard on us all. We could not eat our supper, and we kept busy with our prayers and supplications. Our nerves and emotions were at their edge. The smell of the fire had filled the room. No one else but us seemed to be moved by what had happened, and the meaningless conversations of the other inmates continued. I remember that during that night, my sleep was more like a heavy nightmare, and I kept picturing that young beauty melting like a candle in front of our eyes. The smell of her burning flesh had filled my nostrils and remained in our blankets for a long time after that horrific incident.

Other Memories of Al-Zafaraniyyeh

We had become accustomed to the daily routine of waiting long days and longer nights for a trial date. Our interaction with the other detainees was minimal, and we talked to them only if necessary. Those who had been there for a long time came to realize that we were different and compassionate; therefore, they began to develop a liking for us and to wish us well. This was reflected in their kind words.

Among those inmates was an older, dignified lady who had been jailed because her son, who was a lieutenant in the army, had defected and escaped to Syria. The government considered him a traitor. That lady spent most of her days praying and lamenting. She had been jailed as a hostage so that her son would be forced to return to face his punishment. She was among those who had witnessed our good conduct. Therefore, she always wished us well and prayed for a good outcome to our trial. She was a religious lady and accepted the fact that we recited different prayers from the Muslim prayers, but she also believed that we all prayed to the same God and were all under His mercy and care. We heard later after our departure that she had remained in that prison for a long time but was eventually released because of her deteriorating health.

One very cold and stormy night, with the wind blowing through the open window and the barred gate, we heard a rumor that the Al-Fthailiyyeh detention center, where our Bahá'í men were incarcerated, was in danger of flooding from the Tigris River. There was the possibility that the detainees would be moved somewhere else. That area of Baghdad had many incidents of flooding due to the new dams on the Tigris. We also heard that the jail had become very crowded, and, for lack of space, some of the younger detainees, including young Bahá'í men, were forced to sleep outdoors in an open area with only a roof that did not protect them from the cold.

I stayed awake that night worrying about my beloved son Abir and the rest of the dear young men being outside in that cold and rain. My heart felt squeezed in agony, and there was nothing I could do but beg God for His mercy so we would receive our sentencing soon, and my son could go back to his college in Sulaimaniyyeh to finish his studies. We checked the next day on the flooding situation and found out that the danger was gone. Therefore, I thanked God that my son was still with my husband and the rest of the Bahá'í brothers, watching over each other.

The Story of the Elderly Woman

Among the detainees worthy of mention was an elderly woman. Her advanced age had printed deep impressions on her features; she looked like a carved statue on which the artist had carefully and skillfully engraved her tired old face. Not even one tooth remained in her mouth, and her back was hunched in the shape of an arch. She was no longer able to walk on her two legs, so she reverted to walking on all four, as she did when she was an infant or the way ancient humans must have done. Her charge was crossing the Iraqi-Iranian border illegally, which she did to beg for money so she could afford the bus fare to visit the holy shrines in Najaf. Sometimes illegals infiltrated the borders on foot to obtain added blessings by visiting the holy Shiite shrines in Iraq. Supposedly, the more sufferings they endured, the bigger the blessings and rewards they would receive.

These illegal visitors would therefore take a chance and hope not to get caught. If they succeeded, they would make their journey by begging along the way to reach the holy shrines. They would bring a pouch (most of the time sewn inside their clothes) full of their savings or jewelry and leave it as an offering between the golden bars that surround the shrine of the Imám Husayn. Once they did this, they felt comforted that their prayers would be answered. Sometimes they would make an offering, promising God to do a specific good deed if He granted them their wish. The promise would be carried out. Mothers often left gold in the shrine in anticipation that their sick children would be healed. The shrine would then be filled with gold, sparkling like the sun.

There is a designated caretaker in the shrine of the Imám Husayn who collects the offerings, and the money goes for the maintenance of the holy places and perhaps for helping the needy. The old lady who crawled on all four had hoped to visit the holy shrines, but her bad luck prevented her from reaching it, and she was captured by the border patrol. At that time, the tension between Iraq and Iran was at its highest, and the border was heavily patrolled. Violators were detained and returned to their country.

The old lady, who was accustomed to begging, was not submissive to her captives like the others who were captured. Despite her advanced age, she protested and screamed the whole time. Some of the cruel detainees laughed at her and teased her so she would scream some more, and some guards came and insulted her and the Shah of Iran. Their behavior, in return, upset her even further. There were times when the guards even resorted to violence and kicking her in order to quiet her down.

That unfortunate soul did not fully comprehend the reason for her arrest, and she tried twice to make an escape. She proved that she was courageous to stand up for herself and braver than those who could walk on two legs! One early morning, she took advantage of the front gate still being open (I don't know how that happened), and crawled away. She sneaked out all the way to the outside door, then to the street where freedom was! We heard a loud commotion of yelling and swearing, so we went to investigate. We saw through the bars a rather funny but at the same time very sad scene. Two guards had picked up the old lady, each holding two of her limbs while they swung her and laughed. The old lady was screaming and shouting profanities in Persian. The detainees could not help but laugh, while she was simmering in anger. We pitied her, as her hopes to gain her freedom were dashed.

Just a few days later, she attempted another escape, this time in the middle of the day. She must have been attentively watching for another chance. This was during the period when lunch was being brought in. The guards were busy bringing the food, and the detainees were crowding to take their only substantial meal. In an exceptionally brave move, she sneaked out by crawling quietly to the street again. She was captured and brought back again, carried by her four limbs like a rag doll, surrounded by laughs from all around her from the guards, who questioned if she was mentally competent enough to escape the prison entirely. As usual, they swore at her and cursed the Shah of Iran, as if she were an informant of the shah and her entry to Iraq was politically planned.

A week later, they took her in a van and threw her across the border to face an unknown destiny. To us, she was an example of how humans risk everything to be free of bondage and captivity. Also, we admired her faith, as she had risked her life to visit the holy shrines of the Imáms.

Birth Inside the Jail

Noise had erupted above the normal level again at the Al-Zafaraniyyeh hall. One of the detainees was a Kurdish woman who was in her ninth month of pregnancy. She went into labor late in the afternoon after the prison's administrative office was closed. The nearby clinic was closed as well. No one was left except the officer on duty and a few guards. The news of the possible labor spread around. Some thought it could have been bad food or indigestion caused by the lentils that were not fully cooked in the soup that evening; others suggested she be given some warm tea and so forth. The labor pain was consistent, so the officer on duty was notified. It took a while, but he finally came with a careless attitude, looked at her for a minute, and left.

A long time went by, and her contractions became closer and closer together. The yelling for help continued, but no one seemed to care. As the sun began to set, the woman in labor screamed louder and louder. Finally, the guard came to inform us that an ambulance had been called, but it had yet to arrive. Everyone tried to comfort the woman by telling her help was on the way, but the poor lady was Kurdish and did not understand Arabic. She was in real agony, as it was her first birthing experience. Our girls volunteered to put bed sheets around her mattress for privacy, but she was too agitated to have anything cover her. She was lying down near the gate, and the foolish guard was coming back and forth. Therefore, our girls kept on covering her. One of the Bahá'í ladies (Bahiyyeh Mesjoon) was a nurse and an expert in childbirth. She had known all along that the woman was in labor, but she feared taking the responsibility as a prisoner herself to assist in such a risky task, so she had initially hesitated to help. When I asked her about the kind of risk involved and why she was hesitating in assisting the Kurdish woman, Bahiyyeh told me something I had not known about her—that in the past, she had worked as a nurse in a women's prison. She added that the prison authorities take total responsibility for the safety of each prisoner; therefore, she feared stepping in their sphere of responsibility. I understood her position and hoped for help to arrive, but it did not. The loud screams continued, and so did the agitation of all the prisoners. The guard kept on coming in to check and asked if anyone among us knew how to assist her. For him, being a simple man from a village, childbirth was a natural thing that only required a woman or two to assist in the process, with no need for an ambulance or a doctor. At that point, all eyes were on this Bahá'í nurse, as she could provide the only possible help for the lady in labor.

All pleaded with Bahiyyeh to help that poor woman who was in a tough labor. Bahiyyeh agreed on one condition: that she receive an official authorization from the prison officials. She later received this from the officer on duty. She ordered water to be boiled—which we prepared on the small stove—washed her hands several times, and asked the crowd to step back and away from the woman in labor, who was nearly naked. With the help of a prisoner who spoke Kurdish, she was able to comfort and instruct the woman in labor. The situation was very unique and exciting for our young ladies, as a very special guest was about to arrive! After several agonizing screams, and with Bahiyyeh's assistance, we then heard the screaming of the little baby!

The baby was healthy and beautiful. We ran to give Bahiyyeh clean sheets cut to make blankets, diapers, and other sheets to warm the mother, as it was a very cold night. After Bahiyyeh cut the baby's umbilical cord with a small knife that she had sanitized thoroughly on the stove, the baby was quickly washed and bundled in blankets. The umbilical cord was tied with a thread that one of the prisoners had used for threading (for removing body hair), which was sanitized first by boiling it in hot water. The mother was very happy with her newborn, and she felt hungry and begged for food.

We laughed at the change of mood, and Bahiyyeh fried some eggs (we had saved them for tomorrow's breakfast), which she cooked in date syrup! The new mother devoured it all and licked the pan! After that, she slept well with her beautiful new baby. This is how this newborn came into this world, sharing his mother's suffering but bringing the smile of new life into hearts where pain had resided. A while later, the ambulance finally arrived, while the mother was in deep sleep! Bahiyyeh gave the paramedics her report that the delivery was natural, and both mother and baby were healthy. The paramedics did not find any need to take them to the hospital, so they left.

In the next few days, Bahiyyeh continued her postnatal care for the new mother and her baby, and we all continued to enjoy having a new life in that sad place and looking at the baby's beautiful and innocent face. We asked our Bahá'í visitors to bring clothes for the baby, which they did. Soon after, the mother and her baby left the prison in a police car heading to her court appearance or to an unknown destination.

The Teens at Al-Zafaraniyyeh

As I have previously described, the hall was crowded with many prisoners, who were mostly in the prostitution business. Among them were teenagers who were orphans and others who had been abused and had run away from their families. They had then been coerced into becoming prostitutes. Other teens had been arrested for theft or had been involved in fights and were most likely going to be persuaded by the older prostitutes, who were very clever recruiters, to join them. The recruiters would sometimes entice the young with a life of money and luxury, and at other times, frighten them about what might happen if they returned home and faced cruel and even fatal retribution from their families.

Sometimes a promise to marry someone to protect them would also be a means of persuasion. This is how many of the young teens would be lured into prostitution. Some of the "recruiters" would penetrate prisons by design to look for young victims. I remember one night I was suffering from insomnia and worrying about the fate of my children and what would happen to them if our captivity were to be prolonged—if it was God's will—what would happen to my son, or whether we would be spared the suffering of further imprisonment.

The head of the prostitutes, "Fifi," often liked to stay up late listening to her cassettes or dancing while everyone else was sleeping. At that time, the hall was very crowded, and my mattress happened to be very close to a woman who seemed, during the day time, to be very dignified. There was also a very young detainee, a twelve-year-old girl, who had been raped by a neighbor and taken by the police for her protection (from being killed by her own family). The woman next to me whispered to the young girl to come and lie down by her side, so she did.

I could hear their conversation very clearly, and at first, I could not believe my ears. The honey-sweetened talk that that woman started using soon became an evident means of luring the little girl toward prostitution. The little girl cried with terror from listening to the woman frighten her about how she could be killed by her family. Then the woman continued to tell the young girl that she would provide a safe haven and a happy life for her. I swear that I was shivering while hearing that, as if the little girl were my own daughter. I felt a need to hug and protect her, but I could not do anything to protect that innocent lamb from the fangs of the evil wolf. I could only pray to God to protect the girl.

The next morning I could not be silent, despite the fact that, in order simply to protect ourselves and remain dignified, we (Bahá'ís) had all decided to keep a distance from the others and their problems. I just could not let this incident go, so I asked the wicked woman to leave the little girl alone and let the police take care of her.

She answered me in a very harsh tone, "Can you guarantee the safety of this girl and that she won't be slaughtered by her family?" At that moment, I decided to stop my pursuit because I was fully aware of the unfathomably cruel traditions some of the tribes followed in the "honor killing" of innocent victims of rape, to save the family's reputation, instead of punishing the criminal. Even those who escape death live to be shunned by society or forced to marry someone old and be forever abased, all to save the family's face from shame, as if they are ridding themselves of a deadly disease.

Often, girls run away to escape death and ask for help from the police. I
noticed that there was a lawyer who visited our jail often. He would quietly
talk to some of these young victims. I asked one of the prisoners about him,
and she said he tried to arrange marriages to the victims of rape with "good
doers." I wondered who those "good doers" were and who paid these lawyers,
but I received no logical answer.

The little girl of eleven or twelve that I mentioned was beautiful, thin,
and small. She had been raped by her neighbor, and there had been a fight
between the two families, so she escaped to the police for protection. Even
with that sad story, some of the detainees were doubtful of her account and
accused her of seducing her neighbor! I don't know why I felt such great
empathy toward her.

The first thing that she learned from the other detainees with their encouragement was to put a cigarette in her mouth. Cigarettes were offered to her
for free, and I went to her and told her lovingly that cigarettes were harmful
to her health and that she was too young to smoke.

She imitated the other prisoners by saying, "I smoke to ease my suffering."

I said, "Rely on God in your pain, because the cigarette will not take away
your pain."

She looked at me, unconvinced, as if her smoking was in defiance of her
family's lack of support and an expression of her disappointment.

In the following days, this little girl started to look like a doll smudged by
makeup and lipstick. She was convinced by the others to wear heavy makeup
in a conspiracy to wipe off the innocence forever from her young face. One
day, a lawyer came to talk to her behind bars. He told her that her parents
had agreed to keep her safe, but the other prisoners were giving her all kind
of opinions. Some said go home, but the majority warned her of what might
happen—the possibility of a knife waiting to cut her throat. She trembled in
fear and cried, and grabbed her cigarettes for comfort.

Deep inside, I was burning with pain for this little girl and felt helpless
to help her in her dilemma. I don't know if the other dear Bahá'í prisoners

remember that little girl or if time has dissipated her memory, but her story left a deep, sad impression in my heart forever. More than ever, I resented a society that looked at the victim as a criminal. At times, a rape victim's family could even force the victim to marry the criminal who had raped her, instead of the rapist receiving a severe punishment. Perhaps a quick death would be kinder in some of those cases, rather than a lifetime of suffering.

I also remember another story about a young girl at Al-Zafaraniyyeh prison.

The Cradle

The main character in this story is an eight- or nine-year-old little girl. She had lost her mother and stayed under the care of her father and siblings. The father had to go to work all day, and he had strict rules that she stay at home. One day she disobeyed him by going out to play in the street. The father feared that she might get into a dangerous situation, then he would be blamed and accused by the neighbors of being an inadequate and bad father. So he tied one of her arms every day with a chain attached to what had once been her brother's cradle. He left her food in the cradle and went off to his work. She stayed chained to the cradle like an animal day after day until the father came back in the evening. One day she became fed up and decided to seek some freedom. She carried the wooden cradle above her head—which was not an unfamiliar sight, as many of the poor carried their belongings on their heads—and headed out to the street. She walked to a blacksmith and asked him to break the chain, which he did.

A while later, she realized that her father was going to be extremely angry with her, and she feared his punishment. She decided to carry the cradle on her head and go to a police station, where she began crying and pleading for help. When the father was called and found out what she had done, he became very upset and insulted her in front of family members that had arrived at the police station. He threatened in the company of his relatives to punish her; therefore, the police decided to detain her in Al-Zafaraniyyeh for protection. Weeks after we left Al-Zafaraniyyeh police headquarters, she was still there, and had made friends with other children in that infested place.

We had awaited our trial while being incarcerated in Al-Zafaraniyyeh police headquarters. The trial was rescheduled a total of nine times. Some of the dates were canceled just prior to our leaving for the Revolutionary Court, but others were canceled after our being taken to the court and waiting for long periods of time. On the ninth time, our fate was finally decided.

This concludes my narrative about the Al-Zafaraniyyeh prison days. I will now explain the details of the long and exhausting last trial day in the Revolutionary Court and the dreaded day of the sentencing that decided our fate.

After our appearance in court, we would be sent to the horrific Abu Ghraib prison.

Sentencing Day: Deciding our Destiny

As God willed, the day of our sentencing had finally arrived. The office of the Al-Zafaraniyyeh Detention Center informed us that we were called to appear before three judges of the Revolutionary Court, for what would most likely be the final verdict. Early that morning, we got ourselves ready. The majority of us could not eat breakfast, because after being in prison for so very long, we felt as if hope—like drops of water—were leaking through our fingers. We had been confined by the authorities in that gloomy pit for no reason or fault of our own. The only motive of our captors—though they never admitted to it—had been to try to force us to recant our belief.

We were transported to the Revolutionary Court in a truck. Each one of us reverently and quietly, with suppliant hearts to the All Merciful God, said our prayers until we reached the courthouse. We met briefly with the male Bahá'í prisoners, and we were surprised to see also among them those who had been in solitary confinement for two weeks in tiny cells atop the roof of what used to be the Bahá'í center in Baghdad. The governing party had seized it years before and converted it to a place for detention and torture.

I cannot describe to you how I felt at that moment, when I saw the Bahá'í men trying their hardest to portray a brave appearance in our presence, gathering all their strength while awaiting their fate after being confined in agonizingly tiny spaces. They looked very thin and frail, and their jackets seemed several sizes too large. I was very moved by that saddening sight and the hardships they must have endured, but despite seeing them in this state, I was thankful they were alive, for we had not heard any news about them during that hard and critical period.

Among them was my aging father. My reunion with him was extremely emotional. He had lost a lot of weight and had very dark circles around his eyes, as if he had been punched in the face, and I could not help but sob at the sight.

I embraced him tightly and asked, "Have they beaten you?" (I swear this is what he looked like.)

He replied, "It's the lack of sleep and the discomfort of the tight space for such a long and hard time."

I asked another elderly gentleman the same question, and he smiled and replied, "It is the tightness, the hardship of the constricted space we were in."

We found out later on that the flat roof of the Bahá'í center had been converted to house detention cells for the Bahá'ís, Freemasons, and others. The cells were made of wood, and each cell had a small opening at the top for air. They had put six of the Bahá'í detainees (my father Abdul-Razaq Abbas, another Bahá'í, Ihsan Abdul-Wahid, Selman Haleem, Dr. Abbas Baghdadi, and Kamil Abbas) all in one small cell where these wronged ones could not fully extend their legs when they tried to sleep. Therefore, they just closed their eyes while sitting with folded legs, with their shoulders touching, then tried to sleep. The door was locked day and night. A small meal and some water were passed to them through that small opening.

One day, they were given soapy-tasting water (or perhaps the bar of soap had fallen in it); therefore, they remained thirsty until the next day.

They were thankful that it was winter and not summer when the temperature on that roof could reach close to sixty degrees Celsius (about 140
degrees Fahrenheit). This is how the integrity and grace of the building
that used to be our place of worship was violated and desecrated. It was
turned into a place for torture, where the cries of those being tortured
were heard from long distances (according to the residents of the area);
whereas at one time, beautiful chanting had echoed from the walls of
that sacred building that had been blessed by the visits of Hands of the
Cause (a select group of Bahá'ís, appointed for life by the Guardian of the
Bahá'í Faith, Shoghi Effendi, to serve the Faith) and many other dignified
visitors from abroad.

Later on, when my father visited me in prison, he told me that while
locked up in that cell, he would be called for interrogation and they would
ask him, "Do you know where you are?"

He would reply, "Yes, I am in the Bahá'í center of worship."

Then they would mock him and say, "That is what it used to be! Now it is
a center for the Al-Amn!" They would then ask him to identify all the people
in old photographs found in that building, and he would reply, "I'm an old
man and don't know who the people are in those very old pictures." He told
me he could barely recognize anyone because of the dimness of the light and
his strained vision caused by sleep deprivation.

This is how difficult the period they spent on the roof of the Ḥaẓíratu'l-
Quds was. Later, during Saddam Hussein's era, that building was destroyed
and flattened to the ground.

Going back to the day at the Revolutionary Court—we stood with great
uneasiness; anxiety had taken over our nerves as we awaited the unknown.
The guard in charge started by calling each one of us in a loud and terrifying
voice: "Defendant so and so." Then he would move on to the next name, and
the next. Each one of us would come forward with his/her head raised high
and feet steady, as if receiving his/her strength and courage from the lights

of Bahá'u'lláh's dominion. This is how we—submissive to the will of God, the One, the Omnipotent—entered the courtroom and stood in front of the judges' podium.

One of the three judges (his name was Al-Allaaf) read a very brief statement from each of us and asked each one, "Is this your statement?"

No one dared to say that the statement was not read to us prior to that and perhaps it was written in an altered fashion—none except for Dr. Abbas Baghdadi, who was courageous enough to say to the judge, "Yes, this is my statement, except it is not exactly as you read it."

The judge strongly reprimanded him by saying, "Does such and such judge have a personal animosity against you?"

Dr. Abbas answered no, and discontinued talking.

When it was my turn, I was asked if Bahá'í rituals and practices were held at my home. My answer was that we do not have rituals in the Bahá'í Faith, but rather what we call Feasts (hospitality gatherings) between family members, and that is all. I was not allowed to explain further, and the judge moved on in a hurry to the next defendant, as if he had a rushed, superficial obligation to fulfill.

It was said by observers to the case that our sentences had already been decided and written ahead for the judges to read. I remember that later on, at the beginning of our imprisonment period during our visitation, one of the lawyers came to visit a relative of his, and he was fully aware of the situation of the Bahá'ís and their harsh sentences. He came close to me and said, "Trust me on this: your sentences were handwritten by President Ahmed Hasan Al-Bekr himself and with green ink! Each name had a predetermined verdict and a written sentence next to it. The trial, the defense council, and the prosecutors were nothing but a show for the general public."

I would like to mention that the interrogation had been verbal only and never recorded by hand. Dr. Abbas Baghdadi was the only one given a piece of paper to write down what he knew. His motto was "safety in truthfulness"; therefore, his answer regarding all the affairs of the Bahá'í community was very detailed. Because of this, there was a space for officials to interpret his writing as they wished. I came to realize later on that their interpretation was always personal and based on suspicion. While in prison, I once said that we were honest and law-abiding citizens, with no ulterior motive against the government or the nation.

I heard one of the officials say in response, "Our principle is to be suspicious first and investigate later. If a tree was shaken by the wind, we would first suspect that someone hiding behind it was the cause!"

When the judge was finished reading the brief statements, we were ordered to leave the courtroom and go to the lower level of the building until it was time to receive our verdicts. It was only natural that feelings of apprehension in anticipating the verdict had overtaken us all. Nevertheless, we tried to push them aside by encouraging one another with comforting words and forced smiles, due to the seriousness of the situation. We decided to rely on God, as all that comes from Him is good.

A short while later, we were asked to appear before the judge again to hear our verdicts! The court started first with those who were to be sentenced to a fine (among them was my son Abir, a few young women, and a few men). The fine was five hundred Iraqi dinars (approximately $1700 at the time).

Hearing the judge read my son's name among that group eased my anxiety somewhat and made me ready to personally receive any verdict after that. I am ashamed to remember that although I was supposed to be so proud and brave if my son received a prison sentence, human weakness and motherly love can, at times, take over, especially in times of injustice, oppression, and defense of loved ones. May God forgive my feebleness.

After this, the men's verdicts were read. Life sentence for this one, life sentence for that one, life sentences for all twenty of them, including my husband Seddiq Abdul-Majid. The verdicts came down like lightning bolts. None of us said a word.

We stood in sadness awaiting the ladies' sentences, and then they started! Iqbal Al-Wakeel; life sentence! Dear Lord, our hearts were ripped out of our chests for the cruel verdict, especially since prior to that day, the prosecutor himself had found her innocent! She and the other young ladies had committed no crime except going to a birthday party. The other young ladies received the following sentences: Kawakib Husain: fifteen years. Nida Sabour: ten years. Warqa Abdul-Razzaq: ten years. Fatimah Abdul-Razzaq: ten years. The older ladies (Fakhriyyeh Mirza, Bedriyyeh Ghulam Husain, Hajir Al-Wakeel, Bahiyyeh Mesjoon, and Anisa Abdul-Razzaq) each received ten years of imprisonment. Despite the harsh verdicts, each of us walked silently, exiting the courtroom, except for one of the ladies who was the oldest and in her sixties. She was so intensely affected by the severe verdict that she could not walk, so we helped her climb the stairs. She swore she wanted to tell the judge to straighten the sign behind him (which was truly crooked) that read, "Justice is the foundation of dominion." We asked her gently to remain calm and rely on God.

We gathered in the lower level of the building after we said our good-byes to those who received a fine for a verdict. The Bahá'í friends outside the court were in their utmost preparedness to pay the fines for all and to sacrifice in a way that my pen fails to describe. Their fast response in paying the fines attracted the attention of the officials and angered them. One of them said, "Look at their tight-knit bond!" Another said, "Where did they get all this money and so quickly?" I heard those remarks myself.

We were taken to another underground room for fingerprinting. My beloved son Abir followed us there, and went to his dad and grabbed his hand and put it in mine. This was a habit he had had since he was a little boy whenever our family took walks together. He would come between us, grab our hands, and put them together, and we would laugh.

I remembered his habit and started to sob then without intending to. I told my husband, "We've caused our children to become orphans. No mother and no father."

His eyes filled with tears, and he replied, "We are leaving them in God's care." We said good-bye to our son and asked him to take good care of his

sisters; he agreed to do that. To tell you the truth, I had no knowledge about
the system in Iraqi prisons and the rules on whether visits by families would
be allowed. I imagined it would be a long time before I could see my children.
I worried about leaving them on their own while they were still at a young age
and needed their parents' care. Sometimes parents worry that their children
might not be able to become independent, and we forget that God cares for
all.

We completed the very lengthy procedure of having our fingerprints
taken, as if we were hard-core criminals. When my turn came, the officer
in charge uttered bad and false remarks while smudging ink on my fingers,
taking many prints of each finger and twisting it in every direction possible;
then he did the whole palm. Every time he was done, he would bring more
copies. I lost count of how many copies in all. All I can remember is that I
almost lost my patience out of utter exhaustion, all while listening to his bad
remarks and accusations about how we had sold our conscience to foreign
governments and were haters of our revolutionary government, all for the
sake of greed and money. We had sold our belief in the Islamic Faith and
gone astray, and we had ruined not only our future but the futures of our
children, he said.

The other officers present in the room were listening in agreement and
backing him with more negative remarks. One of them was saying to the
young ladies among us, "You will leave prison in ten years looking like 'old
maids' and never be able to get married because no one will want to marry
you." Another would say, "What forced you to choose this awful fate and
gloomy future?"

At first, I replied to the officer taking my fingerprints and said that I was
not as well-off as he thought and that, as God is my witness, all I had was a
handful of dinars in the purse I was taking with me to prison. He did not care
and continued his bad remarks; therefore, I chose to stay silent. My husband
was across from the table where I sat. He had a very sad look on his face and
put one hand on his face while witnessing what was happening. I remember

that so well, as if it were only yesterday. At that time, my husband had not completely lost his sight; therefore, despite his poor vision, he was still able to reasonably recognize people and his surroundings.

When the procedure was over, our hands were covered with dark ink all the way to our wrists. I took paper tissues out of my purse and with great difficulty started rubbing off the ink. By the time we were done, it was between late afternoon and evening. Our exhaustion had reached its limits. We left the lower area of the courthouse and went to the upper level, where all the men were taken in a special transportation truck (with iron nets on the sides) that was used for transporting prisoners. They were accompanied by armed guards and heavy security. We had no time to say good-bye to our families or to the men.

Our turn to ride in the trucks with the iron nets came next, and it was our first time riding one of those. They were very different from the standard police trucks that used to transport us back and forth from the Al-Zafara-niyyeh detention center. We were accompanied also by armed guards and security officers (of Al-Amn), who tried to appear pleasant at first.

Our loved ones—family members and friends—were still waiting outside. They had been there since the early morning and had been standing on the sidewalk across from the Revolutionary Court throughout that entire cold day in March. Among them were children and others above fifty or sixty years of age. Seeing us climb into the truck stirred all kinds of emotions in them and us. Tears poured, and all began to sob, despite our efforts to control our feelings for the sake of love and kindness to our families. We tried our best to give them courage, so they would be able to bear the pain of those moments that placed us on a separate path from them and sent us heading to an unknowable future.

We attempted to paint some faded smiles on our tired faces to lift up their spirits. We waved to them through the metal mesh on the sides of the truck. Some were able to hold it together and waved back, but most were bitterly sobbing because of the harshness of our verdicts. My pen is incompetent to draw a picture of those emotional moments. I could read the lips of everyone calling "Allah'u'Abhá" (God is the Most Glorious). Some of them were totally overwhelmed by the shock of the cruel sentencing and exhausted after standing the whole day out in the cold.

As the truck began to move, the painful sobbing and wailing rose all around. I remember seeing my brother Suhail, who had put both hands on his head, sobbing very hard, totally taken over by the painful outcome of the circumstances. He was saying good-bye to three of his sisters. It was truly a sight I could never forget. Every time I think of it, my eyes overflow with tears. Another scene I could never forget is that of Dr. Iqbal's mother, Bahiyyeh (may God rest her soul), who was running along the side of the road, agonizingly shouting, "It is OK my darling, don't worry my darling; Bahá'u'lláh was imprisoned, and so will you be." She was repeating that phrase in a way that tore my heart to pieces for her pain and agony, especially since Iqbal was her only child.

We drove towards the Abu Ghraib prison, located to the north of Baghdad. Despite our exhaustion—both physical and emotional—hunger, thirst, and all that we had been through during that day, we felt an immense need to create an atmosphere that could ease the tension of the situation. While still on that ride, the younger ladies started to joke, then to sing uplifting Bahá'í songs, and we joined them. The guards and security men accompanying us were totally astonished. We continued to sing until we reached the prison of Abu Ghraib. By then, the sun had begun to set.

The Prison of Abu Ghraib

We were awestruck by the sight of the high walls and the horrifyingly huge iron gate of the prison. It gave us chills. Upon our arrival, we were inspected by three heavily-armed guards. Then the truck drove us a long distance inside the premises of the prison to the women's prison building. By then, the sun had completely set. The women's prison was a large building with tall walls, a large iron gate, and armed guards. We got off the vehicle, and as I was

The prison wall of Abu Ghraib

stepping onto the threshold of the gate, I loudly voiced, "In thy name, O Bahá'u'lláh, I enter this prison!" Then I suppliantly said, "Be thou my helper, O my Lord!"

Near the gate there was a water vessel made of clay (called Hib) that the guards drank water from. We gathered around it to get a drink to quench our thirst after an exhaustingly long and horrific day. The security guard that had seemed fairly pleasant during our trip changed his demeanor as soon as he met the administrator of the women's prison. With a frown on his face, he informed her of the seriousness and danger of our status and how we should be handled as such!

I heard, without intending to, his cautioning and warning words that called for firmness and strictness. The other inmates were out in the courtyard. They gathered around us with curiosity, as they always do when a newcomer arrives. Most of them expressed sympathy and astonishment when they saw how dignified and well-dressed we looked. The administrator ordered them

94

to step away from us. We reached the gate of one of the prison wards and entered a long, narrow hallway with several prison cells on each side. Each tiny cell had been designed for one person only (for solitary confinement). They were about one meter by two meters in size. Night had arrived as we walked in, accompanied by a middle-aged female jailer dressed in a special uniform of a long khaki dress, a khaki coat, and a black head cover.

This is how our nearly three years of imprisonment at the Abu Ghraib prison, and three years at Al-Rashaad prison—which was located at the very southeastern tip of the city—started. The gates were locked, and thus began that pivotal moment separating a life of freedom from the other world of a strange existence.

We were fortunate that the prison's cook was one of the prisoners in our ward. She was a very kind lady and an old acquaintance of one of the Bahá'í ladies (Bahiyyeh Mesjoon) who, in the past, had worked as a nurse in that same prison while that lady was a cook. At our arrival, the cook warmly welcomed us, embraced Bahiyyeh, and cried. She tried to comfort us by saying that perhaps our sentences would not last long, as she had witnessed many prisoners, including prisoners of conscience, be released after only a short while. Knowing we were very hungry, she hurried and prepared for us a meal of boiled eggs, potatoes, and a small portion of leftover fish from lunch. We had been in great need of someone who would sympathize with us and offer us some food. Seated on the floor, we gathered around the food and said some prayers.

After that, we headed to the tight, small cells, with two ladies to occupy each cell (which was meant to be for one occupant). We later learned that we were temporarily being placed here in these solitary confinement cells. We found some old blankets inside each cell, and other inmates donated some pillows and mats. The light in the hallway was very dim and therefore very dark and frightening. That section of the ward seemed empty except for one cell that was covered with a black blanket. The other inmates told us there was a harmless crazy woman there and not to worry about her! Despite hearing this, I was still worried and fearful. I was experiencing a great sense of defeat and resentment, and I was full of anxiety thinking of my daughters and what the future would hold for them, as they had to live with my aging parents.

That night was one of the hardest nights of my life. I felt like a bird forced to be confined to a cage. I remembered when we had Iraqi nightingales in our home. We used to receive them as gifts from some of the believers from the town of "Al-Awashiq," which was famous for its beautiful singing nightingales. They gifted us young nightingales (chicks) so they could become accustomed to living in captivity and begin to sing. By contrast, mature birds can never get used to their cage and thus will not sing.

I remember once we had an empty cage outside our house in the Al-Athamiyyeh district. The cage's door was open, and a large nightingale entered it. We were so thrilled to capture it and tried to feed it and give it water, but it refused to accept its captivity and, in protest, kept banging its head on the sides of the cage until it began to bleed. We had no choice but to set it free. It flew away making screeching noises that could have been in praise of its freedom, or perhaps curses aimed at us for capturing it.

These thoughts and emotions overwhelmed me during that fearsome night. I stood by the small window while looking at a distant dim light coming from the courtyard of the prison. I was that nightingale at the moment it was captured and the cage door was closed on it, and I was thinking of my daughters and son and how I was forced to be separated from them. I would have been just as distraught as that nightingale had it not been for God's tender mercy, which extinguished the flames blazing in my heart. I turned myself wholly toward Him and asked that He save me from my awful inclinations and bring peace and comfort to my heart. I stayed in that state of prayerfulness until dawn arrived, then I threw myself on a blanket outside that prison cell because I could not bear being confined inside such a tiny space with anyone. I needed solitude to reflect and to try to get some sleep. Even after lying down on the floor outside, I could not sleep more than a few minutes, during which the All-Merciful God granted me droplets of peace and forbearance. I was awakened by the voices of one of the jailers and of the supervisors as they instructed us to get ready for the morning count of prisoners. We were still in our previous day's dresses and hurried to quickly wash our faces, then went out to the prison's courtyard and stood in line with the other inmates of that prison ward.

The jailer started to read the names: Prisoner so and so, Prisoner such and such. It was the very first time that we were honored with this new title instead of Miss or Mrs. so and so. It truly was a title that stirred all kinds of emotions in me, for it signified pride and honor, as well as oppression and tyranny. I felt as if I were in a coronation ceremony to crown me, and while feeling the heavy weight of my crown, I recognized the ultimate honor and glory it held for me.

When the counting was done, we returned to our ward to find a commotion generated by inmates who were going back and forth, transferring their belongings to a different location. We were told that we were going to be moved to another ward to be by ourselves. Our ward was given the name "The Bahá'í Ward," and this is how it continued to be referred to throughout our imprisonment. We even received letters addressed to our ward by that name, including some for those inmates who joined us later on.

The ward was emptied and prepared for us in a hurry so that we would not associate with the other inmates and talk to them. It was as if we were an infectious disease or a calamity that had been inflicted on that prison. When we arrived at that ward, we found it to be an empty, long hall with large cells to the side, each with enough room for three beds. The front of each cell had iron bars and a barred door, and the cell had unpainted cement walls. The ceiling and floor were cement as well. The barred front of each cell faced the hallway wall, which had two small glass windows surrounded by a reinforced concrete structure. Looking out of those windows, one could see the rear courtyard of the ward. Inside each cell was a small Middle Eastern-style toilet (a squatting toilet, no seat) surrounded by two low walls, about one meter in height, with no door for privacy. Our bed was a flat metal board with four legs. It wobbled and squealed every time we tossed and turned.

We spread out into four rooms. My two sisters and I were together in one room. The gate was locked as soon as we entered the ward. The place was absolutely filthy and was filled with trash, empty bags, dust, and other disgusting items left behind by the previous inmates. Despite the hardship we were facing, we found ourselves glad and comforted by being by ourselves in that ward. The young ladies began to freely and happily move around, joking and bringing happiness to our hearts. My younger sister Fatima climbed the bars of the cell and pretended to be Tarzan chasing chimps and calling them with a funny voice, which entertained us and made us laugh, with a mix of joyful and sad tears. After that, we gathered for prayers of gratitude to thank God for liberating us from the previous depressing isolation ward.

Later on, old blankets—filthy and totally worn out—were brought to us. Each of us received two blankets—one as a cover and one to sleep on for bedding. At that time, the season was cold, so we asked if we could kindly have a third blanket, and we were each given one. The third blankets were just as dirty as the previous ones. During the day, we put those blankets on our shoulders to keep us warm, for the place had neither heat in winter nor air conditioning in the hot summers. I remember dear Hajir woke up screaming one morning because she had found a mouse near her foot due to the filthiness of the covers and the place. When I finally got a chance to wash the clothes I had been wearing for several days in a row, I wrapped one of the dirty blankets around my waist and fastened it with pins so I could wash my skirt. After it dried, I wrapped the blanket around my top so I could wash my shirt. We wore the same clothes that we had put on for the day of the trial over and over for a whole month. I also had to keep wearing my medium-heeled shoes all day, because I had nothing else to wear.

Where we hung our wet clothes (we pleaded with the guard for permission) was the mesh wire fence surrounding our ward's courtyard. The guard had to unlock a gate to allow us in. Days later we could bear those filthy

blankets no more and were able to get a bar of soap from the small prison
shop. My sister Warqa was the first to wash her blanket, and after it dried,
the rest of the ladies followed by washing theirs. This is how, a week later,
we finally were able to have blankets that we could bear smelling. We had to
obtain permission from the office to buy some aluminum dinner plates and
soap from the prison's little convenience store.

I remember years later, right before our release from a different prison
(Al-Rashaad prison) to which we were transferred later on, the sight of a
big pile of dirty blankets covered with flies brought tears to our eyes from
remembering our first days of imprisonment. The blankets were burned, taking with them the traces of unforgettable humiliation.

The morning following our solitary imprisonment, we were asked to
accompany the lady guard to the prison's office, where we were thoroughly
strip-searched to make sure we were not hiding anything dangerous, such as
a knife, scissors, drugs, or perfumes. None was found except a nail clipper in
one lady's pocketbook. They took that away. After that, they documented
any distinctive characteristics or signs of recognition for each one of our faces
or bodies. Then we were taken to meet the prison administrator, who was a
lady with a pleasant appearance. Each of us introduced herself, and when it
became evident to her that we were all well-educated (a doctor, a principal,
a teacher, high-level employees, and college graduates), her facial expression
changed to that of respect. She explained to us the rules of the prison and the
importance of being utterly obedient, and we assured her of our compliance.
She then said, "It's unfortunate that your sentences are long, and there is no
chance of changing that because they were decided by the Revolutionary
Court." The effect of her words was very harsh, as we were hoping deep
inside that at some point we would have either a suspended sentence or a
reduction that would enable us to leave prison.

When we were finally taken back to our ward, hunger had taken over. We
had not had anything for breakfast. Our young ladies started joking with us,
saying that fancy dishes would be presented to us soon. We gathered by the

small windows to look at the cells of the other prisons (we were separated by a large puddle of still water and a small courtyard). The prisoners seemed to be dishing from a large pot placed on a table, then heading toward a waste container to dump their food in. We laughed as we predicted the quality of food we were about to receive as our main meal of the day. After a long wait until three o'clock in the afternoon, the guard finally came with a prisoner carrying a container of yogurt and some dark and heavy bread. She said that this was our "bounty" (that's what food is called in prison) for today until our names were officially registered on our meal plan.

The surprise meal was not celebrated at first, but then it was accepted, and we were thankful to God for His favor. We said our prayers, ate, and saved a portion for dinner. We had also learned that each prisoner, independently, had to prepare for her dinner, whether by saving food from a previous day or from lunch. The next morning, we heard our names broadcast on the microphone. We were asked to prepare to go for a medical checkup at the prison clinic. The doctor happened to be the sister of one of my childhood friends, and she had known me as a neighbor. After examining us, she reprimanded us with a stern tone, saying, "You wanted to impose your beliefs on us by influencing Muslim girls in schools and on a large scale!" When I explained to her exactly what happened and that we never promulgated any of our beliefs, she discontinued her remarks but remained in doubt.

Later in the afternoon, we heard from some of the guards that our families had brought us some bedding. The prison administration had refused our relatives entry but was allowing us to see them from behind the wire fence. We hurried and glued ourselves to the fence, which was separated from the main entrance by another courtyard, and we waved our hands to family members—young men and women who were carrying plastic containers and covers in hopes of delivering them to us. They were all standing at the walkway that connected the office to the prison.

We raised our voices as much as we could so we could greet and hear each other. Our faces and the tone of our voices exhibited obvious sadness, but

we received encouraging words from them, despite the distance separating
us and the crackle in our voices caused by the tears, especially when I asked
them about my daughters, and asked them to let my daughters, my husband,
and my parents know I was OK.

The next day at noon, we received our first main meal for the day, the first
of the prison's bounties. It was a large, old, and beat-up black aluminum pot
full of watery and plain tomato marga ("marga" is usually made of vegetables,
meat, spices, and tomato paste thinned with water), but with a few pieces
of potatoes floating on top, and that was all. We joked and wondered how
we could fish for those pieces of potatoes in that big watery pond! We sat
together, chanted a few prayers, and thanked God for His favor, no matter
what. Each brought her aluminum dish and scooped what we could eat, and
we left some leftover in the pot.

When the supervisor came and saw the pot, she became unhappy and
said, "Didn't you like the food?"

We replied, "Yes we did, but we were saving the rest for dinner." By the
time dinner time came, we had lost our appetite for that watery marga,
which by then had a thick layer of hardened grease. We did not know what
to do with it, especially since we could not warm it up. We could neither
eat it nor discard it, and that was a problem! Finally, a kind jailer came by,
and we asked her nicely if she could please take the leftovers because we
had had our fill. She agreed to take it away, and we could finally breathe a
sigh of relief.

The first several nights we spent at prison were frightening and depressing. We would gather in one of the cells, recite our prayers, then chat. The
nights went by, and we continued to recite the same memorized prayers. The
younger ladies at times sang some songs (one famous Iraqi old song went like
this: "I have no fault of my own except the fondness of my Beloved") which
at times we joined in singing to lift our spirits high. Otherwise, we would
have become prey to sad thoughts of separation from our families, and of
how we wished to leave that barred place.

The security on our ward was very tight. A female jailer would quietly enter the ward, sneaking up on us day and night, which used to startle us. As time went by, and with our love and respect, she grew to be a friend. She came to realize that we had pure motives and that we worshiped the one true God. We became comfortable with her sleeping in our ward (in a special room) as the other jailers did in the other wards. Since there were many problems associated with those wards, she was comforted by the fact that our space was quiet and trouble-free.*

A few days later, we were given yogurt in small, square-shaped plastic containers. We were happy to keep them to use as cups to drink our tea. Iraqis very much enjoy drinking tea in the morning. Therefore, when we heard that the prison was serving tea in the morning, we requested to be included. Our request was granted, except that by the time the tea reached our ward, it was cold, especially because the pot would be left at the gate for a while until our jailer would arrive and give it to us.

One day, when the prison's chief administrator came by, we asked her permission to have a small, portable kerosene stove—just as we did when we were in the Al-Zafaraniyyeh detention center—so that we could warm our tea. But she rejected our request by saying, "Those who sacrifice very important matters should not be concerned about little matters, such as warm tea." We accepted her answer since it was told in a gentle manner. We realized that warm tea was not all that important, especially since we would have been drinking it out of recycled yoghurt containers with sharp edges.

---

* The women's prison, one of the components of the vast prison of Abu Ghraib, was composed of several detached buildings (wards) that had their individual fenced courtyards. A prison wall surrounded all the wards. The women's prison officers consisted of an administrator, who gave orders to the supervisors, who directed the jailers. Jailers were typically less educated than supervisors, and they made sure everything ran smoothly inside the wards. At the very top was the prison administrator, who oversaw the running of the entire prison.

A few days later, we were served red rice (rice cooked with some tomato paste). The rice was our complete meal. We were still very happy to have it, except we found that it was full of little stones and other small objects harvested with the rice. Rice often has small stones or dirt mixed in, and it needs to be cleaned before rinsing and then cooking it. Otherwise, the stones are very hard to remove afterward. One of our girls (Kawakib) joked by saying, "Today we are having rice à la rocks!" We would receive that red rice twice a week, and in between we had one kind of vegetable that was floating in some unappetizing broth. I would not be exaggerating if I told you that some of the food was so bad that even homeless dogs would not come near it. We never dared not to eat it. Otherwise, the jailer would get very upset and reprimand us, even if we assured her that we were full.

Anisa with her sisters

The Story of the "Purslane Weed"

One day, the cook came carrying a wooden cage on her head full of small bunches of purslane weed, a common vegetable in Iraq (we call it *berbeen*, and it has small plump leaves. It would be used as a salad or made into a stew). While walking, she was throwing a bunch of purslane into each cell. We were astonished to see her doing this, and as soon as she passed us, we burst out laughing. The younger ladies jokingly remarked that it reminded them of feeding time at the zoo, when the zookeeper tosses food through the cage bars. Purslane became our next day's breakfast, with rye bread. Scallions would be distributed to us in the same way. We would eat them a lot, as it was useful to boost our immune system during the winter.

Our First Bath

We asked if we could have a full bath, for we could not bear having partial sponge baths only. It had been a month since our last bath at Al-Zafarani-yyeh prison. There was a gas heater near our ward, but it was nonfunctional. Therefore, we were finally allowed to have a little kerosene stove, which was put in an empty cell for us to heat up some bathing water. We hung a blanket for privacy, and that is how we each took a turn to bathe. We dried our bodies with small towels we were allowed to purchase from the prison's store. The young ladies wanted to have beautiful hairdos after their baths, especially my sister Warqa, who had beautiful silky hair. She was able to find an empty cardboard box, which she cut into tiny strips that she rolled and tied with a rag to make rollers. We collected all the hairpins we had in our purses, and that is how some of the ladies could have their beautiful hairdo. Nida's thick, straight, beautiful hair did not need curling, and Dr. Iqbal had lovely and very long hair that she put into a braid at times or let down. Eventually, she had to shorten it because it became difficult to wash, especially since water was scarce. In the summer, we did not need to heat water for bathing and were OK with leaving a plastic container of water outside in the hot sun to use for bathing in the afternoon.

You might be wondering how one plastic container of water can be sufficient to bathe with, but I can say that harsh life circumstances teach us humans how to become accustomed to any situation. Cleanliness was a true bounty in the sizzling summers. We had to spread our sheet on the burning hot cement floor, and the hot air blowing from the ceiling fan roasted our faces and bodies. The unbearable heat would radiate from the cement walls around us as well.

Our Ward Lavatory

If you put aside all the mental stress a prisoner suffers due to his being isolated from society and facing an unknown destiny, you will still find many physical and health challenges that are repeated on a daily basis, and they are hard to become accustomed to. One of these challenges was the tiny toilet area that had a short wall—less than a meter in height—in a corner facing the entry of each cell, with no top and no seat!

For someone with joint pains and stiffness like myself, it was extremely hard to use. Please excuse me when I say that it was a place of utter torture for me for the whole three years we spent there. It was supposed to be a place for "rest," as in "restroom," as translated in many languages. Lacking privacy and comfort, it became a place for continuing agony, especially since sometimes the younger ladies would come to socialize. Our customs prevented me from asking them to leave the cell, which caused me health problems for several years. Later, when we were transferred to a different prison and had a separate restroom area, my son Abir was able to bring me a simple seat to use, and therefore my agony ended (please excuse me again for mentioning that).

The Scarceness of Water

Scarceness of water was another difficulty we suffered from. The faucets in the sink only supplied us with water at certain times during the day. Sometimes hours would go by, and we could not get a drop of water to drink. Therefore, we had to find a way to store water in disposable water jugs so we could use it for drinking or washing. Prior to that, we were forced to get water from a dirty basin in the ward's courtyard (some of the stray dogs used to find their way inside the prison through a small gap in the wall and drink from it), so we could wash our toilets, since there was no flushing mechanism in them. I remember once trying to peek through the gap in the wall to see the wheels of the cars passing by. At that time, I could still bend my body enough to do that.

You may not be able to imagine the extent of our need for water on those extremely hot days when the temperature would exceed 130 degrees Fahrenheit (in the shade) and was much higher in the sun. My depiction of the topic of water here is not a poetic one. I will not be describing the beauty of the flowing water of rivers and waterfalls and how the life of all living things relies on it, but rather about how important water was for our survival.

It was our first summer there sleeping on the hot concrete floor, with hot air blowing day and night from a loud fan that became louder at times, as if lamenting the misery of former prisoners. The only relief we had was from wetting our faces to ease the suffering or getting a quick bath with a bit of stored water. When the water stopped during the day, the protests of the prisoners, especially mothers who needed to wash their babies' diapers (which were dirty rags of cloth), would become loud. The odor of the hanging diapers, even after they were rinsed, would fill the air and made it unbearable to breathe. The water was brought to us by water trucks, which at times arrived at night. The news of their arrival would spread, bringing such excitement that it exceeded that of Eid (a holy festival). We would each run to fill our containers, all standing in lines for our turn. Ordinarily, the older ladies were excused from that task, but I was still in good enough health that I wanted to share the responsibility with our dear younger ladies, despite the long distance between our ward and the main gate of the prison where the water truck would be. The water would come out through a wide hosepipe that sometimes sprayed water on us while we were filling our containers. As usual, the young ladies used to ease the difficulty of the situation with their humor.

*Bahá'í ladies in Abu Ghraib prison. Back row: Warqu Abdul-Razzaq, Fatima
Abdul-Razzaq, Kawakib Husain, Iqbal Al-Wakeel, Nida Sabour. Front row: Bahiyyeh
Mesjoon, Bedriyyeh Husain, Anisa Abdul-Razzaq, Hajir Al-Wakeel*

5 / Memories of the Abu Ghraib Prison

A Frightening Day

Days had gone by since our being placed in a private ward and breathing a sigh of relief from the nosiness of the other prisoners. But one day, the guards came to instruct us to leave the ward so our pictures could be taken! The order was suspicious and somewhat distressing because, in the past, we had seen pictures of criminals or people unfavorable to the government posted on TV by the authorities in order to publicize their crimes and their supposed disloyalty to the state, to stir the anger of the public. We used to watch those individuals (prior to our imprisonment), totally humiliated with shaved heads and mug shots from different angles (front and side). Then charges and threats of severe punishments were broadcast by the authorities.

We put on our clothes in a hurry, unable to utter a word about our fears and anxieties, not even to ask the reason for the photos. We had only been there for over a week and were still not comfortable enough to voice our fears to our captors.

The female guard seemed extremely stern. She made us stand very close to each other in front of the outside wall, and the photographer took multiple shots of us. Then we were returned to our ward. The door was shut, and we were shaking from fear, still wondering what the reason behind the event could be. We talked about what we had seen on TV and the many citizens who had been hunted like prey by the angry government!

However, a few minutes later, our conversation turned to hysterical laughter, which, as I mentioned earlier, was our coping mechanism. This, as explained by the science of psychology, is what humans revert to when under stress. We joked and wondered how we would look with shaved heads! Would we look better in a mug shot from the front or a side view? What would be the reactions of our families and friends to seeing our pictures with the men from the Al-Amn and hearing their accusatory remarks? And, most importantly, what could we anticipate the government to do to us after we had already been sentenced? We remained worried about the photos for days but had not dared to question anyone until the day we gathered enough courage and finally did ask the woman who was the guard. Her reply was that the photos were for the prison's official documents only and that the group picture would be cut to size into ten pieces (separating each prisoner); that way all would be proportionate!

May God forgive the prison's office if the proportionate size of the photos was worth the fear they put us through! May God also be our helper for all those ordeals we had to endure, and the effects they left behind. Those incidents might seem insignificant now, but for us then they were considerably strenuous on the nerves.

The "Tishreeb" Dish

The traditional Iraqi dish called "tishreeb," or by some called "thireed," is a simple meal consisting of slices of wheat flat bread over which people pour the broth of lamb cooked with onions and spices such as turmeric and dry lime. The meat is usually cooked slowly on low heat for a long time until extremely tender. The meat is then added on top of the soaked bread.

We had reached a point of total boredom and repulsion to the bad food offered to us once a day. One day, the news came that "bounties" of lamb meat were being distributed among the prisoners. Perhaps they were offerings from kind Samaritans or just extra inventory removed from the kitchen so the person in charge would look efficient at her job. We were told that each ward was responsible for cooking their own meal. We decided not to miss out on that opportunity, so we asked if the kind cook would please supply us with a cooking pot, an onion, and a few spices. The only remaining issue was the heat!

I took the meat and was able to cut it with the top of a can that I bent to one side for a safer grip. I tried to cut ten equal-sized pieces for the ten of us, as we had always done with our food. There was an empty room / cell designated for our guard at the end of the dark hallway of our ward. The cook suggested we ask the guard for permission to use the electric stove in that room.

We made our request. After a long hesitation, and after we gave her our promise to use the stove only for cooking, the guard agreed. I took the pot to her room, started the cooking, and continued to keep an eye on the stove until the delicious smell of the food started to fill our ward. For the first time in weeks, we were able to enjoy a very tasty, memorable meal!

Our First Visitation with Family

Upon our arrival at prison and on a visitation day, the ward's courtyard became filled with family members of some of the prisoners. Visitation with family members and friends was a right granted to every obedient prisoner who was compliant with the prison rules. It was also taken away from those who committed violations. For the offenders, the period of suspension was decided by the prison's office. We had heard that some of the political prisoners had been deprived of this privilege, and we were hoping that we would be included with those who could see their family.

I had a deep longing and yearning to see my children. My beloved son Abir had returned to finish college at the Sulaimaniyyeh University, and I very much wanted to hear his comforting news. I was also aching to see my little one Ruwa and listen to her fun, detailed stories, which she enjoyed telling after returning from school. She used to follow me around the house telling me those stories, and I always enjoyed very much listening to her. What distressed me the most was worrying about my beloved daughter, Alhan, who had fallen ill from a bad cold, with fever and complications from a cough. She had never become sick for years before that. With suppliant hands I begged God to be allowed visitation with my family so I could find some tranquility and comfort.

It was glad tidings indeed to hear from the prison office that the next visitation would include families of the Bahá'í women. Our happiness had no limits, and our yearning for that event increased every day. On the day before the scheduled visit, we began preparing ourselves to look our best, so we would not shock our families or draw their sympathy and sadness.

The pair of high-heeled shoes that I had been wearing day and night for two months in a row had started to show signs of wear and was covered with scratches, So I hurried to the stove that we used to heat our bath water, collected some soot, and rubbed it on my shoes with a piece of paper. They became black and shiny.

My skirt had also become wrinkled, so I placed it under my blanket, and lay over it at night to flatten the wrinkles. My two-piece suit also needed ironing, so I also used our aluminum teapot to heat and use as an iron. Necessity is the mother of invention!

On the day of visitation, we were allowed to have our families join us inside the ward and not have to mix with the rest of the crowding visitors. We woke up very early and gave our thanks and grateful prayers to God for bestowing on us the favor of seeing our families.

The time of our reunion finally arrived, and it has become eternally engraved on my memory. After a long wait of eagerly standing by the window of the ward, I saw the friends and family members pouring in and coming inside the courtyard adjacent to our ward. I saw my parents, my brothers, and my daughters Alhan and Ruwa.

We all ran to the gate of the ward, but it was still locked, although it was past 10:00 a.m. Our families had been waiting at the gate of the prison since 8:00 a.m. and had had to undergo intense searches that took a long time. I remember wishing very much that I could destroy that locked gate so I could embrace my daughters immediately.

The guard finally arrived and unlocked that gate.

I felt a spectacular array of emotions. I wanted to show through my embrace how my heart felt toward my daughters. I remember I picked up Alhan as if she were a little girl. I was so happy to see her and to know that she was feeling better. I embraced my little Ruwa so tightly, like a mother would do if someone were trying to snatch her baby away from her arms. My mother came to me with her usual calm demeanor, and I could see signs of pride visibly glowing from her beloved face. She embraced me and said, "This is the will of God and His Cause. We all must be patient in the path of The Beloved." My father looked as though God had granted him all his wishes—by seeing his children join the caravan of the oppressed and those who suffer for the sake of God. It was as if he could see in the faces of his three daughters the faces of the first believers. He used to recite their stories to us—the stories of those who bore such suffering and anguish to raise the banners of the Cause. My father began to comfort and encourage us by reciting prayers and quotes that drew our hearts to the Blessed Beauty, Bahá'u'lláh.

The visitation was like a rally that many family members and friends attended in solidarity with those of us in prison. We all shared the happiness of being able to see each other and the sadness regarding the fate we prisoners had received from our harsh and unjust sentences. Each one of us prisoners greeted tens of visitors. The Bahá'í community, despite the hard circumstances of that fearful atmosphere and always being closely watched, was still very eager to visit and offer their support. We were brought different kinds of food, fruits, and canned goods.

When visitation time ended and we had said our good-byes, the guards instructed us to go inside the ward, and they locked the door. All of the guards and prison employees had witnessed that very moving, large display of visitors and the emotions of all of us and our families.

We divided all the food equally among us—a system we had always used throughout our imprisonment. We were very conservative in the consumption of the food to make sure it lasted until the next visit. One small can of beef would be divided into ten pieces and would become our lunch. The same thing would be done with a box of cheese, and that would be our dinner. Even a small melon would be divided into ten pieces.

I remember once Dr. Iqbal's family brought her one fruit, a quince, the only fruit that their tree produced that year. We joked about how we could possibly divide such a small fruit equally among ten people, so I suggested that I make it into jam. I did so, and we were all able to share it. Our families had expected to see us dressed in the depressing-looking prison uniforms, just as they had seen on the male Bahá'í prisoners the previous week. The men had been dressed in those raggedy old uniforms, and some of the uniforms had been several sizes too large. The men had had to tie ropes around their waists to keep their pants from falling down. Some had even had pants cut at the legs. It had been extremely painful for the relatives to see the men in that dreadful state. But to their surprise, we were still dressed in our nice clothes, for the prison had not yet assigned prison outfits for us.

The fact that we had our own clothes on kept everyone's spirits up. The visitation time lasted for two hours, which was spent in the greeting of everyone and the "how are yous" and did not leave me enough time to ask my daughters detailed questions about their lives. It was the first time they had been left to live on their own after receiving such good care from their parents in every aspect of their lives. Each of my daughters assured me that she was OK and that there was no need to worry about them. I felt that my daughter Alhan—despite her young age—had assumed my role in taking care of her sister Ruwa, and knowing this brought me great comfort. I was also consoled to know that Abir had returned to his college in Sulaimaniyyeh. I was waiting for the school year to end so he would come back and care for his sisters as

much as he could, just as we had discussed in our last good-bye in the basement of the Revolutionary Court on the day of sentencing.

There was plenty of food on the day of visitation, so we were told to give a
share to the guards, as the prison's regulations demanded. We did so, and we
also gave a share to other prisoners, since we did not have the means to store it
all. We asked our families to bring us some Styrofoam boxes to use as refrig-
erators; this is what the other prisoners did. We also asked for toothbrushes,
and a pillow and pillowcase for each of us.

During the following two weeks, we continued to exchange news and stories each one of us had heard during our family's visit, and we felt a thread
of hope connecting our isolated world with that of the outside, as if we lived
on a small planet, dissimilar and lagging behind the rest of the universe.
We learned that every insignificant piece of news became magnified until it
became the talk of the whole prison. Similarly, every disagreement between
the prisoners turned into a fight with fists, tools, and curses that ended up
with prisoners facing punishment and isolation.

The Importance of Visits

In the first few months of imprisonment, we had hopes of receiving an
acquittal or a suspension of our sentences, as had happened to some of the
political prisoners and prisoners of conscience. But as the time went by,
despair threatened to enter our hearts. Nevertheless, we continued to be
supportive of one another, so our daily matters would go smoothly, and we
always stayed in compliance with the prison's rules.

We counted the days until the next visit, as though it were a festival—for
it was our only contact with the outside world. When a prisoner is made captive by another human being who does not understand her circumstances,
the prisoner will feel oppressed and suppressed. And perhaps prison is the
harshest punishment invented by man for his fellow man. But despite it
all, we resisted those feelings of despair and pushed them aside by saying
prayers and using humor whenever the opportunity arose. For over six years

of anguish and suffering, this is what we continued to do. The faces of the prison employees were full of astonishment as they watched our cheerfulness and contentment. It was hard for them to understand the fact that we were in prison because of a noble and sacred belief, which was the reason behind our acceptance of the imprisonment and the shackles. When they asked how we were doing, my answer would be, "We are thankful to God under all conditions and are awaiting His mercy, for we are innocent and have not violated any law. Therefore, we hope to be released."

On the visitation days, we would wake up at dawn, start our day with prayers, and prepare a light meal to be shared with our loved ones. In the early months, we met in our ward's open courtyard and sat on the concrete seats, where we spread out our blankets. We sat near a pool of water and a few trees where we could sit with our visitors.

At our second visit, we gathered near the ward's fenced courtyard and saw our families carrying bedding that they had brought for us. This caused us extreme happiness, especially for me, since I had started to have back problems. But time passed, and we were will still awaiting their entrance.

Suddenly the supervisor came in very angrily and asked us all to go to the office! As is to be expected under such circumstances, we feared the unknown! When we appeared before the prison's administrator, we found her annoyed as well. She said if it were not for the trust she had in us and her sympathy, we would have been at the mercy of the Al-Amn agents by then. When we asked the reason, she told us that one of the young ladies among our visiting family members had in her possession a poem glorifying the Bahá'í Faith and showing pride in what the Bahá'í prisoners were enduring for their faith.

Gloom overtook us at first, and each one of us began to apologize on behalf of that young lady. We explained that we had nothing to do with what apparently was a young person's adolescent and passionate zeal, and we promised the authorities that it would not happen again. The administrator answered that if it were not for the fact that we were a trusted, law-abiding, and educated group of women, we would have faced a penalty of no visitations, or even a worse punishment. Joy turned to fear and melancholy as we were handed the poem to discard.

Our visit with our families became shortened by that event. Instead of thanking and embracing the beloved young lady who brought us the poem, we had to let her know that she almost caused us severe punishments. Forgive me, my beloved lady, I wish I adored the blessed Faith to the extent that you did. I so wanted to take you in my arms, kiss your innocent young face and your hand—the hand that wrote the lines of glorification and praise to this noble and lofty Faith. Forgive me, my dear one, for the circumstances were much harder than the incident. After the visit, each one of us took her bedding, and we were happy to have clean covers and comfortable mattress pads. We felt the warmth of our homes and were comforted by the smell of our beloved families. The prison's orders were to keep the black blankets of the prison on our beds all day, but at night we would hurriedly and happily remove them.

There were times during our visitation days when the wait to see our families would be very long, and we would have to be patient until all our dear family members were inspected. The number of inmates was three to four hundred (sometimes more and other times less). The inspection process included searching the belongings, the clothes, and even the underclothes of each visitor. Our families also had to go through such inspections whenever they visited the men's prison.

When we were eventually allowed to visit the men, we had to be subjected to these inspections as well. The inspections were carried out to look for drugs, propaganda against the government, sharp objects, and personal letters, all of which were prohibited. Since a prisoner is the government's trust handed to the prison, it is the prison's responsibility to ensure his / her safety from harm. Therefore, the inspection is for the protection of the prisoners, especially since a prison is considered by some to be a place of corruption for a woman and a source of shame. There are families that feel disgraced that their daughter is a prisoner and might want to harm her to rid themselves of that shame, even if they are fully aware of her innocence. Other families might try to sneak clothes in so that a prisoner could disguise herself as a man and find her way out of the prison with the departing visitors. Or a male prisoner might try to disguise himself as a woman, especially since some women wore a hijab that fully covered their faces and body.

When security became tougher and personal identifications were requested and stored by the prison, some of our friends became afraid of being targeted by the Al-Amn, so they stopped visiting. Therefore, our visitors became limited to family members only. Our visits were intimate and warm, as all of us felt like members of one family. We were thankful to God for showing us mercy during these times. Not only were we allowed to wear regular clothes instead of prison uniforms, we could use metal storage boxes to store our belongings, which was great for a place infested with mice and insects.

My feelings during these visits were a combination of happiness at seeing my loved ones and exhaustion. I had to be social and polite with my parents, brothers, and friends, and as a result, I had less time to be with my children and to inquire about their life and well-being. Also, my children had to divide their visiting time between seeing me and seeing their father in the men's prison. The entire situation left me weary, especially since I had so many questions for my children but not enough time to have them answered.

Each of us tried to comfort and encourage the others to remember God's bounty and the honor He bestowed upon us with this imprisonment, and to never give up hope. We said our good-byes with the hope of seeing each other at the next visit. After everyone had left, we all felt the need to rest. We would gather and spread newspapers on the floor so we could equally divide and share what had been brought to us by the families. One time, we deboned a chicken that one of our families had brought us and, as usual, cut it into ten equal shares.

At the end of June, we were allowed to buy blocks of ice, as was done with the other wards. Each time, we would wrap the ice block with cloth and put it in the Styrofoam box where we stored some plastic bottles of water or leftover fruit. As time went by, each of us was allowed to have her own Styrofoam box. We were also allowed to have soda, which we bought from the prison store.

Our Independence in Cooking

After suffering long months of awful meals, we sent a request to the office for permission to receive our share of the "prison's bounty," as it was called, and cook it ourselves, just as some other wards were allowed to do. Each ward had its own kitchen with a cook (one of the prisoners). What I mean by a "kitchen" is a room with a kerosene cooking stove on the floor, two pots, and a frying pan. We explained that our request would save the prison the hassle of transporting the meals from a long distance.

The office accepted our request, and we were allowed to have a small kerosene-operated stove, which we asked our families to buy for us. Two weeks later, the family of Mr. Badi Ghulam Husain donated a kerosene stove, but the prison's office rejected it because it was larger than what was allowed! We waited a few more weeks until we were able to get a smaller one. We all shared the expense of buying the fuel, which we stored in the bathing area of the prison. That area also became our dishwashing area. The only problem left was how to acquire a knife. Up until that time, we had been using the cover of a cheese tin as a knife. We asked Um Musa (as you recall, "Um" means "mother of," and Um Musa was one of our jailers who was very kind) to buy us a small folding knife, but she could not find the smallest size, and the prison's office refused to allow a knife of any other size.

I had volunteered to be the designated cook, and I had the greatest difficulty cutting the meat and the vegetables with the cover of a tin can, especially when I made kebab. Every so often, I had to rest my arm several times before continuing with the cutting. Making "dolma"—stuffed grape leaves and other vegetables—took a very long time, as I had to clean the rice and chop the meat for the stuffing.

After a long search, Um Musa finally found us the smallest folded knife in the market, which the prison's office finally agreed to allow us to use. We had to guard the knife so no one would steal it. It was a big responsibility to have, and we would be greatly penalized if it were lost. Later on, when we had to mix with other prisoners, we had to hide it in a place where no one would know about it. If we forgot at times where it was, we would be in a great state of anxiety until someone remembered. Food required a very long time to cook on that small stove, but we were very thankful to have meals that were similar in taste to what we had eaten at home. For example, we were now able to eat our spinach free from all the sticks and grass that had been inside it before. Our younger ladies became encouraged to cook, and so did the other ladies. Each would take a turn in cooking, and a schedule was made. The younger ladies became quite skilled and creative in making all sorts of dishes and salads, all from the "bounties" that were distributed by the prison. Sometimes we would ask Um Musa or Um Khalil (another very kind jailer) to please buy us a couple of tomatoes and other salad vegetables when they did their personal shopping.

The Prison's Storage

There was a locked door in our ward, and small mice would come in from under it. When we asked the guard about it, she said it was an abandoned storage room. We asked if it could be opened so we could clean the area. After long negotiations with the office, the guard came with the key. We gathered to witness an unpleasant surprise, for it was filled with dust, trash, a large amount of broken glass, and old dirty prison uniforms from previous inmates. The shelves were covered with dust and broken tools. The space was utterly disgusting. The mice had reproduced and multiplied, which made my body shiver. Their newborns were red in color, and there were a lot of them.

While the others backed away from that filth with disgust, I was determined to put my efforts into cleaning that storage area. At the time, I was healthy enough to do the job, so I put the baby mice on an old newspaper using a wooden stick. I took them to the courtyard as far as I could from our ward and left them to face their fate. I proceeded to clean the space of all its contents, and I would go back and forth to the common dump in the courtyard to deposit all the trash there. Then I cleaned the shelves with soap and water.

It was a massive effort, and only God knew its extent. We left the shelves to dry, then lined them with pages from old magazines and stacked all the cans and goods our families had brought to us during our visits. When the guard came the next morning to do her inspection, she was greatly surprised to see what had happened. She hurried to bring her colleagues to take a look at the Bahá'ís' storage and said, "This is the finest storage room anyone could wish to have!" And this is how it became the talk of the entire prison.

The Prison's Official Uniform

In the first month, we wanted to receive our prison uniform so we could wash our clothes, but as I mentioned, one was not provided. Instead, pieces of fabric—a black and white plaid—were distributed to each one of us so we could make our own uniform. At that time, uniforms looked like a long, wide gown, similar to a nightgown. We decided to make our uniforms in a different, more modern style, especially since most of us were good at sewing and knitting. Kawakib, for example, was very skilled in making her own and her family's clothes. I also used to make my own dresses and others for my daughters. Nida also was skilled at sewing, and so were my sisters Fatima and Warqa. The other ladies—Bedriyyeh and Hajir and Bahiyyeh—all knew how to sew.

We started the sewing process and designed very dignified outfits. (I still have a picture of us wearing them.) The younger Bahá'í ladies wanted to use sewing patterns, as they had been accustomed to do in the past. However, we were not allowed to go to the sewing room that many other prisoners were permitted to use (some prisoners even learned sewing as a profession so they could use it after being released from prison).

At the next visit, my great aunt Khairiyyeh visited us and volunteered to donate a very old, hand-operated sewing machine—a Singer brand, perhaps one of the first models of its kind. We were extremely happy to hear the news and hurried to request permission from the office. We were very pleased to receive the approval right away. For the prison office, it was a good solution that allowed us to make the uniforms without intermingling with the rest of the prisoners, which we were not allowed to do.

The sewing machine arrived at the next visit with lots of spools of threads and the Burda magazine (a European magazine for fashion and sewing). It was warmly welcomed as a very precious gift, despite its old age. (I remembered it from my childhood when this kind and faithful aunt lived with us.) Each of us chose a style suitable for herself, and we took turns using the sewing machine. When the uniforms were finished, we wore them and received the admiration of all the prisoners. We were the first to wear beautiful and fashionable uniforms that the rest of the prisoners began to imitate. I still have my uniform in my closet. Fabric used to be distributed to us every winter and every summer for making new uniforms. I asked my daughter Ruwa to ensure that my uniform, which I cherish, be placed on me when I leave this world.

The prison's regulations required that we wear our uniforms from morning until the late afternoon, when work ended for the staff. After that time, we were free to wear what we wished. Thankfully, we were not forced to wear a headscarf, as was expected in the old days, or in the prisons of Egypt and Iran.

The Holy Day of the Martyrdom of the Báb

It was a blazing hot day when this revered Bahá'í holy day arrived. We had decided to fast during that day. At the time, our main meal was the prison's "bounty," which was given to us at lunch time. We decided to save it for dinner. We started the day with dawn prayers, then had a light meal and missed having tea with it. At the commemoration hour, which is noon time, with absolute reverence we faced the Al-Qibla (a point toward which Bahá'ís turn to pray in 'Akká, Israel). With bitter tears, we read our prayer for the bloodshed of his holiness the Báb, as well as for the injustice we were suffering.

I remember the unbearable thirst I was experiencing in that intolerable heat. Before being put in prison, I used to consume a lot of liquid. In the hours prior to the time we broke the fast that day, I could not move at all. When sunset arrived, we gathered for prayers, this time with very different emotions than we had experienced on similar occasions in the past. It was as if I were sharing a minute portion of the suffering His Holiness the Báb had experienced, since we were at the mercy of those who persecuted the Cause of God and its followers—all because of prejudice and nothing else.

Our fasting that day was memorable. It lifted our spirits like a charge of spiritual energy and faith supplying us with more steadfastness, dedication, and submissiveness to the will of God.

Cleaning the Ward and the Courtyard

The prisoners held the responsibility of cleaning their wards, including the hallways, and each took turns doing the job. Some were assigned to clean the large courtyard area that surrounded the wards. After each of the visits with our families, we were asked to clean the area where we had met with them that day. We would also help other prisoners with the washing and sweeping, which was done with a small hand sweeper made of woven palm leaves. This task required a lot of bending, and it dispersed plenty of suffocating dust, especially since some of the visitors came from farms and villages with muddy shoes and left behind leftovers and garbage.

After sweeping and collecting the trash, we would carry water in buckets and wash the ground and the concrete seats very well. I was always sad to see our young ladies doing such hard labor, especially since the yard was so large, and bringing water required such hard effort—all under the supervision of the guards yelling their orders. One time, when I saw Dr. Iqbal looking very exhausted, I deliberately called her name with a loud voice so the guards would hear: "Doctor Iqbal, Doctor Iqbal, do you need to rest a bit?" I don't know why it was so hard to be under the watching eyes of the guards while we were working. It was as if we were watching a film about prisoners being forced to do hard labor with guards watching them. I said, "Dr. Iqbal, let me finish what you're doing because you are very tired." I then looked at the other young ladies who were showing utter exhaustion and said, "You were never accustomed to such hardships in your homes."

The guards then pulled away and left us to do the work in peace. As for the long hallway dividing the wards, we were allowed to pay one of the prisoners to clean it. She was a middle-aged Iranian woman who spoke a mix of Arabic and Persian or sometimes got creative in combining one language with the other in a very humorous manner never heard before. That kind lady's name was Nena Jan. We all liked and joked with her, and we always listened to her simple stories that came from a well-meaning heart. She was as simple and good-hearted as a young child.

Surprisingly, she had been accused of being a drug dealer. She had lived in the city of Karbala and had guided Muslim visitors to the holy shrines. She swore she did not have more than a small amount of drugs in her possession when she was arrested, but someone had taken advantage of her simplicity and diverted the police's attention to her instead of himself. When she was asked at court about the amount of drugs she had and if it was a kilo, she did not understand the question and replied "yes." Therefore, she was sentenced to seven years in prison and then to be deported back to Iran. Being deported was Nena Jan's greatest concern because she feared going back to Iran; she wished to stay in Karbala.

There was a poor man who used to visit Nena Jan from Karbala and would bring her some fruits. We asked her who he was and she said "sedeeqish," a mixed word of Persian and Arabic meaning "my friend," which sounded funny. This is the answer she gave the office as well. We laughed because such relationships are neither common nor accepted in her culture, but despite this, Nena Jan did not care!

Nena Jan remained loyal to us all the years we were together, and she always prayed sincerely for us to be released. There were many funny incidents with her strange imagination, such as when a helicopter came close to the prison's courtyard and caused a cloud of dust and loud noise. Nena Jan came running to us, saying, "They've come to rescue us!" She then ran outside calling, "Come in, come in, all is clear!" When the helicopter left, she became dismayed, cursing her bad luck. Whenever she heard a song on TV that had the word "prison," she thought it was a government code for a release soon to take place for the prisoners. Therefore, she would happily run like a child. She amused us with her innocence, and we loved her good heart.

Our ward soon became filled with new prisoners. Nena Jan used to obey the prison rules in a literal way and would run as fast as she could to join the morning count. One time, she was taking a bath when she heard the supervisor's call for the count; she ran outside naked to join the rest of the prisoners. The morning count was a very important daily event, and those who were tardy would receive a punishment, such as no visitation. Therefore, everyone had to respond quickly to the supervisor's call, as if they were in the army. Nena Jan hurried naked to join the count and caused a storm of laughter. Even when the supervisor asked her to go back and put her clothes on, Nena Jan refused to do so until she heard her name being called in the count!

We took turns cleaning our ward and cells, and we individually washed our clothes. At first, we hung them to dry using old hosiery, tied together to the fence around our ward's courtyard, for a clothesline. The clothes had to be removed before the start of the day. After a while, our families provided us with a rope for the clothesline.

Meeting with the Head Administrator of all Prisons

Sometime during the first few weeks, we were visited by the chief administrator of prisons, who checked how we were doing. We all stood in the long hallway to meet him. With a disappointed tone, he started by saying, "We thought that Bahá'ís believed in Islam and were, in fact, a sect of Islam and were all Arabs. It turned out that you are all Ajam." The word *Ajam* means *Iranians*, and at that time, relationships between Iraq and Iran were very hostile.

We replied by saying, "We are all Iraqis." Among us were those who belonged to known Arabic tribes, so each of these ladies gave their names, and added that we believe in Islam as a divine religion and hold a great reverence to the holy Qur'án and all religions.

He replied: "You believe in a woman called Qoot Al Quloob" (who was a Lebanese entertainer, a singer).

We smiled and said, "You mean Qurratu'l-'Ayn" (which means "the solace of the eye," a title of Ṭáhirih, an early believer, a prominent figure, a poet, a theologian of religion, and an example of women's strength and leadership in Persia in her time who was eventually executed for her faith). We explained all of this and how Ṭáhirih therefore deserved all our respect.

The head official then ended his visit without asking us how we were doing or if we had any needs.

Another Visit

We also had a visit from the administrator of our former Al-Zafaraniyyeh detention center, where we had spent two months before sentencing. His name was Mr. Jum'a. Truth be told, we were treated fairly and kindly by that administrator. He had allowed us to use some blankets and bedding to sleep on, and he would also allow us to receive cooked meals for lunch from our families instead of the degraded, low-quality jail food. One time, as I mentioned previously, he also gave me permission to see a specialist when I was ill, and he sent me with a guard in a taxi (that I paid for). He told me that he allowed it out of trust and faith in me. I will always remember his kind act and pray that he is rewarded by God.

Our respected visitor Mr. Jum'a expressed his regrets for the sentence we had received, and he asked why we had not submitted a plea for clemency or leniency and mercy to the government. I replied that the chief administrator of prisons had informed us that the court's decision was final. Mr. Jum'a became quiet and did not go any further.

We had known that the only way out of our captivity was to recant our faith, and that was by all means an impossibility. I had heard from my late brother—God rest his soul—that a friend informed him that President Ahmed Hassan Al-Bekr had asked: "Why will the Bahá'ís not recant their belief and ask for a plea to be released? Do they consider themselves better than the many dignitaries who pleaded for clemency and whose pleas we took into consideration?"

I do not believe the president or the others could imagine the magnitude of how difficult such a choice is for those who strongly love and cherish their belief.

The Chicken Cage

I would be exaggerating if I said we were in perfect harmony the whole period of our imprisonment and that the bonds between us were ideal. The prison's conditions, our diverse upbringing, and our questioning of why we were there—what crime we had committed, and when we could be released—were all contributing factors that, at times, could threaten to lead us toward disharmony.

Among the ladies, I was probably the most eager to go home to my family and resume my responsibilities toward them, and I felt that I still needed to contribute more to their safety and well-being. Behind bars, the atmosphere was very disheartening. We tried to overcome our impatience and despair by deepening our faith, praying, and talking ourselves into being more patient and steadfast. At times, we had differences of opinion that caused some uneasiness. Matters that otherwise would be of little significance outside the prison became magnified because each one of us had a need for reassurance and care from the others! For example, simple conflicts sometimes flared up regarding eating customs and the kinds of food we would eat, as well as sleeping habits and bedtimes. These disagreements usually involved matters that each one of us was accustomed to at our homes. We had to accept and compromise on the habits and practices that had brought us comfort before we entered the prison.

For example, when we were at home, we had been able change into comfortable clothes whenever needed. But this was not allowed in prison, and we had to keep wearing our prison uniform until the late afternoon and bear it under hot weather, just in case we were inspected by the supervisors. At home, we could rest our backs by sitting in a chair, lifting up our feet, having a cup of tea, and enjoying simple little comforts that we were deprived of in prison. We would picture those little comforts as if they were high hopes that we longed to have again!

How numerous the times that we had to drink—either from the faucet or from a plastic container sitting on the hot cement floor—warm water that tasted terrible. The prison office would distribute ice in June, yet the hot weather always started two months before then. When we were allowed to have a Styrofoam cooler, I saved some water early in the morning while the water in the faucet was cool, and I conserved my intake until the evening.

We also had to sleep at specific times, and sometimes we were not tired. At other times, we would be able to finally get to sleep, but then we would be required to wake up early, even if we had not gotten enough sleep. And, of course, there was the disagreeable food we had to eat when we were not able to cook our own.

These and many other issues contributed to clouding our moods. However, we made an effort to act lovingly toward each other, and we tried to live as if we were all sisters. Perhaps in a household, sisters might have disagreements that would linger for a while, but in prison, we had to immediately overcome any differences no matter what, and we had to train ourselves to adapt to the variations in our customs and characters. We put a lot of effort into achieving harmony and accord, and if we were faced with pressure from the prison officials, we gathered for prayers to recharge our calmness and patience and receive God's tender loving care. This is how our good conduct with one another became distinguished among those in the prison.

One time, during a difficult situation, I recalled a story from my child-hood. At the entrance of the garden of our old house by the Tigris River, there was a room that had a large chicken cage where I enjoyed spending time and watching chickens of different types and colors. I noticed that when we let them out sometimes, they would run with liveliness and joy, picking insects in the grass. But when we called them in, the chickens tried to escape, which forced us to gather them up and put them back into the cage.

After they were inside the cage, all the chickens would turn quiet and gloomy, and then they would start pecking each other. At times, fights would start over one grain of seed. At other times, one of them would step on another that was trying to sleep, or a fight would start for no reason except the awful sense of captivity.

I thought of that chicken cage every time we felt the agony of captivity, and I wished that we were together in more pleasant circumstances, such as a vacation or a celebration—but it was similar to a chicken cage. Each one of the older ladies had worked tirelessly her entire life, cared for her family, and was advanced in age and in need of medical care. The younger ladies were missing their families and their love. Therefore, we older ladies had to offer them some of the love they yearned for.

One day, dear Kawakib came to me, and she was very upset. Kawakib was an excellent college student who had embraced the Bahá'í Faith in difficult circumstances shortly before being imprisoned while the Bahá'ís were under surveillance by the Al-Amn. She said, "Aunt Anisa, I want to confide to you something personal. When I embraced the Faith, I had this vision of an ideal and perfect society, yet I see us far from that model."

I understood from what she said that she had experienced some hard feelings, perhaps because of something trivial, which because of the prison circumstances became magnified and important. I said to her, "My beloved daughter, it must have been the lofty principles of the Faith that attracted you to it and made you hold on to them and bear the shackles of imprison-ment, even though it affected your life and future."

She replied, "Yes."

I continued, "My dear one, we are only human and trying our best to avoid disagreements and error so we can live as one family while defying these difficult circumstances. I wish you had come to this Faith in better circumstances, when we were under the shadow of religious freedom, practicing our beliefs, and praying in our Bahá'í center. If you had come then, you would not have witnessed the agony and repression on our faces, but this is that 'chicken's cage.'"

I then told her the chicken cage story. We laughed and embraced each other, and she returned to her old happy and vibrant self. Years later, after our release, I had the pleasure of attending Kawakib's wedding to a fine young man. Many Bahá'í friends were present at that wonderful celebration. God bless you and thank you, dearest Kawakib, for refreshing our soul with your beautiful and warm voice as you chanted God's prayers and sang beautiful songs in that chicken's cage that was called Abu Ghraib.

Bahá'í prisoners at Abu Ghraib

The Lady Who Had Tuberculosis (TB)

Two to three weeks after we were put in a ward of our own, the jailer brought in an elderly woman with a frightening cough. Nida and Kawakib were ordered to move to Fakhriyyeh and Bahiyyeh's cell, which became very crowded with four beds, but it was an arrangement all of them had to accept.

The newcomer had been accused of dealing drugs, as had her husband who was imprisoned in the men's prison, where she later could visit him on visitation days. We had heard stories about addicts sentenced to prison and how agitated and hysterical they would become during their first days of imprisonment. They would refuse food and display other sad reactions caused by their withdrawal. This woman tried carrying opium hidden in the hem of her long dress during one of her visits to see her husband, but the inspectors were very skilled at figuring out such tricks of smuggling, and one of them became suspicious of this prisoner and decided to do a thorough search. The search enabled the inspector to find the hidden opium tablets in the hem of this woman's dress.

The wife was charged and sentenced to hard labor, but when the other inmates did not tolerate her, she was transferred to our ward as if it were a situation we were obligated to deal with. At first, we were displeased, but we were unable to utter a word about it, for we had no choice but to accept it. We were unaware of her health condition at the time. Her presence among us was undesirable, for we were accustomed to talking to each other and reciting our prayers as one family. But now we had to remember there was a stranger among us.

The new inmate had a horrifying cough. When she calmed down a bit, we came to greet her from outside the room, but she resumed her coughing. At first, we assumed she had a cold or the flu. The room was dark, and she refused to turn the light on. I came close to her room at night and saw her expectorate mucus on the floor. That situation lasted for a whole week while she was with us, and still no one told us anything about her condition.

I consulted with dear Dr. Iqbal and told her about my concern and suspicion about it being tuberculosis, and she said, "It is possible. She is an old lady who is on drugs, and perhaps the drugs harmed her lungs."

The phlegm on the floor was terrifying me, for I knew the seriousness of tuberculosis. As the waste dries, the bacteria are carried in the air to other areas. I feared for the innocent young ladies, since they were more vulnerable that we older ladies, and they had their whole lives ahead of them.

The second week went by, and I continued to be anxious, so I decided to approach the supervisor with my concerns. It turned out that my suspicion was accurate. That prisoner had tuberculosis! I almost lost my mind. I asked to see the chief administrator and was given permission. I asked her politely to transfer that sick lady from our ward because it was not an "isolation ward" at a hospital. That is exactly how I said it. I added that we, the older ladies, were not fearful for ourselves but rather for the young ladies among us.

Thank God the meeting was a success, and the sick lady was moved to another ward across from us, the prostitution ward. After the lady was moved, a prisoner came with a bucket of disinfectant and cleaned the floor, and only then could my mind rest. Thank God we were safe from a deadly microbe and could go on living our normal lives again. It was peculiar to sentence such ill people to spend their life behind bars. Even if such a person were forced to seek treatment for a while, he or she would go back to finishing their sentence in prison.

The prisoner with tuberculosis remained in the prostitution ward. We heard that for drugs she substituted chewing on tobacco leaves that she mixed with Noura (Noura "calcium hydroxide" is a building material used in making mortar), and her health continued to worsen.

The Kurdish Prisoner

After that sick inmate left, we imagined being by ourselves again in that ward, especially since the other prisoners were instructed not to mingle with us. But our assumption was wrong. A few days later, the supervisor and two jailers came in with a slim young woman in her twenties. She was pale, fair-haired, and pleasant-looking, her facial expression showed a mixture of courage and defiance. She was shoved into a room that we had used as our eating area during the first days of our imprisonment.

We Bahá'í ladies were ordered to gather, and we were told that the newcomer was a Kurdish rebel who had been sentenced to death and that we were not to come close to, talk to, or make any contact with her. The gate was locked, and the guards left. It was our first time hearing the term *death sentence*, which left a horrible impression on us. Because of the strict orders from the prison, we whispered to each other and said we must not to come close to this miserable soul, despite the fact that no one was overseeing us in that ward. We did not want any association with her, and we greatly feared the Al-Amn men, especially since the Kurdish conflict was a very sensitive matter. The Kurds were in a state of war with the government.

The young woman's cell, however, was on the way to the outside and across from the washroom; therefore, it was impossible to avoid seeing her in the morning and several other times during the day. Even if we avoided a conversation, we had to smile at least and say, "God is the All-Merciful." This expression is commonly used in Iraqi culture to comfort someone, and it could not be misinterpreted by anyone. We were concerned at times that perhaps we were being spied on through hidden microphones, as we had been told by one of the inmates. If one of us loudly said something, we humorously came up with a code word (which was "hairpin") that meant, "Be careful, and stop talking."

The Kurdish prisoner was left with her agony and loneliness. She asked the jailer if she would bring her a copy of the holy Qur'án, from which she used to chant the verses of God every evening before going to bed. She would also always eat no more than only a small portion for her dinner.

She stayed in that condition for nearly two weeks—close to us day and night, like an alien bird in a segregated cage within a larger cage. We so wished that we could comfort her or offer her some of our food, but the orders from the prison authorities were greater than our wishes. We were told to be extra cautious because she and her fiancé had plotted to plant a bomb inside a movie theater.

One miserable morning, the executioner himself arrived in our ward, accompanied by the supervisor and two guards to take this young lady to her execution. She had a red shirt on, but I have forgotten the color of her skirt. Her door was unlocked, and she left her cell without any emotion, resistance, or feelings of a breakdown. She walked peacefully in front of everyone, and through the window we watched her walking with her head held high. The situation was horrifying to watch, as it was her eternal good-bye to this world while she was still a young lady in her twenties.

Shortly before noon, the supervisor came to tell us Bahá'í ladies about the execution of the prisoner and her fiancé. She said, as if she were telling us the story from a movie, that they were both killed at the same hour, in the same quad. The supervisor recounted the event without emotion, and I have no idea why she chose to tell us the details of that execution and all that had happened. We felt compelled to listen to her while she was condemning that young lady's courage for asking to kiss her fiancé moments before his execution! To her, that was considered a vulgarity beyond anything! She continued to condemn that prisoner for asking to kiss her fiancé instead of asking for God's forgiveness!

We were in a state of terror listening to her, but we had to stay silent. Her story about the execution became more horrific as she continued to say that after the hanging rope was pulled and the doctor came to verify her death, he found that the Kurdish woman still alive because of her low weight. Therefore, the order came to hang her again. When she reached this point of the story, my patience had run out, and I almost told her that in such a situation, the sentenced should have been left to her fate to continue her imprisonment. But I chose to be quiet, and the dreadfulness of the story continued to worsen. She continued to try to scare us by saying that the doctor had had to remove the executed girl's eyes for medical reasons! She went on and on repeating that they were terrorists who deserved to be executed. Please forgive me, dear reader, for the horrible details, but this was a small portion of the suffering we had to endure.

We lost our appetite that day, and we kept looking at that empty cell and the holy Qur'án still on the bed. We pictured her reading from it every night, and we pictured her thin body swinging from that rope, freed from the miseries of this world and aiming to reach God in His realm of mercy.

Sleeping in the Ward's Courtyard

In Iraq, the heat always starts to rise during the month of May. Therefore, many people hurry to sleep outdoors on top of their flat roofs to enjoy the coolness of the night.

In our prison during this time of year, the cement cells would start to heat up, and the walls would begin to radiate heat. We were given permission to use the ceiling fans, whose age exceeded ours. These fans were so ancient that they had started to moan like an old person, with protests when they were switched on and again when they were switched off. They burned our faces with hot air, but they also dried our sweaty skin somewhat and gave us a bit of relief. We noticed that some of the inmates in the wards facing ours were able to clean their area of the ward's courtyard and take their mattresses there to sleep at night. We wished to be able to do the same, since sleeping inside had become nearly impossible. We sent a request to the prison office, then sent another, until we were given a permission to sleep on the grounds of the ward's courtyard. We were very happy and hurried with cleaning the ground where we would sleep. Cleaning it, however, was extremely difficult to do because it was paved with small and uneven bricks that contained many gaps and holes filled with dirt, ants, and other insects.

But we were undeterred, as the prospect of sleeping outdoors, away from the intense heat indoors, motivated us to continue our cleaning efforts. We carried containers of water to wash and cool off the bricks that were raging with heat. We put our reliance in God, and each of us carried her mattress out at eight o'clock that evening and placed the prison's black blankets first under each mattress, to avoid getting the mattress dirty.

Everyone sat outside under the heavenly dome, and we enjoyed gazing at the stars and remembering the nights we spent on the roofs of our homes with our families. Our joy at being outdoors was somewhat ruined by worrying about scorpions and insects that might crawl over us while we were sleeping. I remember some of the Kurdish detainees hummed special conjurations and spells for deterring scorpion's bites, and this practice gave them a sense of comfort before sleeping. Also, the presence of snakes was common in prison because the sandy areas around the prison contained many snakes. I always shivered even when looking at pictures of snakes.

The long months of summer extended until mid-October, and the ground remained very hot. The probability of being bitten by insects was high. Therefore, we asked the prison if we could sleep on metal beds that would keep us off the ground, but our request was rejected, since no special favoritism was permitted.

Many similar requests followed to convince the office that it was in the best interests of the prison to care for all the inmates and to give a good impression to those visiting the facility. Besides, what would the harm be in allowing the prisoners to sleep on a metal bed?

Our request was finally approved, and we were allowed to use lightweight metal beds similar to those used by the military. The beds were to be folded and carried inside every morning, which we did. The following year, we were granted permission to keep the metal beds outside (inside our ward's fenced courtyard) during summer, where we slept peacefully without having to worry about insects. We were also able to buy mosquito nets suspended on sticks on all four sides. The young ladies among us enjoyed staying up late chatting inside the nets, as there were no supervisors watching.

Another New Prisoner in the Ward

Weeks after the Kurdish prisoner was executed, a new Kurdish prisoner was brought to our ward. She had been accused of circulating leaflets and propaganda to incite opposition against the government. The cell next to the one my sisters and I occupied was prepared for her. She was placed there, and the door was locked. The guards left without any further instructions for us not to talk to her.

We gathered around her cell to find out what was going on and to try to ease her anxiety. She did not speak much Arabic, but she tried her best to communicate with us. She asked for some cool water and a few more items. Our young ladies hurried in the most loving way to get her what she asked for, and we continued to ask her about her situation. (By that time, we had confirmed that no one was listening in on our conversations).

Her name was Zekiyyeh, and our girls gave her the nickname "Zegzoog." As the days went by, she started to trust us and showed us marks of torture on her body caused by beatings. Her feet and toenails were also black with bruises, and she still moaned occasionally from the pain. After a while, her toenails fell off, and new nails started to grow. Her body also had marks of cigarette burns. We were so thankful to God for sparing us such torture. Zekiyyeh grew to like and trust us, and she developed a friendship with our young ladies and exchanged jokes with them from behind the bars of her cell. Weeks later, she was allowed to leave her cell and attend literacy class. We continued our friendship with her until many of the Kurdish prisoners were granted release after the end of the Kurdish-Iraqi war.

Visiting the Men's Prison

We noticed that at times some of the prisoners—sometimes accompanied by their children—would get up early in the morning and prepare to leave the prison. We asked where they were going, and their reply was, "It is visitation day at the men's prison." Some had relatives who had also been imprisoned—

Siddiq Sulaiman and his brothers

for example, when a husband and wife had committed the same crime, such as theft, murder, or smuggling drugs and weapons.

We became hopeful of being granted permission for such visits, and we presented to the prison office a request—signed by my sisters Warqa, Fatima, and me—to visit our brother Munis, my husband Siddiq, and our uncle Kamil. Bahiyyeh Mesjoon presented a similar request to visit her cousins Ihsan and Nimat 'Abdu'l-Wahid.

Permission to participate in the next visit was granted, and we were over-joyed. We got ready on that day, wore our prison uniforms, and took with us some food and canned goods. Our dear Nida, who was visiting her father Nimat Sabour, was also with us. Accompanied by the jailer, we headed to the men's prison.

The different prisons were inside one large prison complex. We walked in the blazing sun for nearly half an hour until we reached the gate to the men's prison. We entered several branching hallways, where we were care-fully searched by the guards and then thoroughly inspected again by a special female supervisor. The search included the food we carried with us to make sure we had not brought any forbidden items with us.

We were taken first to the office of the prison administrator, who asked about the reason for our visit and about our relationship to every person we had asked to visit. After that, we were taken to the end of a hallway and given black blankets to spread on the floor to sit on. The men were called, and we were very eager to find out how they were doing.

After a very long wait, the men finally arrived, not knowing the reason for their being brought there. Uncle Kamil was anxious and waved to us from a distance, inquiring, "What happened?" I rushed to tell him that everything was fine and that we were just there to visit them. Everyone was able to relax, and we all began to enjoy our visit. We exchanged stories in quiet voices, since the guards were nearby.

After half an hour of conversation and the exchange of simple gifts and phrases of encouragement and reassurance, we said our good-byes and hoped to see each other in a following visit. We sent our greetings and regards to the other prisoners, as we had heard a lot about their suffering in the very crowded conditions.

We walked back again under the hot summer sun, with its blazing rays burning our heads and roasting our bodies, and we all felt tremendous thirst and hunger. I remember how the sun that day left burns on my skin that took a long time to heal.

As soon as we reached the women's prison, the searches and inspections started all over again. After that, we were warmly greeted by the other ladies, as if we had returned from a pilgrimage. They were eager to hear how our Bahá'í brothers were doing, and they asked about each one individually.

A New Prisoner on our Ward

It seemed as though God's will for us was to go through further smelting with new tests in order to prove our submission to Him, despite the daily tests we endured with patience and steadfastness.

Visiting family at the men's prison

A new elderly Kurdish woman, around eighty years of age, with a hunched back and facial marks suggesting a life of hard work in the countryside, arrived at our ward. As usual, she was brought by the jailers and the guard. The old lady was carrying the usual blankets, with a jug of water. She was shoved into her cell, and her door was locked with obscenities and curses. Conditions such as these always made us avoid asking any questions and proceed with caution instead. The officer started to talk about the crime and the charges of this newcomer with a condemnatory attitude of indisputable nationalism and said, "This old woman carried explosives to one of the military camps."

The Peshmerga—the military forces of the autonomous region of Iraqi Kurdistan, who were defiant toward the Iraqi government and hid in the mountains—had used this woman and enticed her with a small sum of money, possibly five dinars ($15), to carry for them a container of buttermilk to sell at the camp. Since that woman was very poor, ignorant, and naive about war and politics, she had agreed to accept the attractive offer (as we later understood from her using simple language and gestures).

As soon as her door was locked, the Kurdish woman began to mumble in her language and moan like a wounded animal, in a voice full of pain and longing to be freed. Her voice remains in my ears to this day. She was a villager accustomed to living in the open, to leaving her hut to farm and care for her animals, and now she found herself confined behind those bars.

We gathered around her to offer some comforting words, but she was unable to understand anything. She could only point to heaven, and groan continually like an angry lion. We offered her some food and water, but she refused them and continued to moan. The next day, our Kurdish friend Zekiyyeh (Zegzoog) took a chance with the supervisor and tried to gather some information about this new lady. Later on in the afternoon, she briefly told us that that poor lady had no clue about her crime, why she was in prison, where her family was, and when she would be able to return to her village!

We had to become accustomed to these kinds of events, and we feared that she would be executed. In the following days, her moaning would subside during the day but would continue loudly at night, which became a source of gloom and depression for us. Gradually, she started to become comfortable with us, as we told her in Kurdish, "Khuda Kareem" (God is merciful), which is a common phrase that is meant to comfort others.

One day, bad news arrived that her execution would take place the very next day. Our hearts were pulled from our chests in terror, and we did not know how to act toward that miserable soul. Fortunately, she was not informed, or else she would have been extremely agitated. As usual, we gathered for prayers, and perhaps God conferred upon her His mercy.

The next morning, we awoke at dawn for prayers and prepared a breakfast for her, while she was unaware of her fate. I remember making her two boiled eggs with a large piece of bread, which she very quickly consumed. The young ladies made her some tea to go with it. We did not know if we should cry or be sad for her because she was happy and eating with such an appetite after being informed she'd be taken to see her husband, who had come to visit her! She was like a lost child happily finding her father after a prolonged separation.

Finally, the decisive hour arrived, and the jailer, the guards, and the executioner—who looked like an ordinary man—had all arrived. In these situations, the news of someone's impending execution would spread throughout the prison, and everyone would come out of their wards to watch the final scene.

When the committee arrived, the old lady became extremely happy. She gathered all her humble belongings, fixed her attire and hair cover, and put a shawl on her shoulders. The poor soul walked with the hope of meeting her husband, not knowing that she was about to meet her Maker, the most merciful God. That is how that pitiful woman became a victim of her ignorance, and of those who had taken advantage of her for political initiatives—something she could never comprehend, since she had been living happy and content, having no other ambitions except a life of simplicity in her small hut.

As I have previously mentioned, when tough and fearful times intensified, and feelings of sadness overcame us, we tried to bring peacefulness and calmness back to our hearts and minds. This was a natural process to preserve the balance of our emotions. We reminded ourselves how that poor woman was preparing herself for a romantic reunion with her husband and was happy, but then we humorously blamed ourselves and said that perhaps we had fed her too much that morning. Our sad tears would then be accompanied by tears of laughter. I consider our laughter an expression of an intense emotional release, which happened every time we were faced with difficult circumstances that seemed to be beyond our capacity to bear.

A month after the execution of that pitiable woman, her husband arrived to visit her after a long journey from Kurdistan. He was carrying a little basket with a small melon and a few cucumbers inside. The journey of more than six hours had exhausted him. That poor man with the raggedy clothes had no knowledge of what had happened to his wife and why she was in prison in the first place. When he learned of her fate, he started to hit himself on the head and repeated in his Kurdish language, "Why? Why?" One prisoner (Zekiyyeh) who knew Kurdish explained to him what had happened, and he left the place crying in agony, leaving behind his basket and the food.

After this incident, we had to resume our usual life.

6 / Tears of Sorrow, Tears of Joy

The Flood of Kurdish Prisoners

When the prison office became reassured that combining the Bahá'í ladies with the other prisoners posed no threat and that Bahá'ís were neither promoting nor imposing their beliefs on others (as we had been accused of doing), our ward began to include a diverse group of other minorities, including Kurds. At the beginning, a large number of Kurdish prisoners were placed into an empty cell, then a second empty cell, then the isolation sector, which was adjacent to our area and only separated by a small hallway.

The newcomers were a mix of elderly and young women, all accused of cooperating with the Peshmerga—the military forces of the federal region of Iraqi Kurdistan—and the rebels. The allegations against them included concealment of weapons, conspiring with and covering up for the rebels, transferring ammunition hidden within merchandise carried by mules, and delivering messages and letters to other groups of rebels. Among the prisoners were also illegals who had come to visit the holy shrines without authorized documents. The ward became crowded with activity and loud noise and frequent visits from the jailers, who wanted to make certain we had no suspicious intermingling with the other inmates. It was nearly impossible not to intermingle, as we all lived in attached, open cells and interacted with

145

each other in a single environment. So we were free to roam throughout one area. The other prisoners continually needed items such as dishes and clothes, which we helped get them. Their families lived far away—north of Baghdad—some were six to eight hours away by car depending on which villages they came from.

Warm relationships began to develop between us and the Kurdish ladies, and we received much admiration and respect from them. They were sympathetic to seeing our young ladies there. Some who were fluent in Arabic told us about the humiliation and foul language they had received from the police during their interrogation. One woman confided to me that one of her interrogators had threated to rape her, and she fell on the ground kissing his feet, begging and beseeching him with his mother's and sisters' honor until he let her go after kicking her. We heard many such stories, and we thanked God for His tender mercy that we had received no such treatment.

Our relationship with the Kurdish prisoners remained a positive one. We did not wish to mention our belief to them, since we were prohibited from doing so and also were under close watch. Despite this, they came to realize that we were faithful to God, revered the Qur'án and the Prophet Muhammad (salutations be upon Him), and all the other Messengers of God, since They had all come for the betterment of humanity.

After the 1975 Algiers Agreement (an agreement between Iran and Iraq to settle their border disputes and conflicts), the conflict with the Kurds ended. The Vice President of Iraq at the time, Saddam Hussein, and the Shah of Iran agreed on the terms for the border between Iraq and Iran, such as in the area of Sutt Al-Arab, and the shah discontinued his help to the Kurds.

After this agreement was in place, the Iraqi army took full custody of northern Iraq, which was under the power of the Kurdish rebels. Although the Kurdish prisoners were extremely displeased by the shah's actions, they were still hopeful of being released from prison and returning to their homes. Their release eventually did take place for all of them except one lady—her name was Um-Nesreen—with whom we had built a good friendship. Eventually, after our transfer later on to Al-Rashaad prison, she did get released.

I still remember her beauty, her pleasant demeanor, and all her wonderful stories. When we asked her how she maintained the vibrancy of her beautiful golden and shiny long hair, she swore that she only washed it with Tide detergent! We laughed in disbelief, but she insisted that she would pour a bowl of diluted Tide on the head of each of her children, rinse it, and their bathing would be done! We continued to laugh in disbelief, but she continued to swear by her words. Please do not try this method at home!

Um-Nesreen was very fond of us. She swore she would tell everyone she met how she had never seen such honorable and sincere people as us. May God give you His blessings, O Um-Nesreen, for we have loved you very much.

The Prisoners in Confinement

After the release of the Kurdish prisoners, a large number of new prisoners began to pour in. Some were crowded in the attached quarantine area adjacent to our ward. As I described earlier, it was a long and narrow hallway with small cells for solitary confinement on each side. Because of the large numbers of prisoners, two or three people would occupy each cell and sleep on blankets. Among them was a young Iraqi lady belonging to the Syrian Baath party. She was in so much distress that she could not walk. After receiving love from us and encouragement to walk, she began to feel calm and comforted until she regained her emotional and physical health. She started sewing, a skill she was proficient at before entering prison. She asked us nicely if we could lend her our hand-operated sewing machine. At that time, our young ladies had become skillful in sewing—for a modest fee—dresses for the jailers and employees and uniforms for other prisoners.

The cells became crowded with other prisoners who were charged with various crimes—such as espionage, illegal residency by migrants from Al-

Ahwaz (southwest Iran), and many others. Among them was a beautiful young woman in her twenties with the Persian name Gul-Bahar. She had been accused of engaging in espionage, as well as running a house of prostitution. Her appearance showed poise, innocence, and politeness. She was shy and respectful while talking to us and sought to gain our friendship. But because of the serious accusations against her, we had to be extremely cautious and obedient to the prison's rules. At times, contact with her was unavoidable, such as responding to her greetings or answering a passing question about daily matters. Still, we always kept our association with her within boundaries that we did not cross.

A while later, a new young inmate was brought in without any accusations against her personally, but her father was a member of a resistance movement. He had escaped; therefore, his daughter was taken hostage so he would be forced to return. I so wish they had brought that wonderful girl to stay with us, instead of putting her in the crowded confinement area, accompanied by dangerous prisoners. That young lady with the good heart cried a lot in her first days and was consumed with sadness after being taken away from her family, home, school, and friends. In addition, she was worried about her father and his unknown fate. She became a prey to some of the untrustworthy prisoners, who approached her under false pretenses of befriending and comforting her.

One of those friendships was with Gul-Bahar. As a mother and a teacher, I have always been protective of my students, who were about the age of the young inmate. This young lady became a source of my constant worries, and I wished I could do something for her so that the prison would not become a new school for her to learn misconduct. Many young and naive inmates, who enter prisons with simple charges, would eventually be led to more serious misconduct upon association with corrupt inmates. Some would later on escape their family's wrath, and, in fear, hide in suspicious homes that to outward appearances provided shelter for them but then robbed them of their dignity. They remained under the control of abusers until the end of their lives and were continually bought and sold as a commodity, with no hope of escaping that life and seeking safety.

One day, during a visit to the men's prison, while waiting for our Bahá'í men to arrive, I was standing close to the prison's office building. The supervisor of the men's prison called for me through one of the guards. To reassure me, he pointed to me in a friendly way to enter the room and be seated. His look was free from any hostility or harshness, as others in his position would have had.

He asked me whom I had come to visit, and I answered, "My husband, Siddiq Abdul-Majid."

He replied, "I do understand your circumstances, and here we consider the Bahá'í men to be the symbol of obedience to the law and good conduct."

I replied, "Sir, the majority of us are well-educated, some with academic degrees and high qualifications."

He replied, "Yes, I am aware of that, and I am extremely pleased with their conduct. I hope that your sentencing is of a short duration so each one of you will soon return to your respective home."

I thanked him for his kindness and good wishes and in return wished him all the best in his role as the administrator of a prison that contained thousands of inmates. He then asked me about the young prisoner, the student about whom I have previously written. He was aware that she had been placed in a cell inside our ward. He said she was from his town and that he knew her story.

I replied that I was burning inside with pity and sorrow for her. He nodded his head in agreement, and I continued to say, "In the holy Qur'án, God said that every soul is accountable for its own action" (I am paraphrasing here. It means no one else should be accountable for another person's faults.)

He replied that it was unfortunate that this lady had received her father's punishment.

149

I said, "We would have taken her under our care, were it not for our difficult circumstances (not being allowed to mingle with the other prisoners), of which you are aware."

He nodded in agreement, and I left to join my colleagues in meeting our men.

The girl's condition had become an obsession of mine every time she showed signs of rebellion and carelessness that were due to feelings of being punished for no fault of her own, and also for missing the final exams of her last year of middle school!

My suspicions began to grow regarding Gul-Bahar. She seemed to have two sides—one was soft-spoken, polite, and shy, and the other was cunning and attempted to lure other girls to suspicious homes and prostitution.

One day, I decided to call the new, young inmate to our cell while my sisters were busy with the other young Bahá'ís. I spoke to her with a motherly voice and said, "Daughter, why don't you send a petition for clemency, through the prison's office, to the Women's Union? Perhaps they would offer you their humanitarian help."

The Women's Union was a political group and a division of the Baath party. They had a direct connection and influence with its leadership. If they found something suitable that would benefit the regime, they influenced the higher authorities to act, and they could convince party leaders to reconsider a prisoner's case.

She happily agreed.

I hurried the same day to write her a detailed petition that showed her disheartened emotional state due to separation from her family and being denied the opportunity of finishing her studies. Besides, her father's return was uncertain, and only God would know if and when it would ever happen. Of course, I composed the petition on her behalf, as if she were the one writing it. I added that at her critical age, and being in the greatest need of her mother and family, prison life was very unhealthy for a girl such as herself who knew nothing about the life of crime. I pleaded, on her behalf, to the Women's Union to put a great humanitarian effort into releasing her.

Only two weeks after writing the petition, and on a happy day I will never forget, a decree of pardon came for her. We congregated together to hug and congratulate her! Sounds of joy were all around, and I thanked the Lord for answering my prayers and rescuing her from the evils of that contaminated place. On the day of her release, I said a tearful good-bye to her as if she were a daughter of mine. God bless you, my dear, and may you enjoy your freedom and the love of your family.

I am also thankful to God that three years later, I was able to help another prisoner to gain her freedom. I wrote another petition that was sent through the prison office to the Women's Union. That poor woman was caring for her children after her husband's death, before she committed an illegal act out of total ignorance. She came to me one day crying bitterly and saying that her children were dispersed in several homes of their relatives and that she did not intentionally mean to do anything wrong to deserve her fate.

I wrote, on her behalf, a petition for clemency, which the prison allowed her to present in person, accompanied by a guard, to the Women's Union. When she returned, she told me that the Union was very sympathetic and that some of the members had even cried and had promised her a positive outcome.

Not long after that a pardon came, and she was able to return home to her children.

The Passing of Dr. Abbas

Not long after entering the prison, we lost a dear colleague, Dr. Abbas Ihsan, after he was infected with a lung disease. Shortly after he was moved from prison to an outside hospital, he passed away. We were extremely saddened by this news, especially since he was still in his fifties, with a delightful character, firm in his faith, and very knowledgeable in the field of geology, which he had taught in one of the universities in Baghdad.

The cause for his arrest was that he had purchased a small residence in the same alley where the blessed house of Bahá'u'lláh was located. In addition to the trial lawyers hired to defend the Bahá'í prisoners, another lawyer was hired to defend him and his brother Dr. Jameel. With great proficiency, the lawyer presented her defense by asking the court to take into consideration the honorable status Dr. Abbas held as a professor doing many services and valuable research in his field, and that he was greatly admired by his students and colleagues. She asked, "Isn't it the right of any Iraqi citizen to purchase a house with his personal money in any area in the country without it being a felony?"

He was the only one among the detainees to be given papers to make his confession, on which he freely wrote anything that came to his mind concerning the Bahá'í community in Iraq. After that, he received a life sentence, which left a wife and four children in a difficult situation.

We gathered on the day of his passing to read prayers. Sadness and quietness spread over the ward. The prison office had heard of the news and had sent us their condolences. That was how the suffering of the first of the Iraqi Bahá'í prisoners in our group came to an end. May God immerse his soul with His infinite mercy and raise his station. We had heard from our men that when Dr. Abbas was first detained, he did not have a pillow in his cell, so as his pillow he used an empty bird's nest that he had found.

Getting Permission to Walk Outside the Ward

Four long months had passed since the beginning of our incarceration, during which we were confined to our ward and could only walk along the narrow hallway that was in the center of it. On rare occasions, we were allowed to be outside, within the confines of our ward's fenced courtyard. It was a joy to see some of the inmates be able to walk outside our designated quarters, and we wished to obtain that same privilege one day.

Being able to go outside held a feeling of liberty, as if this outside area were not part of the prison. One day, the administrator of the women's prison paid us a visit—perhaps it was her second visit. We found the courage to ask if we could walk outside our ward. She granted us permission, and we were allowed to go out one hour every morning at ten, when the gate to the outside would open for us. We considered this time to be a very joyous event.

I remember the chief administrator saying, "Staying inside the dark ward is harmful to your eyes, and it is your right to be outside." She was right, as our eyesight was beginning to suffer because of the dimmed surroundings and our aging. She also offered any other kind of help we might need, so we thanked her sincerely. In truth, she had feelings of admiration toward us, but she had to do her job and follow the instructions that came from the central office of the Al-Amn, such as preventing us from any association with the other inmates and prohibiting certain foods, brought by our families during visits, from entering our ward. As instructed, she was always adamant that our visitors had to carry their identification, which we fully understood. She was doing her job in the best way she could.

When she left her job to take on another, we were very sad to see her go, for she had earned the respect of all the inmates due to her kind conduct toward everyone. I remember going to say good-bye to her on behalf of myself and the other Bahá'í ladies. I became emotional telling her how we would always remember her with fondness. She thanked me, shook my hand, and said that she, as well, would never forget the fine group of people the Bahá'í ladies were, and that she hoped that we would receive a pardon soon.

The day after that visit from the administrator, the guard came with her key exactly at ten in the morning. With a smile upon our faces and great anticipation, we were ready to leave our cage for a broader world where we could, if only for a short time, breathe the fragrance of freedom and feel equal to other inmates already enjoying free mobility outside their wards after business hours. That is how we were able to go out to the large outer courtyard and a wider pathway parallel to our ward. The walking distance was designated for us, and the time allotted was to be one hour. The walk left a positive mental and physical effect on us. The news among the inmates spread as fast as lightning, and many hurried to watch the Bahá'í prisoners walk in the courtyard, as if we were putting on a show!

Some Memories from the First Period of Imprisonment

After a while, biweekly visitations with our families and our men in the men's prison—which was about a half hour in walking distance—became permitted. We eagerly awaited these visits, put on our best appearance, and tried our best to conceal our troubles. I greeted my children with good composure and a smile on my face so they wouldn't notice the suffering caused by our separation. They, as well, greeted me with joyfulness and concealed the anguish of being away from their parents and their home—a home that had provided an embracing shelter for our tight family, bonded by love and obedience to God. Our home was, as much as possible, open to all our loved ones, such as family and friends. During our visits, we avoided any overly emotional dispays, although our feelings were clearly visible on our faces. In my children's looks, I could read lines of pride that God had honored them with their parents' imprisonment for His sake.

Our imprisonment was a heroic event for my beloved daughter Ruwa, who was a young girl of twelve. I remember once at the end of our visit, my little one fondly clung to me, just as she used to follow me all around our house from one room to another and tell me exciting stories about her school. My little one pleaded with me for her to stay for just one night, and suggested that one of my brothers could pick her up the next morning. She was persistent in her plea, as if she wanted to share my feelings of imprisonment.

I explained to her that what she asked was impossible and prohibited by the prison's rules because it would be a big responsibility. Upon her insistence, I headed toward the office; perhaps there was a way to grant her that request. I said, "I know that I am asking for something unreasonable, but I wanted to tell my daughter that I at least had tried for her sake."

The administrator's answer was, "Anisa, have you forgotten that this is a prison and not a hotel?"

I replied, "Yes, madam, but I wanted to tell my daughter that it was the office that refused that unreasonable request."

That is how I said a more passionate good-bye to my daughter, while seeing the disappointment printed on her beloved, innocent face.

I spent my night awake, picturing my daughters sitting beside me with joy, my beloved Alhan busy using her creativity to make a beautiful, miniature doll or skillfully painting a beautiful landscape with fine detail, while Ruwa was playing the organ with melodies that she had learned by heart. After this, my imagination took me north, where my beloved son Abir had gone back to finish his college education—for which I was thankful to God—after being absent for the long period of incarceration. The horror of the place, the dimness of the light that, with great difficulty, penetrated the cement wall around the window where I was standing, and a loud screech piercing the silence of night coming from the nearby ward of the prostitutes, followed by the usual foul language signaling the beginning of a fight, woke me from my imaginations.

These fights would often lead to inmates fiercely hitting each other with fists or slippers and pulling each other's hair, and they would not end until the tough guards intervened. Sometimes even these guards would curse in repulsion.

With all this happening, I headed to my bed, supplicating my hands to God and asking Him to protect my children, for I had left them in His care. I also pleaded to the Greatest Holy Leaf (Bahíyyih Khánum, sister of 'Abdu'l-Bahá), of whom I had been very fond since my childhood, to protect my children.

A Visit from the Women's Union

During the time we were by ourselves, a directive was imposed upon us to remain unseen by those who visited the prison. There were times when delegates from other countries would visit to study the conditions of the prisons and the inmates, or come for humanitarian purposes or cooperative efforts between prisons. During these events, we were told not to leave our cells for any reason until all visitors had left. At times, the visitors would be told that our ward was empty, and at other times, when the visitors were Iraqis, they would be informed that our ward was designed to house political opponents to the government. Once the visitors had departed, we would hear of their identities from the supervisors.

Once, when I was on my way from the washing area that we had converted into a cooking area, it happened that the visitors were arriving. One of the guards noticed me through the fence while I was heading back to my cell. She ran to me in a hurry and asked why I was in the hallway of the ward while visitors were present. My apologetic reply was that I had to go turn the stove off because it was my turn to cook. The rules about not leaving the cell for any reason at all were firmly recited to us again!

As time went by and the ward became too crowded with inmates who had been accused of various crimes, visitors were allowed to enter our quarter. One day, delegates from the Women's Union, accompanied by a member of Al-Amn, an officer, and a guard, came for a visit. We were ordered to gather in the hallway, along with other inmates.

In a stunning coincidence, one of the delegates from the Women's Union happened to be an ex-student of mine from a high school where I had taught child education (child rearing, child psychology, and health education). When she saw me standing unexpectedly among the other prisoners, she fell into an overwhelming state of shock. With a face expressing astonishment and sorrow, she came closer to me and asked, "Ms. Anisa, what has brought you here?"

I said, "Special imposed circumstances!"

I noticed the irritated look on the face of the man from Al-Amn, who tried to redirect the conversation and distract my ex-student. But she continued expressing her regret and empathy and said that seeing me there was the last thing she had expected.

I said, "Take a look, my dear, at the teacher who taught each one of you how to be honorable and exemplary mothers to your children, so they would be raised to be praiseworthy and virtuous. Where is she standing now?"

Though our conversation was private, the Al-Amn man hurried to divert the conversation by asking another inmate a question, but my student went on insisting that I submit a petition to the Women's Union as soon as possible so a reconsideration of my case could transpire. I told her there was no hope for our release or even a reduction of our sentence, but she insisted that it could happen. She then left me in huge turmoil, with an awakened glimpse of hope that had been dormant in the depths of my inner being.

I wrote a petition that explained my circumstances and my daughters' need to have me with them, especially since they were in a critical stage of their education, and that our house had been locked and abandoned. I pleaded with the Women's Union to reconsider my sentence (which was exactly what my ex-student had asked me to write). I told my brother Suhail about it, and he promised to take the petition to the Union. Two long weeks passed while I remained a victim of turmoil, torn between my emotions and a sense of duty. One moment I would scold myself for sending the petition without including my colleagues, while at another moment I would forgive myself because my circumstances differed entirely from those of the rest (none had younger children that were left parentless). Besides, a petition such as this one is a very common procedure in prisons and would either be considered or rejected. There would be no compromises on my side (God forbid); therefore, I need not have scolded myself about it.

The day of visitation had arrived, and in my morning prayers I beseeched God—all praise be unto Him—to bring on whatever was best for the family, and I prayed that I would be of those who are firm and steadfast no matter the circumstances. My brother finally arrived with signs of disappointment clearly visible on his face. He told me there was no hope. He had handed my petition to the Director of the Women's Union and had heard her clearly disparaging the Bahá'í beliefs and restating all the accusations, such as treason and others. My ex-student told him of her empathy and disappointment in not being able to help. The news of the rejection was very normal and had no impact on me, for I had prepared myself during the prior two weeks and had laid all my affairs in God's hands to manage them as He wished.

During our continued family visits, I watched as my daughters seemed to gradually say good-bye to their childhood, as if every day that had gone by was equivalent to a year of their maturing. They would fortify my soul with courage and would ask me to take good care of myself and to never worry about them. Each had now started her life's journey in the best manner, and they were conscious of God's loving care along that journey. Oh how I longed, dearest ones, to come back and care for you, but the price for that—recanting my faith—was too high for me to consider, no matter how strong my love for you was in my heart. There is a grander purpose and a loftier cause, much greater than my emotions—and to this lofty cause I had offered myself. I had taken this path, and I would continue on it, no matter how long and agonizing it might be.

This was my position and the position of every one of my Bahá'í colleagues. Each one of us was determined to endure until the end, despite the moral and material hardships we were facing. Some of us were employees, others were retirees, but our salaries had been taken away from day one, despite our urgent need for buying items such as clothing and other necessities. We relied on the humble assistance of families in buying what food we needed—such as eggs, fruit, and yogurt—for simple breakfasts and dinners, which were not always available to us through the prison's unreliable weekly distribution system of "bounties."

Some of us were subjected to confiscation of our possessions, and Doctor Iqbal was asked—and her family was forced—to repay her financial aid to the medical school where she was a student. Hence, our fate was, and remained, under the mercy of God, and we would often sacrifice our need for essentials from outside the prison. I had an allowance of five dinars (at the time equivalent to $15–$17) per month, but I had to spend this small sum on food for breakfast and dinner.

The Inspection

I mentioned to you in the past that our families were always subjected to careful inspections by the guards, who were skilled at finding prohibited items smuggled in by visitors. However, there were also systematic, unannounced searches conducted in our cells. The search could last either a short or long time, and we would be ordered to leave the cells. Ordinarily two or more female guards would come in; each would search our beds and belongings, even when they knew we had nothing to hide. If ever a teacup made of glass or a small bottle of perfume that families had given one of us as a gift were found—even a small piece of paper with a prayer written on it—a big deal would be made out of such a small violation. They would come out victorious, as if dangerous weapons had been found! They would then start a process of questioning and interrogating everyone. The truth is that although we were cautious not to violate any rules, some incidents still occurred.

One time, a piece of paper with a prayer for protection was found under the pillow of one of our ladies. She was questioned about it, and she explained that it gave her comfort while sleeping. The office let that incident go but gave the order not to let it happen again. I worried about the office finding such scraps of paper that our young ladies kept for memorization. I must say that despite the terrorizing atmosphere of sudden searches, I still kept strips of paper with special phrases, stories, and parts of letters from my children after they left Iraq so that I could memorize and recite them to their father during our visits to the men's prison. I also gave my mother (God bless her soul) some of them to keep. There was nothing in my papers whatsoever that I feared to expose. Time went by peacefully, and none of us were punished for any violation.

A Very Crowded Ward

The ward became congested when two sisters, one with a four-year-old child; another woman accused of spying and distributing pamphlets against the regime in the northern region; an illegal alien; and another prisoner accused of running a house of prostitution were all brought in. As a result of these new arrivals, the ward started to feel like a beehive, and our ward's courtyard also started to feel crowded. (By now, the prison office no longer restricted or scolded us for talking to other inmates).

Cleanliness inside the hallway and the ward's courtyard became impossible; therefore, we had to assign individuals to take turns. The smoke of cigarettes coming from most of the cells started to fill the place. The ward also became filled with foul odors coming from the open toilets inside the cells, which had no water for flushing. To prevent any appearance of favoritism toward us, Nena Jan was prevented from entering our ward to help with the cleaning, so all the cleaning fell on our shoulders.

Our cleaning—although it was a tiring task—was very thorough, but when the other inmates cleaned, they did only a bare minimum of work. Their idea of "cleaning" consisted of using a hand sweeper—called a Muknaseh—that was made of dried palm leaves from date palm trees. Using the Muknaseh simply scattered irritating dust polluted with dirt around the ward. In addition, we were forced to contend with the odor generated by several-days-old food brought by visitors. Whenever the food was heated, a suffocating stench would be diffused throughout the ward that killed everyone's appetite.

The presence of all those people might have somewhat lessened the feeling of segregation that we had had in the past, but there were times when we wished we could have been alone and have our privacy again. I will dedicate part of my book to stories from some of the characters we encountered at that time, as these individuals had become part of our daily life. We were moved by the accounts—as if they were our own—of each one of these inmates, although hearing their sad stories increased the emotional suffering we endured in that place.

A Hideous Day I will Never Forget

We were delighted to be given permission to sleep outdoors in our ward's fenced courtyard, where we could enjoy Baghdad's night breeze and gazing into the sky instead of at the depressing ceilings inside our cells. However, our comfort began to diminish as the number of inmates and their children began to increase. Inside the courtyard, there was an Eastern-style bathroom, with a squatting toilet that was very filthy. We tried our best to avoid using it at night, as it had no water and was abused by the mothers and their little children, who were allowed to deposit their waste everywhere. The stench coming out of it became unbearable, but at the same time it was unbearable to sleep inside our hot cells. We informed the office and asked them to find a solution to keep our only bathroom clean. The office directed the other office at the men's prison to send one of their prisoners as a cleaner. The cleaning man had no other way but to pass through our hallway and in front of us, carrying an open pan full of waste, with a swarm of flies hovering above. Soon large swarms of flies started to invade our ward at a huge and intolerable rate. The cleaning man left afterwards, thinking his task was done, but the outbreak of flies intensified. I went outside to the ward's courtyard to find the filthiest sight I have ever seen! That miserable prisoner, as if forced to do the job, had spread the human waste everywhere, and there was still on the ground a pan full of waste which the flies had covered. The ground and the walls of the bathroom were smudged with waste.

I ran to my lady friends telling them the news. The gate of our ward was locked, so we pleaded with inmates in other wards to notify the office. But they said not to expect any help from anyone, and each left. I became very concerned about our health, especially the health of our girls. Therefore, I had to choose sacrifice. In that sizzling hot day, after the gate was opened, I carried the filthy pan through the hallway to the end of our ward's courtyard and disposed of the contents there. I was furious about what had happened and continued to clean the filth that the imbecile had left behind on the bathroom walls and floor. I brought old newspapers and rags, and carried water back and forth until that horrible task was over. Little by little, the flies started to disperse and abandon the area, after attacking my face and drinking my falling tears.

I ran immediately to the bathroom of our ward to dispose of my clothes, which were filthy beyond words, and to disinfect my body with soap. After that was done, I felt that I had accomplished an important task that protected the health of everyone. Therefore, I began to calm down. I was not expecting any praise from anyone, not even a thank you. It was a sacrifice that someone had to do so everyone could sleep outside again at night instead of in the unbearably hot cell with the squeaky, noisy fan that continued to complain about the cruelty of time.

The Children of the Prisoners

It would not be any exaggeration to say that the smile of a child can bring joy and serenity to my soul, and I consider a child's smile to be the most beautiful picture, painted by the wondrous Creator, in the album of the universe. A teardrop of a child stirs all kinds of uneasy and sad emotions in me. What angers me the most is the abuse or humiliation of a child. The world of childhood captures my whole heart, and I dream of a world of happiness, stability, and health for the children of the entire world.

It was an unpleasant shock for me to see such a large number of children accompanying their mothers behind bars! Some were infants, while others were older, perhaps four or five years old. It was destined for those unfortunate souls to suffer pain and neglect. A mother would be sentenced for many years—sometimes even a life sentence—and the child would be kept in her care, especially because some of the prisoners had no families to care for the child, or their families refused to do so.

As I have previously mentioned, for many families, having a family member who was a prisoner was often considered an embarrassment that brought shame to the family, and a family member who entered prison was often seen as polluted. Even if a kind relative became sympathetic to the prisoner, the rest of the family and neighbors would look down on the prisoner's child and shame him about his mother, especially if the crime was related to honor or murder. The child would be considered a source of bad luck to anyone who cared for him.

Often, a mother would bring her child with her to prison for these reasons, and the child would live with her behind bars and remain deprived of the barest necessities for physical and emotional development. A child in prison is forced to accept and abide by restrictions—such as not being allowed to move freely, play, and make noise as other children do—because he is not living with his mother at home, where she can be tolerant of his disturbances.

In the prison, every time a child cried for some reason, the other inmates would shout and complain, and the child had to be stifled. Sometimes a mother would run out of patience and endurance, and she would curse the child that was adding to her misery, and frantically hit him as if emptying some of her load onto his little body or head. How many the times I witnessed such cruelty!

Once I saw a mother abusing her son by picking him up by his hair and putting him down several times while he screamed in pain. I was watching her from our ward's fenced courtyard and raised my voice so the angry mother could hear me. I told her, "Don't be cruel, and let the child go," while deep inside myself I was saying, "You beast, motherhood has disowned you!"

I saw her face-to-face another time and gently asked her, "What sin has this innocent child committed while he's deprived of so much and needs your loving care?"

She said, "It's that miserable luck that brought us here."

The only thing I could offer her then was to console her with words.

Despite the fact that children are considered an added burden to their mothers in prison, and despite the occasional cruelty they endured, their mothers remained mothers and tried to compensate their children for the harshness they had to endure. Sometimes they would get them candy— which the children would devour in an instant—from the prison store, or they would buy them some triangle-shaped cheese. Sometimes a mother would give a whole box of cheese to her child to eat piece after piece until it was gone. I witnessed that in our own ward.

The prison's rules regarding children were that a child would accompany the mother in her cell until around three or four years of age. Then the child would be taken a few days a week to a large room inside the prison to be with other children. The room was almost bare of any source of enjoyment for a child.

One day, we were allowed to walk farther than the area of our ward, and I saw from a distance the room where the children were taken. I could see a few plastic toys placed on a shelf, but I did not see any toys in the hands of the children. Instead, they were sitting quietly like statues, perhaps in fear of the teacher, who was one of the jailers. The look on their faces was that of dumbness and lacking all childhood enjoyments. The teacher's job was mainly to watch the children while their mothers were busy in sewing or Islamic studies classes, cleaning wards, or helping in the kitchen. Some mothers would be working on some handmade items, such as small purses decorated with beads or bead necklaces, or knitting washcloths out of wool, all to sell for a small profit during the scheduled visitations. I still have a small purse and a necklace from that time.

If a mother's sentence was long, she would be forced to give up her child to a willing relative or an orphanage. The day a prisoner gives up her child is a day of mourning and wailing—not just for the mother but for the other prisoners. The child that was a burden to the mother and the other inmates becomes the center of love and attention and becomes very difficult to part with. At such sad occasions, the inmates share their empathy. Each tells about the pain she carries in her heart, and crying and wailing is abundant as they say good-bye to the child. The mother curses her bad fortune, and the child is bewildered, not knowing why he/she is being taken away from the mother, the only person they have had in this miserable life, to leave for another miserable community with unfamiliar people and strangers. Children still need their parents—even if they have not been kind people—in their lives.

At times, a child would be brought for visitations. Some children would grow up and finish school, and still the mother would be in prison serving her sentence. Without a doubt, an orphanage provides a far better environment for a child than a prison. Orphanages provide education, sports, and even occupational training, such as in mechanics and in rug making. (Woven rugs of goat hair made by inmates in Iraq are very famous for their beauty and durability.)

The children of prisoners are sad victims of society. Fate has brought them to a situation not like any other, where they are deprived of at least one parent. Often, only a few months into her sentence, a prisoner would hear that her husband had left her to marry someone else, even if the crime for which she was serving time was to cover for her husband (either out of fear or submission to traditions), and the guilty husband had orchestrated the whole plan.

We met many oppressed women here who were coerced into assisting their husbands to commit crimes such as theft, drug trafficking, or smuggling. When captured, the woman would confess, either out of fear or submission that she had acted alone and would even defend her husband or brother. Sometimes, being naive would be the issue, such as when the husband promised, for example, that the stolen money would be for both of them and that he would be patiently waiting for her when her sentence was over. He would visit her a few times and would bring gifts of sweets and fruits.

Then, the woman would be shocked to hear that the man she had sacrificed so much for had remarried. If they had children, then the children would most likely be victims of neglect or cruelty by the stepmother. These prisoners would often share their sad stories with us, and hearing these stories would add even more grief to our own. For them, however, it was an emotional outlet that eased their suffering.

I remember two beautiful inmates who were accused of smuggling drugs and were caught on the border. They were co-wives who were married to the same man (In Islam, a man can legally be married to up to four wives), and each had a child with the same husband. The husband had promised each of his two wives that he would divorce the other wife. The two women, accompanied by their children, suffered imprisonment, and the children were deprived of attending kindergarten. The husband, who was captured as well, tried to escape from the men's prison's wall by tying sheets to use as a rope, but his attempt failed. He was severely beaten by the guards, and many years were added to his sentence.

Despite our love for the children in prison, it was not permissible to be close to them. I remember one day, while I was inside the ward's courtyard and hanging my laundry out to dry, I saw some children playing in the outer courtyard. I tried to befriend them from a distance, but they ran away like terrified mice. I was astonished by their odd behavior because children are naturally curious about people. The second time I saw them, I took some candy with me. Very cautiously, one of them came closer, then another. I asked them why they ran away from us.

One of them said, "The supervisor threatened to put us in a dark room with goblins if we ever came close to you!"

I said, "You can see that we are not scary, but that's OK; be obedient to the supervisor."

There were many children in our ward that I will talk about at another time.

The New "Home Visit" Governance

The second year into our sentence in Abu Ghraib, delightful rumors quickly spread that a new law had been issued by the authorities that allowed prisoners with good behavior and light sentences of ten years or less to visit their families for a week, once every three months. At first, we were doubtful about the validity of the rumors, but after a while they were confirmed by the prison's office. It was among a list of corrective laws suggested by world organizations dedicated to improving the conditions of prisons and prisoners. These laws had been implemented in other countries and had proven to be positive.

The news brought some hope, and we started to wonder if fortune would smile on us and if we would be included. Perhaps for a few days, we would be able to leave this place, to be with our children and the rest of the family, and to see Baghdad's streets, and enjoy being free!

We did not dare to ask anyone if the new law would indeed include us because we were fearful of being disappointed. But the jailer of our ward spared us the humiliation of having to ask and told us, with regret, that the Bahá'ís were excluded! Among the others excluded were those accused of murder and espionage, and thus we were always equated with those criminal groups, as we had been on several other occasions. Naturally we did not discuss the issue; however, we still felt disappointed.

For me, the disappointment was intense, as I had dreamt of being with my children. Our normal time for visitation always went by as quickly as the blink of an eye, and my children had to divide their time between visiting me and visiting their father. As I mentioned earlier, out of politeness, I also had to share the time of my children's visits with other members of my family or friends, and I could not allocate more time to spend with my children alone.

The new law made the extended period for visitation available to most of the prisoners, but some chose not to leave out of fear of punishment or retribution from their families or others. Some had been disowned by their families and never received visits from anyone, and some received visits from suspicious people who would arrange, for the prisoners after their release, a different kind of life away from their families or country. Those characters were skillful in manipulating prisoners who were fearful of the unknown after their release.

Our exclusion from the home-visit law intensified our feelings of oppression, especially after threats came from the authorities that our captivity would be extended even further than the sentences the judges had given us. In those hard circumstances, and with broken spirits, we continued to encourage each other, while imploring God to increase our steadfastness and endurance. The miracle of serenity and comfort would always come to our hearts and would inspire us to fall back on using jokes and amusement to deal with such situations. Our young ladies were witty, quick, and had a great sense of humor that turned gloomy situations into laughter and positivity.

The new law of visitation continued to be in effect until the end of our incarceration. I remember a day, while we were in the Al-Rashaad prison (the prison that followed our incarceration at Abu Ghraib), when the prison's chief administrator came to examine our ward. It was the day for home visits for many of the prisoners. After we were greeted, I asked for permission to express my opinion, which was granted.

I said, "Sir, we have been incarcerated for over three years, and everyone can testify to our good conduct, outstanding manners, and obedience to the law."

He said, "Yes, there is no doubt about that."

I continued to say, "Then wouldn't it be fair for us to receive the same treatment as the other prisoners in earning the right for home visits, when all of us have given sincere service to this country?"

The tears that flooded my eyes as I was talking seemed to deeply move him, and he said, "Yes, yes, I will look into that."

A glimpse of hope entered my heart, and I went back to envisioning myself one day visiting my family at home and embracing my children.

Weeks passed, then months and years, and no one knew if the chief administrator had truly tried to help us but received no support, or if he had simply forgotten his promise as soon as his official mandatory visit ended.

My Tooth Extraction

When I was taken to prison, my teeth were in decent condition, but two months later, I had a severe toothache in one of my molars due to a modest cavity. I asked permission to see the dentist in prison. The dentist surprised me by saying that the tooth had to be extracted. I pleaded with him to fill it instead, but he refused. I had heard from other prisoners that extraction was the most common dental treatment inside prison. He immediately brought a needle to administer anesthesia. Just minutes after the injection, he proceeded to extract the tooth. I had not started to feel the effect of the anesthetic at all, so I pleaded with him again to give me a few minutes, but he did not care and continued with the procedure.

Only God knows the extent of the pain I suffered, which was beyond what I could bear. I started to scream, but my cries did not affect him one bit. It was as if he were a carpenter pulling a nail from a wall. My tears started to pour down my face from pain and anger, because that dentist would have never behaved in this manner with his own clients outside the prison. The pain I endured and the humiliation I encountered could be consoled with nothing except with tears. I went to bed, and my jaw started to gradually become numb a half hour after the procedure. I continued to doubt if the anesthetic amount was too little or if it was old and ineffective. I wondered if the dentist's conscience was clear after treating me with such cruelty. Thank God I did not have to see his face again until our discharge from prison. In the following prison, I had another cavity that I asked the dentist to fill. This time, the dentist agreed to fill the cavity, and the filling lasted me until the time I needed dentures and willingly consented to having a few of my teeth extracted while I was living in the United States.

My Children's School

Despite the repetitiveness of life in prison and the long days that seemed without end—as if the wheel of time had stopped during our imprisonment—we endured partly by connecting with events outside the prison life, such as our families' lives. We took advantage of simple happy events to celebrate among ourselves, or we shared the sorrow of those who suffered distress. In general, prisoners sympathize with each other despite the occasional disagreements. The sense of oppression creates ties between prisoners as if they are a forsaken community.

I celebrated my children's academic achievements and their passing their final exams at the end of each year. My son Abir, due to his arrest, had lost four months of his school year, which resulted in a delay of his final exams until after the summer break. My daughter Alhan was in eleventh grade, and my youngest daughter Ruwa was in eighth grade. Each had been self-reliant in managing their affairs, despite the material and incorporeal difficulties. Regardless of the hard circumstances, each of them was able to finish the school year with good grades, and that was a source of joy that I considered a gift from the gracious Lord that eased my suffering and alienation.

I decided to celebrate their success, even in a humble manner, so with the little money that I had, I bought some beverages and some simple sweets from the prison's store. The whole ward celebrated my joy and happiness. Standing proud, I received congratulations, hugs, and kisses from my Bahá'í friends and the other inmates.

God granted me another joy when my son Abir was able to finish his academic year with good grades as well, after putting great effort into making up for the time lost while incarcerated. I then had a similar celebration for his accomplishment, and the Kurdish inmates were very happy to know that my son was attending university in Sulaimaniyyeh, Kurdistan, so they danced their traditional Kurdish dance called *Dabke*. It is a dance that Kurdish women participate in, wearing their very colorful and beautiful Kurdish dresses, and normally they are joined by Kurdish men. It was a joyous day I will never forget, and I thanked God for granting me a wish I had long prayed for.

When visitation day arrived and my son Abir came to visit, the Kurdish inmates were astonished that he could speak their Kurdish language with such proficiency and ease. After that, the Kurdish inmates became close to me, like family, and it was as if Abir were their son. This is how language brings nations together and removes all differences.

Years went by, and this is how I continued to celebrate my children's academic successes. My son Abir received his Bachelor of Chemistry; my daughter Alhan graduated from the Institute of Technology and received a diploma in technical drawing; and my daughter Ruwa received outstanding grades at the end of high school and was accepted into an engineering university to study chemistry.

Because of the hard circumstances we all faced, Ruwa decided to leave the country. Then, her two siblings followed her shortly afterward, and I was left to suffer the bitterness of imprisonment that seemed unending, with the added anguish of our separation, which seemed like a long, dark tunnel without a light of hope at its end.

The Television

When we arrived at prison, we heard from inmates of other wards who passed close to our ward's courtyard and from the cook that there was a large hall where inmates could go and watch TV if they wished to do so. Such a privilege was denied to us Bahá'ís; therefore, we never attempted to pursue it. But when winter arrived with long and cold nights, the dream arose of having a television for us alone, so we decided to approach the prison administration with the idea, and we hoped it would be accepted. In those circumstances, similar to a child in a hurry to get what he has asked for, we were eager for the answer. We dreamt that the television would become a savior, rescuing us from the repetitiveness of our days, especially since our conversations had become tedious and too familiar.

Newspapers were permitted, except that we had no access to them and had to wait until visitation day to obtain them. By then, most of the news had become old. Besides, the newspaper's main topics were all political and propaganda, and they were meant to showcase the revolution's achievements and victories. We only read newspapers for a few minutes, and that was it. For these reasons, knowing that the process required official approval in a specific routine manner, we focused our efforts on trying to get a television. Weeks full of worry and anticipation went by, and finally good news of the approval arrived. The approval was made on the condition that the television be placed in the main hall so the other inmates would be able to watch it as well. Our joy was grand! The door to the hall, which was completely empty of any furniture, was unlocked, and we shared the responsibility of cleaning it in preparation for the anticipated newcomer!

During the family visit following the approval, some of the friends were happy to hear the news about the television, but others were not as pleased. For some, perhaps, being in prison was supposed to be about sacrifice for our Faith, and seeking the pleasures of life would be a sign of a lack of endurance in the face of difficulties; with greater suffering we would make our families and friends more proud!

We—the Bahá'í women prisoners—felt differently. We wanted to be in higher spirits so we could share more pleasant conversations than those of sadness when we met with them. In any case, one of the friends volunteered to donate a television to us but asked Bahiyyeh that he remain anonymous. He also asked her to be the person in charge of the TV, and he sent the TV to Bahiyyeh through a Bahá'í visitor. We were very thankful to the donor, and we did not try to find out his/her identity.

At the next visit, the old television arrived. It was very small, and it was a black and white TV. We were pleased, nevertheless, to have something that could make our long gloomy nights a few hours shorter. Otherwise, we had nothing to do but pray and think of our families, in a routine that was similar to a broken record that left the same emotions in the depth of our souls.

At the time, we made seats for ourselves from the empty egg cartons that the prison's kitchen had discarded. We stacked them firmly on top of each other to a certain height, then covered them with burlap from used sacks. We either sat on them as they were or put a small cushion on top. We continued to use those seats until the time when we were granted permission to obtain very low chairs.

On that happy day of the television's arrival, we eagerly awaited evening. When the time came, we all hurried to take our seats. Some of the other prisoners came running with joyfulness and spread some old blankets on the floor. We placed the royal TV, looking like a tiny rabbit with two long ears (antennas), on a carton seat in front of us. As soon as it was six o'clock, Bahiyyeh walked, calmly as usual, and turned the TV on the only broadcasting channel.

The voice of the news anchor was instantly heard saying, "This is the television station of the Republic of Iraq!" Everyone was ecstatic and in a state of continuous laughter and joyful tears! We were like young children happy with a birthday present. After that, we sat watching the program, which started with cartoons. It was still enjoyable for us adults to watch. The broadcasting appeared grainy at times, so Bahiyyeh with her calm demeanor got up and adjusted the antenna throughout the evening.

It was a happy evening, despite the cold weather and the cold floor where we had to place our feet. After that evening, I started to take a stack of news-papers or an empty egg carton with me to put my feet on, because we were not permitted to bring a heater. We also had to bring our blankets to stay warm until the end of the broadcast (at the time, TV broadcasts in Iraq ended at midnight).

Within just a few days, however, the TV started to show signs of old age. All evening Bahiyyeh had to keep turning it off to let it "cool off," as she described it, and then turn it back on again. We tried to fix it numerous times by sending it to a repair person. Each time, we would have to wait for weeks before it was brought back, and we had to keep holding on to it until we were moved to the Al-Rashaad prison, where we were permitted to get another old black-and-white TV.

I was astonished to see black-and-white televisions still being used, as we had had color TVs since the fifties. We used the black-and-white TV until the time of our release at the end of 1979. I must admit, the television was a vital part of our prison life that made our evenings more bearable, despite the fact that we could only watch the one station broadcasting mandatory political programs that suited the governing party.

7 / The Prisoners of Abu Ghraib Prison

Some of the Characters in Abu Ghraib Prison

If I talk about "Abu Ghraib," then no doubt I must mention certain prisoners with whom difficult circumstances destined us to be locked together in the same ward day and night. Cohabitation and interaction with them, even on a trivial level, were inevitable and left impressions on our consciousness—some positive and some otherwise. They were our prison comrades, whether we liked it or not. I will be giving some of them disguised names, although I do remember all of their names.

Guel-Bahar

The prison guard brought a woman in her fifties with boney arms, raggedy old clothes and dirty narrow pants, and bushy hair tied with a rag. She had an odd smile on her sunburnt face, with a manic and angry look in her piercing eyes. Prisoners gathered around her to investigate who she was and what her alleged crime was, and they were asking her curious questions.

It was said that the newcomer was a spy who had infiltrated the Iraqi-Iranian border. Prior to that period, tens of people like her had come from Iran every day to visit the holy shrines in Iraq. Some traveled on foot to earn extra spiritual rewards, and most were oblivious to Iraqi laws and legalities.

The past Iraqi regimes were not as strict with these Iranian visitors, except for the few suspected criminals, but in our time, as I have mentioned, the relationship between Iran and Iraq was very tense. Therefore, the laws became very restrictive toward all illegal entrants.

When the women gathered around Guel-Bahar, she became very agitated and screamed loud profanities in Persian. The women laughed and left. The prison guard told us that that woman was an Iranian spy pretending to suffer mental illness. Therefore, everyone avoided her, and she remained alone in her cell repeating over and over the same profanities until the following day when she finally calmed down and started to ask for food.

She was bold enough to walk outside her isolation cell and come to our area. We saw her pacing back and forth all day long, wearing an odd smile and still repeating the same profanities. She also had no inhibitions about entering other people's cells inside our ward at night.

One night, I was very tired and went to sleep early. All of a sudden, a noise woke me up, and I found Guel-Bahar in our hallway right beside our cell. I was terrified, but I could not awaken my sisters Warqa and Fatima, who were in a deep sleep. I was worried that this insane woman would enter our space and was concerned about what to do if she did. I left my bed and looked for some long stockings, and I quickly and firmly tied our cell gate so she could not enter. I told our guard the following day so they would take action and prevent her from roaming around at night, but the answer was: "She's crazy. What do you want us to do with her?"

Our ward had become an isolation area for those with mental illness, those with life sentences, infiltrators, spies, illegals, and all those who were rejected by prisoners of other wards, such as troublemakers and unruly prostitutes. All would be placed in the Bahá'í ward, and the Bahá'í ladies had to endure them! Our only comfort were the sacred words, "And if thou art overtaken by affliction in My path, or degradation for My sake, be not thou troubled thereby. Rely upon God, thy God and the Lord of thy fathers" (Bahá'u'lláh, The Tablet of Aḥmad, in *Bahá'í Prayers*, pp. 309–10).

We remained apprehensive of Guel-Bahar, despite the humorous incidents involving her that we witnessed. She was unpredictable and not in control of her behavior. We tried our best to show her kindness, but she was living in her own world, mumbling words in Persian and then screaming profanities.

One day, I was washing my plate in our bathing area, which had an extended basin. Guel-Bahar was sitting by the door. She quietly sneaked in, and I felt her boney hand firmly and forcefully extending inside my clothes in a painful and embarrassing way. I jumped in terror and ran toward the cell, shivering in pain while she burst into hysterical laughter and repeated her profanities. I hesitated to tell anyone about the terrible incident, fearing it would become a magnified story among the inmates. I could not help but quiver in disgust every time I thought about that incident. I did eventually forgive her due to her mental illness, but I continued to avoid and fear her until the end.

A prisoner from Ahvaz (a city in the south of Iran) by the name of "Nusrat" told us that Guel-Bahar had crossed the border on foot and been captured by the border patrol. She had then been then taken to a police station where she had been severely beaten and tortured to the extent of leaving marks on her feet and body, and the beating had caused her to lose her mind. This was the reason she was terrified of seeing the guards and police inside the prison and always ran to her cell covering her head with a blanket in fear of their torture. After the end of the Iraqi-Iranian war, guards came to take Guel-Bahar to be deported. Nusrat assured her that no one would harm her, but Guel-Bahar was extremely agitated. We collected some food and money for her and saw her ride in a caged police car, waving good-bye to all and shouting her familiar profanities, which made everyone burst into laughter.

Latifa

As I mentioned earlier, the Bahá'í ward, as it was called, was considered by the prison's administration to be the most suitable place for depositing all prisoners who were special or problematic. During the time the Kurdish prisoners were being released and others were being deported, a young woman in her thirties was brought in and placed in one of the cells. Her charge was premeditated murder in the first degree. We were not interested in knowing her story, as we had enough gloom to endure, but the ward supervisor volunteered to tell us all about it.

According to the supervisor, the woman and her lover had planned a staged situation where her lover, after murdering the woman's husband, had tied her arms to the bed while her children were sleeping in the next room. He then left through the window. The woman would then tell the police that a thief had entered, murdered her husband, gagged her, tied her to the bed, and then escaped. The police officers did not believe her ludicrous story, and she was arrested alongside her lover. She unsuccessfully tried to take the blame all herself, but her lover had confessed. Out of her devotion to him she sent him small notes, smuggled with visitors to the men's prison, telling him that he should not have confessed because he was a man and that she had tried to protect him.

Latifa was put in the same cell in which the slim, pale, soon-to-be-executed Kurdish woman from chapter 5 had been placed. I am calling her Latifa ("pleasant") because she had pleasant traits such as calmness and peacefulness. It was bewildering how evil could hide under this veil of loveliness and composure, but her face was cold and empty of emotion. There was never a mention of her children, nor did she ever express missing them. Her children had been left with her late husband's family, and, perhaps, she had given up on the possibility of ever seeing them again. Latifa was given a death sentence, which was not implemented until a year later. During that year, and as the days went by, she had hopes that her sentence would be changed to a life sentence. A life sentence was her dream, as it was for all those with a death sentence, for life is valuable in all circumstances. With time, we had forgotten her sentence and distanced ourselves emotionally from the thought of her possible execution.

I remember her so well: her expressionless face, her long hair, her bashfulness, and her immense politeness while talking to others. Perhaps that was genuinely her character but her lower self had overpowered her, or perhaps her late husband had had a hand in her decision to get rid of him. In any case, our relationship with her did not go beyond the basic courtesies. Latifa preferred seclusion and remained in her cell as much as possible. At times, she would walk in the hallway, holding a little radio to her ear, preferring not to use an ear microphone. She listened for an hour to long songs by Fareed Al-Atrash (a renowned Arab singer) broadcast every Tuesday on a Kuwaiti radio station. She gently placed the radio at her ear, singing along with a soft voice while pacing back and forth in the dimly-lit hallway. At times, I would notice a blush and emotions on her pale, cold face while she sang.

Latifa had become a familiar face in our ward, and we became accustomed to seeing her sitting in her cell, crocheting a large wool bed cover with a crochet needle that she was an expert at using. I still remember the designs with harmonious colors that she skillfully made. Her hope was to sell the bed cover for a decent amount of money so that she could afford to hire a competent new lawyer who would request a retrial and perhaps free her and her lover of the crime they had committed.

In reality, hand-knit items from the prisoners never brought the kind of profit that would fulfill such dreams. A cover like that would not sell for more than fifty dinars (about $165.00 at the time), and that amount was not sufficient to hire a skillful lawyer, especially for two individuals. There were a few times when Latifa went on food strikes—refusing all food except two cups of tea per day—and lost a significant amount of weight. She was adamant about her innocence and that the true criminal was a thief who had murdered her husband, gagged her, and then tied her to her bed.

On a difficult day, everyone was shocked to know that her execution and that of her lover were about to take place. There was a loud protest from all the inmates, and we were very saddened by the news because Latifa had become an important part of our ward. We had grown accustomed to seeing her day and night, despite the limited interaction—such as sharing food and little gifts from the extra items brought to us by our families during visits—we had with her. And as I mentioned earlier, she was very peaceful and never a bother.

Early that morning, they took Latifa away, accompanied by the executioner, who was a tan-skinned young man with no apparent cruelty or malice on his face. No one, if seeing him outside the prison, would have ever guessed his profession. Latifa left without a good-bye. Everyone was crying, and no words could be said to her, for what can be said in such a horrible hour? And why was it necessary for the executioner to come, especially when she was being accompanied by jailers and a supervisor? I imagined the executioner was similar to a butcher who came to inspect a sheep before slaughtering it. We watched Latifa's last steps leaving the ward among the wailing of everyone, but the hours went by, and there was no news from the guard regarding the execution.

Right before sunset, the biggest surprise in the history of the prison happened when the guard returned with Latifa. She had not been executed, and no one knew the reason. All prisoners came to the courtyard to see her, and there were loud cheers and ululates that reached the heavens, then the Dabke dance followed the celebration. Everyone was congratulating her and offering thanks to God and the officials for not implementing her execution. When the high emotions finally became calm, the guard came in to return all the prisoners to their wards, and we remained with Latifa, offering her our congratulations and good wishes. A pale smile returned to Latifa's face, and her story seemed as if it would have a peaceful outcome.

But our hope and optimism did not last long, as a couple of days later a bigger surprise, more shocking in severity and impact, came to pass when they took Latifa again to be executed with her lover, this time for real. What we had witnessed in those two days shook our nerves beyond their limits, as we had gone from happiness to dread to the horror of the execution. Stillness and terror filled the place.

This is how we were constantly forced to emotionally react, as we were left with no choice or way of separating ourselves emotionally from those who lived with us under the same roof and shared the long prison days in that miserable place. Later on, we heard from the guard that the reason for postponing the execution had been because one of the judges had not shown up. Without his presence, the indictments and charges could not be read in front of those witnessing the execution.

You might wonder how anyone could sympathize with such criminals who had committed horrific crimes against society and themselves. My personal answer is that punishment is a just, divine law and is not vengeance toward the wrongdoer, but rather a lesson and a preventative measure. But when the criminal is a neighbor, a human being living a few steps from you, someone who respects and interacts with you in the best manner, who conveys to you their life circumstances, who never causes you any harm, and who shares with you the same depressing and isolating prison life—all of these things will cause prisoners to sympathize with each other. Prisoners are effectively castaways, a discarded category of people who are going through hardship under similar circumstances. We all shared one wish—to be free from our shackles.

Um-Muhammad

Um-Muhammad was a middle-aged woman, always dressed in black with a thin scarf for a head cover, who had a calm and cheerful demeanor. She had a mysterious smile—just like the Mona Lisa—that was so enigmatic that no one could guess if she was happy or sad.

On the first day we entered prison, we were told that she suffered from mental illness. As usual, she was brought to our ward. Um-Muhammad's alleged crime was the premeditated murder of her husband, whom she suffocated with a pillow. She repeatedly swore that she had only covered him with a heavy cover because he was extremely cold and shivering. Perhaps the cover was too heavy, which caused him to suffocate and die a martyr of intensive care by a miguided wife.

Um-Muhammad always walked the hallway while wearing her mysterious smile. At times I was envious of her and wanted to discover the reason behind her neverending bliss! One day, she insisted that I come close to her. Despite the fact that I knew she would not harm me, I was still slightly concerned, simply because every now and then she would be sent to the mental hospital. I gathered some courage and came closer, thinking in the back of my mind that I could run away or resist her in case she tried any abnormal or harmful behavior.

I asked her, "What do you want?"

She said, "For God's sake, put your ear close to mine." With pleading insistence, she wanted me to tell her what I was hearing.

I was afraid to tell her that I was hearing nothing, but she rescued me from hesitation by saying, "Here they are talking to me! Do you hear their warning when they come? 'Chirp Chirp Chirp' is the signal of their arrival. They chirp like birds, and then they start greeting me and talking! Don't you hear them? Don't you?" She repeated that question with the excitement of someone awaiting validation of her hallucination and mad fantasy!

I did not wish to dishearten a mad lady, because no usefulness would be gained, and perhaps I would become her enemy. So I said, "Yes, yes I do hear their chirping."

She was very pleased and comforted to hear me say this, and like a little child, she kept on repeating, "Isn't their voice beautiful? Chirp Chirp!"

I said, "Yes, it is."

She then said, "Their beautiful voice is so loud and clear, and yet no one wants to believe me! They are angels, and they talk to me!" She continued her walk with laughter and cheer and enjoyed the imaginary voices in her head.

And so I finally discovered the secret behind her neverending bliss!

Um-Muhammad would be taken every now and then to the mental hospital to receive her treatment for a week or two, and when she came back she would be depressed for a few days until her smile and joy would return. One day, after returning from the hospital, she showed us black and blue spots all over her body. She said that the patients at that hospital had continually pinched her every time she passed by them.

Another time, I saw her collecting watermelon peels from the common dump. I asked her why she was collecting filthy peels, and she said, "That's OK, I will wash them." Another prisoner said she used the peels to treat infections! She was afraid to go to a clinic or a hospital. I wondered if Um-Muhammad's method was her own creation or if it could have been a method inherited from old medicine!

Um-Muhammad remained with us until the time we left for Al-Rashaad prison later on.

"Naiima Deportation"

Our imprisonment was now stretching our patience and endurance to the breaking point because the ward had become entirely filled with comers and goers. One of the prisoners was a woman close to fifty years of age. Thin and quiet, she spoke Arabic with an Iranian accent. She was brought in with Kurdish convicts on charges of illegal residency. She was an Iranian citizen who had been married for thirty years to an Iraqi man and had been residing in Al-Kathumiyyeh (a suburb of Baghdad and a holy town). She was like many foreigners who came to visit the holy shrines, married an Iraqi, and remained without legal documents. Her husband had died, and she was childless. Therefore, she had lost all rights of residency. She was arrested by the police, sent to prison, and put in the deportation section.

In prison, a convict is named by her charge, such as, "so and so theft, or so and so embezzlement, fraud, murder, and so on." Thus, Naiima was given the name "Naiima deportation," meaning she would be returned to Iran even if she no longer had any family there.

Naiima was hoping to be set free so that she could go back to Al-Kathumi-yyeh, where she had made many friends and knew all her neighbors. She had lost all ties to Iran in the past thirty years, but those long years still had not earned her the right to a legal residency in Iraq.

One day, Naiima was ordered by the supervisor to get ready in one hour. The police were coming to pick her up for deportation. She wept and became very nervous. She said, "Whom am I going to in Iran, for I no longer have anyone there. How will I live while penniless?" We were very saddened to hear her words and wept with her, sharing her pain.

We were able to collect for Naiima a modest sum of money and some food and fruits. We said our good-byes, and offered her our best wishes. The prisoners were accustomed to cheering and ululating while saying good-bye to anyone leaving prison, whether the occasion called for it or not. No logic was involved. As the big commotion of loud ululations, applause, and tears went on, we were questioning why the prisoners were cheering. Were the ululations to celebrate the unknown destiny that was awaiting this miserable soul as she crossed the border after being expelled from a country that she had loved? She had spent the best years of her life on its land.

Days went by as we remembered Naiima, who was a kind, cheerful, and mild-tempered woman and liked by all. Only a month had passed since she had left prison when we heard a new commotion and more ululations! What was going on?

Naiima was back, after being rejected by the Iranian border patrol. Every-one welcomed her back with hugs, kisses, and embraces. We offered her our sympathy and thought perhaps it was a good indication that she would be forgiven and allowed to remain in Iraq. Life returned to normal in prison, and she remained hopeful. However, a while later her deportation was reac-tivated; this time she was going to be taken to a different point on the border of Sulaimaniyyeh and Iran.

Naiima gathered her belongings and cried until her eyes turned red. She put on heavy clothes, fearing the cold weather in mountainous Sulaimaniyyeh during winter. Again, we gathered whatever money we could afford to give her. Perhaps it would sustain her for a few days, especially because she was, like many of the prisoners, addicted to cigarettes.

We wished her well, as everyone said their farewell with ululations and cheers. A few days went by, and as suspected by some of us, Naiima returned again, faster than the previous time. The Iranian border police had rejected her due to the absence of legal documents identifying her as an Iranian citizen.

The poor soul came back with stronger optimism, despite all the difficulties she had been through, thinking that she would be allowed to stay in Iraq as a token of mercy. She wished to live close to the holy shrine, and continued to dream of being released. She was relieved that she had still not been deported, and she returned to being cheerful and optimistic.

Bad luck, however, seemed to be clinging to the hem of her clothing. The police returned for the third time to take her for deportation, and she said her good-byes for the last time. She headed to an unknown and dark fate. She was taken to a new point on the border, this time in the southern part of Iraq, near the province of Al-Amarah.

Thus the curtain came down on another sad prison story, as Naiima left, accompanied by sorrow and hopefulness. May God be with you, Naiima, whether you are still in this perishing world or in His everlasting realm. You were denied the chance to live on a small blotch of the land of Iraq, a country that your heart had loved. It discarded you, just like the country your parents raised you in, and you had no one to help and defend you from such misfortune.

Nothing could lift our spirits from the sadness we shared with the other inmates, except gathering for prayers and reading the sacred words of Bahá'u'lláh. These eased the load of suffering that our souls bore. God would always answer our prayers, and He would always grant us the serenity to cope with our circumstances once again. It was as if He always clothed us with a new garment of fortitude and steadfastness in His Cause.

Abu-Tubar "The One with the Cleaver"

In the months prior to our arrest, a series of horrific crimes—crimes we had never heard of in the past—terrified Baghdad. The Iraqi media did not cover the details of those crimes as is typically done in the West; we only heard a brief mention of them in the newspapers. The truth is that serial crimes were very rare, due to high security and the severe methods of punishment used, which in return became positive contributors to citizens' safety. For example, when my family and I were still living in our home, we would leave our outside gate unlocked numerous times, day or night, without any concern for our safety. We even left the doors open to our home unless the weather was too hot or too cold. We enjoyed the fresh air coming from the outside garden, and we walked in the streets at night feeling completely safe.

Suddenly, during those months, news began to spread of a brutal murderer who killed people with a cleaver. They called him *Abu-Tubar*, which means *the One with the Cleaver*. He planned his crimes carefully and expertly, and he was able to escape all attempts by the police and detectives to find him or discover his identity. The number of crimes committed by this butcher began to rise; sometimes the victims were individuals, and other times they were families.

Terror took hold of people in a way no one had ever seen. It was summer, and the people of Baghdad were accustomed to sleeping out on the flat roofs of their homes, under the dome of heaven. Perhaps it is a custom they have always followed since Baghdad was built a thousand years ago. Metal or wooden portable beds would be set up on the roof for five or six months, and people enjoyed the cooler Baghdad nights and the pleasure of sleeping under the beautiful stars of heaven. But the fear that filled the city from near and far caused everyone to be afraid of sleeping in the open, and they began to tightly lock their windows and doors. They tried to think of clever ways to defend themselves with alarms or by hanging metal pots or utensils behind doors to generate noise if opened, and other trivial ways for self-defense. Some of the young men formed groups in each neighborhood to patrol the homes at night. For the sake of amusement, I will mention that my dear Ruwa took a small hammer and a toy mortar and pestle to the rooftop and placed them close to her bed, which was close to mine. It was of comfort to her to know she was protected, and perhaps could frighten the one with the cleaver!

At first we thought we were only hearing rumors, but the continuation of these crimes caused us to quit sleeping out on the roof. Finally, the police forces were able to obtain information leading to the tenacious murderer and arrest him with his wife, who was an accomplice who covered up his crimes. Peace resumed in the city, and horror left the people's hearts. Everyone anxiously awaited the sentencing of "the One with the Cleaver."

One day, news spread inside our prison that the trial of the wife of Abu-Tubar—they called her "Um-Tubar"—had ended, and that she would soon become a guest in our ward! She would be there until it was time for her execution. In cases such as hers, no one knew the length of time until her sentence would be implemented.

We were troubled by the news, for we anticipated plenty of unpleasant happenings in our ward upon her arrival. There would be no way to fully avoid her because the small isolation chamber the office had designated for her was in the way of our coming and going. That chamber was very small— about one square meter—with a sturdy iron door that had a small barred window-like opening on top that is hard to reach. Such a chamber exists in every ward and is designated for inmates who rebel against the rules. Depending on her offense. the prisoner would stay in that tight space and would be forced to sit on the damp floor, sometimes for days. The offender would be given one meal per day that would be passed to her through that barred opening at the top of the door. The prisoner would leave her cell only for urgent matters, such as using the bathroom. That happened only after wailing and screaming, and heaven forbid if the supervisor was late.

Bothersome situations such as we had previously experienced were on our minds as we anticipated the arrival of Um-Tubar. On the next day, the supervisor—a college student with whom we had a good relationship and a mutual respect—came in with a prisoner to clean the isolation chamber in preparation for Um-Tubar.

I came close to her and acted as if I knew nothing and said, "We heard that Um-Tubar will be placed in this chamber!"

She replied affirmatively.

I said, "I would like to keep our conversation confidential."

She smiled in agreement.

I then said, "The administration wished to keep us secluded, especially from any visitors, whether guests or officials."

She agreed.

I continued, "Is it logical to still keep us isolated while Um-Tubar is in our ward, and lots of visitors from Baghdad will be coming to see the woman who, with her husband, has terrified the whole city for months? In addition, hundreds of inmates will want to find excuses to enter our ward to see her! That's just my personal opinion."

The superintendent was quiet for a moment, then said, "They are orders from the office, and I have to implement them."

I said, "I have no doubt about that."

I left praying that God would spare us all the hassle with Um-Tubar.

It was a long wait of several hours, with inmates congregating outside the ward to meet the notorious and frightening Um-Tubar. The awaited moment finally arrived! We could see from the courtyard the main entrance of the prison and watched as Um-Tubar entered. She was a short woman, wearing the traditional black cover (abaya), but we could not see her face very well. Heavily armed police were surrounding her, along with members of the Al-Amn. She was taken to complete the necessary and long procedures of her admission.

With all of us impatiently waiting, the procession finally started, with the administrator of the women's prison in the lead, then the jailers and supervisors accompanying Um-Tubar, who was in shackles. It was a truly horrifying procession. All prisoners were ordered to go inside. As soon as the procession came close to the courtyard that separated our ward from that of the prostitutes, we saw the procession stop, then enter that ward.

It was truly a surprise for us! They had changed their minds and prepared a place for her in that ward, instead of ours. The cell had iron bars, and visitors could see her. We embraced each other in relief. The worry had been lifted, many thanks be to God.

Surely and steadily the visitors started to arrive on a daily basis to see this horrifying woman, whose looks were not dismaying at all. The inmates started to weave all types of tales about her. Some vilified her, while others were sympathetic and believed her when she said she was innocent and feared her husband, who threatened to kill her if she did not collaborate, and forced her to wash his bloody clothes.

When the prisoners were then given permission to see Um-Tubar, I dared to go see her mainly out of curiosity. I had to ask for permission. It was late in the afternoon when, for the first time, I entered the prostitution ward—a place that was never noiseless or peaceful whether it was day or night. I walked towards Um-Tubar's "cage" and saw other visitors there as well. It did truly look like a cage because it had metal bars on all sides. As soon as I came close to her, I saw her arm quickly extend through the bars. She firmly held on to the hem of my dress, pleading and saying, "By God and your pure and blessed hem, I swear to you that I am innocent and had no knowledge of my husband's crimes."

I said, "Put your reliance on God, and if you are innocent, your prayers will be answered. But first, please let go of my hem."

She held on to my dress even harder, pulling the hem and repeating what she had said earlier. But in truth, I felt no empathy toward her, despite her simple appearance. Her face was not attractive in the least, but then again, it was not the face of a malicious criminal.

A while later—I cannot recall how long it was—Um-Tubar was taken by heavily armed guards to the execution courtyard, which was at the men's prison, to face her death along with her husband Abu-Tubar. Stories were told that he boldly walked to the courtyard, asked for a cigarette, and smoked it to the end, right before his execution. The family of Um-Tubar, who were present at the execution, condemned what their daughter had done, and each declared their renouncement of her right before her execution. And thus ended the period of horror that had taken over Baghdad, with the many innocent victims who were brutally murdered, and the many others whose names and addresses were found on a list he had and whose lives were spared.

Other Characters in Abu Ghraib

When I write to you about the period of our imprisonment in Abu Ghraib, I find my memory rich with characters that were woven into our life in that place. I have written about some of the inmates earlier, but I will tell you about another inmate whose memory stays with me until this day. I will call her Rebecca, but before I start writing about her, I want to bring your attention to the common pattern of thinking among the many ranks of society in Iraq, and the harsh traditions—stern to the extent of abuse—that were passed down in families. Fathers in general, and specifically uneducated people, raised their daughters by suppressing their freedom, to ensure their good status, which was extremely important for the reputation of the family or the tribe. Instead of instilling virtues in a daughter and giving her self-confidence and self-respect, parents often treated girls with harshness and would scold and reprimand daughters for the smallest act thought to be not within the stern customs and traditions of the culture. For example, a girl might be reprimanded for the glance of a passing stranger or if a foolish teenage boy followed her. This topic is lengthy and tiring if I mention it in detail. Under such conditions, a girl would grow up with a heart filled with fear of ever making a mistake. When this fear became overwhelming, the temptation to commit a crime to relieve that fear would be difficult to resist.

Rebecca, that sixteen-year-old girl, full of vibrancy and energy, clever and quick, contentious and unwilling for anyone to violate her rights, was detained in Al-Zafaraniyyeh before us. We were shocked to learn that her charge was murdering her younger brother. Newspapers seldom wrote about such stories. Rebecca strongly denied the allegation, and she swore she was innocent.

The story told was that one day she was alone in her house when a teenage neighbor came in to see her. Suddenly her young brother, a twelve year old, entered the house and saw them together. Rebecca feared her family's punishment and her relatives' knife, so she hurried to eliminate her brother before he told on her. We heard her story but could not believe our ears because she appeared to be a very pleasant and articulate person, to whom we became attached as she tried her best to be close to us. She insisted that she clean our area and did not allow others to do it. While she was insulting those who upset her, she was tremendously pleasant and respectful to us. Rebecca was given a life sentence before our sentencing happened, which moved us because we considered her a victim of the severe traditions of her environment. We had no knowledge at the time that we would one day soon meet her again, and our association would be prolonged.

When we entered prison, we saw her right in front of us in the hard labor division. She greeted us crying and wailing, embracing each one of us as if we were her family. She hurried to bring us blankets, spread them on the floor of the isolation area, offered her pity and sympathy, and told the other inmates about our kindheartedness. After we were moved to the "Bahá'í ward," she tried to say hello from a distance by waving her hand above her head and pretending to fix her hair, since she was prohibited from being in contact with us.

After her sentencing, Rebecca rebelled and refused all restraints. We heard stories about her violations and punishments. One time she swallowed a number of needles in an attempt to kill herself. The needles even showed up on an X-ray to which she was forced to submit. She also swallowed beads that the inmates used in crafts. She did not die in these attempts, even when she swallowed many pebbles, but we were saddened by what happened to her and could not give her any help, advice, or guidance.

Rebecca remained for a long time without any visits from family members, and when her family finally started to visit her, she was fearful of their retribution. But they assured her that she was forgiven. She believed them with her simple-heartedness, as she was in need of their love more than anything else. Her fear of her family began to subside.

When the general amnesty law was issued, Rebecca was released. She had forgotten about her crime and her state of affairs with her family, especially since five years had passed. She surrendered herself to her family like a sheep surrendering to a butcher's rope. Her certain fate was her family's knife, which is a legal right—the defense of honor—for which the family is not punished. Or, if a family member is punished, he or she is given a very light verdict suitable to the traditions. This was especially true after president Al-Bakr reinstated this law and allowed light sentencing of only a few months, or sometimes even a pardon for close family members who participated in these "honor killings."

We were very saddened to hear about the fate of a girl we liked and who had become attached to us due to the absence of family love during her imprisonment. She had tried her best to make money so she could treat herself to some cheese or a can of tuna, and had tried to fit in by imitating other inmates in smoking cigarettes. She had offered to clean even the sewer for pennies. Some inmates accused her of clogging the sewers and then cleaning them for money. This experience was yet another one of the sad memories we encountered in that horrible prison.

Baraka and Nadira

Please be patient with me while I tell you the stories of inmates who were part of our daily life and struggles. These were people whom we were obligated to courteously deal with and to whom we had to listen as they shared their feelings and anguish. Sometimes we had to step down to a level that was suitable for their comprehension, upbringing, and social status so that we would not appear vain or superior while interacting with them.

One day, the superintendent came with two sisters who would occupy a cell close to ours. They had a three-year-old little girl with them. Their charge was smuggling illegal weapons to tribes. Other members of their family were charged as well.

One time I asked how they were able to smuggle the weapons, and they laughed, saying, "We put them inside woven baskets (called Zenbeel, normally used for carrying fruits and vegetables)."

Men used their female relatives for this illegal business. One of the sisters told me that the judge called them a gang, and while sentencing them, he pointed at all of them after they were asked to stand in a row and said, "From this end to this point: a life sentence, from this point to here: ten years, and from this point to the end of the row: five years!" It was fortunate for the sisters that they were standing at the end of the row.

As soon as they were put into their cell, they started to smoke with a ferocious appetite. Before they had even finished one cigarette, they would be starting another. Cigarettes never left their fingers, and clouds of smoke started to drift into our cells. Quarrels between the sisters began, due to the bad prison conditions. Perhaps if they had been placed in another ward, they would have found more suitable people who would listen to them, offer them comfort, and ease their loneliness, but our relationship with them was limited because we had very little in common with them. They were from an uneducated stratum of society and spoke a language that was polluted with vulgarities. Luckily for them, the "Home Leave" law allowing home visits had been issued prior to their incarceration, and they were ecstatic to go home for a few days and come back with a few dollars—enough to buy more cigarettes—until their cell floor and the hallway were entirely covered with cigarette butts.

Only a short period had passed since their return from their home visits when we heard the glad tidings: both sisters are pregnant! And this is how, a few months later, each delivered a baby boy, despite the fact that each had several other children at home—one even had a married daughter. Their pregnancies had benefits for each sister. For example, their status improved in the eyes of their husbands and in-laws because they had been able to increase the number of children for their families. This improvement in their family status ensured that their marriages would survive. The sisters were hopeful that each of their spouses would not take a second wife, since—as I have previously mentioned—this practice was common for the husbands of female prisoners.

The babies were delivered, and both were frail and malnourished. Their heads looked like clay soil that is deprived of water and starting to crack. I had never seen babies look like this, despite the fact that I had many brothers and sisters.

Sleep became very difficult inside the ward. One baby would cry, and as soon as it calmed down, the other baby would start crying. Having the babies in those hard circumstances was very difficult. There was no way to warm up a milk bottle or to store it in a clean environment. The lack of nutritious food necessary for the mothers and babies, especially the fact that the mothers were in need of cigarettes more than anything else, was another challenge. Sometimes mothers would sell the new clothes they received from family during visits and buy the cigarettes they were addicted to with that money.

The other major challenge was the absence of diapers. Mothers in the prison would usually make them out of cloth, and the poor used old clothes to make diapers. An even bigger obstacle was the shortage of water; it would be cut for hours at a time, which forced the mothers to keep their children's diapers on wet for prolonged periods of time, then wash them quickly using mostly water. The effect of the lack of soap always became clear from the repulsive odor coming from the hanging laundry inside the net after hours. That was during the hot months, but in winter, the situation was even harder on us and the mothers.

As if the misery of prison wasn't enough for the sisters, news arrived that the husband of the younger sister had remarried! She pretended to be too occupied with her baby and that she did not care, but after her second visit home, she complained about the second wife. In a few months, she was able to convince her husband to leave the second wife, who had a baby as well, and the younger sister brought the stepson to live with her in prison!

This is how our ward came to have four children. The older daughter (her nickname was Nassooreh) had no choice but to stay with her short-tempered mother, who was busy with the baby and left her with pots and pans to play with. She banged with a spoon on the aluminum pot a very slow beat that gradually increased in loudness and speed. The little girl enjoyed the banging, especially after lunch. That was the time we needed to rest, but the little girl needed a release of her frustrations, especially when her mother tied one of her legs to one of the bars in her cell so she would not roam outside the ward. When her banging went higher, so did the blood pressure of everyone.

We tried to talk to the little girl nicely, which made her stop for a few seconds, but then she would resume the banging. If we ever showed the slightest displeasure, her mother would angrily reply, "Leave the child alone. Isn't it enough that she's in prison and adding to my misery?" We tried avoiding any confrontation with the mother, who had a sharp tongue that could strike at any time. And if it wasn't for our treating her kindly, we would have received endless verbal insults.

The children in the ward were extremely irritable and cried often. Just like the adults, they suffered from the gloom and depression of the confinement and the repetitiveness of prison life. They were deprived of the joys of childhood, especially the freedom to play. Their mothers—through hitting them, and scolding them, and forcing them to be quiet and still whenever they wanted—took out on them all the agony they were suffering. This behavior, of course, was unnatural for a child.

Despite everything, we still loved Nassooreh. She was a beautiful child with golden hair, lovable despite her dirty face and clothes, but the annoyance of her banging was hard to deal with every day—it went on for months and years. It might seem to you that such situations were insignificant, and you might ask why we did not help those prisoners and offer toys to their children. My hope is that you can understand that we Bahá'í ladies were not allowed to mingle with the other prisoners, despite the fact that we were confined to the same ward and locked in by the same gate. Later on, two more children were brought in with their mother, raising the number to six children on our ward.

As time went by, and with our persisting love and kindness, the two sisters learned to be respectful toward us and proud to tell their relatives that they were in the "Bahá'í ward." Even the letters they received had the address "Women's Prison, the Bahá'í ward." We tried our best to tolerate the suffocating smell of smoke that mixed with the dirty-diaper odor, especially in winter when all the windows had to be closed. Every time the cell door of the sisters opened, the smell that drifted out into the ward was similar to a stable for horses. We longed to smell the fresh breeze or the fragrance of flowers. How I missed the fragrance of one jasmine blossom from our garden! Believe me when I say that one Iraqi jasmine would have been enough to perfume the air in my cell. It is customary to bring roses on happy occasions, but bringing them to prison during visits somehow seemed inappropriate! It is an unpleasant occasion, I suppose, but people honor their returning warriors with flowers and also place flowers on the graves of the fallen soldiers. Were we not warriors of our blessed Faith and hostages abducted for the sake of bringing terror to the hearts of His loved ones? Were we not worthy of even a single flower?

Yet this is how we remained in Abu Ghraib—we were deprived of even a single flower. We remained deprived of that small, cherished pleasure until later, when we were moved to the prison of Al-Rashaad, where we were allowed to have a small area near our ward for planting some flowers. Even perfumes were prohibited in prison, and a prisoner who was caught with perfume would be punished for hiding something prohibited. Occasionally, we were able to put on perfume that our dear visitors were carrying with them during their visit.

Alyaa

One of the ward companions was a young lady in her thirties who was nice-looking, sharp-minded, always cheerful, very observant, and curious. Despite the fact that she was illiterate, she was accused of espionage and the distribution of leaflets for the Communist party among the Kurds in the north of Iraq. Her clothes were those of villagers or the poor, and she was barefoot most of the time. She had received a life sentence, but her husband was to be executed. He was the one who had lured her to that criminal path. He was a member of the Communist party, and many consecutive Iraqi governments had strictly barred this political party, halted its activities, and prohibited its books.

Alyaa, accompanied with a three-year-old little girl, was brought directly to our ward. She was quick to befriend us, and nothing could hold her back from accompanying us most of the time, even while we were having our meals. Despite putting on the appearance of simplicity and goodness, she was very audacious. We began to feel suspicious about whether her placement was a plan to bring our news, word for word, back to the office, but her good-heartedness made us dismiss the idea that this prisoner had any intentions other than befriending us. She seemed to be sympathetic and kind. We had nothing to hide, and therefore continued our good relationship with her until the time of our release.

After a while, however, I became certain that Alyaa would not hesitate, for any reason, to report us to the officials. She was allowed to leave the ward every day and go to a class, to the prison's store, or anywhere else, and she would visit the prison's office on her way.

My suspicions were in place as one of the kind supervisors hinted to me by saying, "I am surprised you care about someone who's reporting news about you!"

I said, "We offer love to everyone, and we have nothing to hide. We have not committed any violation of the prison's rules."

The supervisor replied, "Be careful, she's a mischief-maker."

However, our kind hearts still refused to treat that woman with anything other than generosity and friendship.

One day, Alyaa came in disturbed and pale-faced. She donned her traditional abaya in a hurry and took her daughter with her. Rumors spread that her husband was about to be executed. Everyone seemed troubled by the news because, as I mentioned in the past, during such circumstances, inmates feel empathy toward each other.

Alyaa and her daughter left the prison accompanied by a jailer to see her husband before his execution. We said our farewell and offered her some comforting words, saying that God is merciful and we must not lose hope. Before sunset, Alya returned absolutely distraught and horrified, wailing and lamenting with only one slipper on her feet. She told us that they had put the standard clothing (a red hood and neck cover, and a gown similar to those patients wear in hospitals) on her husband and were preparing for his execution. As usual, everyone was gathered around her listening and crying in empathy for her loss. The sound of wailing rose even from the other wards, and a cloud of sadness spread over the entire prison until sunset.

Two hours later, news came that the chief administrator of the men's prison had arrived. In interest, we hurried to look outside through the narrow windows of our cells and saw him coming toward our ward where Alyaa was. Fearful and anxious, poor Alyaa went to him anticipating more bad news. Out of curiosity, I listened carefully through my window; they were close by. I heard the chief administrator tell Alyaa that she could save her husband's head, as they had not yet implemented his execution until they heard from her first.

He said, "You must give us the entire details of your case and inform us of all suspects."

Supplicating and pleading with the administrator, she swore to God, that she had no other information besides what she and her husband had already given their captors during interrogation.

But the administrator insisted that she must give them more, or her husband would be executed at once.

She swore again that if she had any additional information, she would not hesitate for a second to save the life of the father of her daughter.

After hearing her, the administrator stopped his questioning and left the prison.

We stayed in a state of anticipation to see what the next day would bring. We beseeched God to cast His mercy upon her and her husband, as we had nothing in our hearts but sincere love toward her. We had always tried to comfort her and give her hope.

The next morning Alyaa, pale-faced from sleeplessness, remained in her cell. She had had a night filled with torment and agonies. We also wondered what had happened, and we beseeched God for His mercy to spare the life of that man for the sake of his wife and daughter. All of a sudden, we heard the sound of ululations coming from the other wards, and we were told that the husband's sentence had been indeed changed from execution to a life sentence! More ululations rose from our ward as well, and we went to congratulate Alyaa. Even the superintendent came to congratulate her while she was in total shock.

Alyaa returned to her old cheerful and intrusive self, meddling in everyone's business and forgetting that horrible day, charged with surprises, when the hanging rope had been around her husband's neck. When the "Home Leave" law was implemented, both Alyaa and her husband were included and went home. Alyaa came back to add another baby to our ward, as she was pregnant! She hinted her wish for our dear Bahiyyeh Masjoon, who was a registered nurse and a midwife, to be her midwife. She begged and pleaded, but Bahiyyeh, who would never hesitate to help anyone, apologized several times and said she did not want any responsibility while she herself was a prisoner.

Bahiyyeh used to be a nurse at the same prison's hospital and had spent many years working in other fine hospitals. Alyaa did not stop pleading with

Bahiyyeh and was able to get consent from the prison's administration for Bahiyyeh to assist with the childbirth.

The night of the delivery arrived, and we spent a second wakeful night with Alyaa—but with a huge difference. The first night had been filled with anxiety and fear of losing the life of a human—her husband's—but during the second, we were anticipating the arrival of a new life and the safety of the mother. But this little baby was going to be with its mother in a cell, while God has created man free to enjoy His bounty on this earth.

That night, we remained with Alyaa. Dear Bahiyyeh made a tremendous effort in assisting her because it was a complicated delivery. At dawn, we finally heard the cry of a newborn, a baby girl by the name of Mejjo. Bahiyyeh was very busy cleaning the baby, cutting the umbilical cord, and tending the needs of both baby and mother.

The Bahá'í sisters all participated in preparing clothes for the newborn, using the sewing machine we had. Alyaa was delighted with the outcome and happy with her newborn and the safety of her husband. We had to tolerate Alyaa despite her nonstop talking and rambling, and the day and night crying of her children, but we were always amused by her cheerful character.

Um-Ahlam

Um-Ahlam was another inmate who shared with us the bitterness of captivity in that ward. She was a woman in her forties with average looks and figure and long black hair, which she sometimes tied in the back with a hairclip and other times let down. After she arrived, she would always dress in all black, but as the days went by, she gradually replaced her black clothes with a more cheerful and stylish attire. Apparently, the deep pain and depression that were engraved deeply on her soul had also started to diminish. Perhaps the atmosphere around her had contributed to her emotional healing, and perhaps we had a positive role in improving her morale, or maybe the passing of the days had eased the shock of imprisonment and helped her accept her new reality. This process normally happens to a person in prison when he or she starts to empathize with the self and protects it from being destroyed by the circumstances so it can survive.

Um-Ahlam was accused of espionage, along with her husband and sixteen-year-old daughter. We never asked about her allegation nor permitted anyone to bring up the subject, but she volunteered to talk about it. She confessed that she—and her husband—had made a mistake and had not thought out the results of their actions, the possibility of imprisonment and the displacement of their children at the homes of relatives.

Ahlam was her eldest daughter. The authorities included her in the charges because she was considered coherent enough to report her parents to the authorities. But while in the care of her parents, Ahlam did not have this kind of awareness. How can one expect a young lady like her, who is respectful of family traditions, to report her parents and then see them be locked up in the darkness of prisons or even executed? That was the reason for Um-Ahlam's deep sorrow as she recounted her dear daughter's tragic story and how she was a victim of her parents' mistake.

When Ahlam, a beautiful and delicate young lady, was given a prison sentence that separated her from her brother and two sisters, deprived her of her school friends, and forced her to stay behind bars in hard labor with a number of criminals, she could not bear the shock. She broke down and started to wilt little by little. She refused to eat due to her loss of appetite, and her spirit turned away from life. Her mother had no means to take her to a psychiatrist, as there was only one small clinic in the prison to refer to for any illness.

Within two months, Ahlam passed away. Her death was another shock for the suffering mother, and the burden on her conscience became hard to bear. The news was just as hard on the father and destroyed him both emotionally and physically.

We were compelled to listen to Um-Ahlam as she told her devastating story with bitter pain. We had to listen because she was by then another number in that ward and was considered a family member. She never stopped describing the beauty of her beloved deceased daughter and how she resembled several famous movie stars and was even more beautiful. Without a doubt, we were sympathetic toward her and offered her words of comfort. We shared her sorrow and prayed that God would help her endure.

Um-Ahlam's worry about her other two daughters, who were staying in the homes of relatives, was a different tragic story. Whenever Um-Ahlam received visits from some of her relatives, these relatives would only bring with them additional problems and worries that they would then pile on to Um-Ahlam. As I mentioned earlier, prison was considered a polluted spot that most relatives tried to avoid. When my daughters came to visit me, I could read on Um-Ahlam's face an ample share of sad and agonizing emotions in her longing to see her own daughters. She told me that she wished that her daughters were staying with relatives or grandparents like my daughters were. I didn't want to explain to her my daughters' and son's circumstances and the struggle they were facing due to the sudden life changes and the imprisonment of both of their parents. That poor soul, Um-Ahlam, told me to thank God that my daughters were with my parents, as she did not know the fate of her daughters and what unfortunate surprising events could be awaiting them.

She had the right to worry because her daughters had stopped going to school, and they had found no encouragement from the relatives to continue. Her older daughter, a very beautiful girl, had been looking for work, and those who intended to help her were characters with whom Um-Ahlam did not feel comfortable. Her constant worry about the safety of those jobs and her daughters made her a captive of anxiety.

Naturally, constantly hearing her voice her anxieties caused me to reflect, deep in my soul, about my own daughters, despite Um-Ahlam's and my completely different family scenarios and the great trust I had in each of my daughters, who had deep faith and great attachment to the lofty ethics we had installed in them. My thoughts differed from those of Um-Ahlam, but we also shared many similarities in our current situation. We were both being held prisoner with our husbands, and we had both been forced to leave our daughters to live in the homes of relatives.

With time, Um-Ahlam came to accept her new reality, and she gradually returned to a more joyful nature. She enjoyed friendships and found in her babbling a relief from her pain. We saw her go back and forth with amusing stories about prisoners in other wards where she was allowed to enter because she was allowed to attend sewing and religion classes. She remained friendly with us, and we maintained a good relationship until the time we left Abu Ghraib.

It was by a coincidence that I met Um-Ahlam after our release from prison years later, and she told me about the agony she had endured after the passing of her husband subsequent to their release. At that time, I was missing terribly my son and daughters, who had left Iraq, and our separation had bitterness far worse than that of the imprisonment. But I am thankful that my children were under the care of the beloved Bahá'ís. When a person compares his difficulties to those who have much worse agonies than himself, he finds his own suffering much more tolerable.

The Jailers at Abu Ghraib

When talking about Abu Ghraib, thoughts about the jailers come to mind. As I mentioned in chapter 4, jailers were employees with individual tasks assigned to each one of them, and they had different roles than the supervisors. Their uniform had a different color as well—it was a long, khaki-colored dress and a coat, with a black scarf covering the hair (for female jailers). The jailers were trained to deal with the inmates on a personal level and tend to their needs.

The name of the first jailer who directed us to our ward upon arrival was Um-Musa (mother of Musa "Moses"). She was a kind, mild-mannered, and quiet woman of faith. Due to her orders, she would occasionally surprise us at night to see what we were doing! Sometimes we would be praying, and at other times the girls would be singing, with me accompanying them. At that time, we were alone in that lonely and uneasy place. Sometimes we would stop singing when she arrived, and other times she would startle us when she stood behind us in the dimmed light, watching and listening.

Um-Musa never objected to our behavior or took a complaint to the office, and gradually, she became a friend with whom we felt comfortable. We continued our good relationship with her until we left the prison. She was a source of comfort, especially during the first days of our imprisonment. We were very thankful to God for her, as other jailers were very stern and would have made the beginning of the experience much tougher on us. God bless you, Um-Musa, in both worlds.

Rafiiaa

We gave Rafiiaa the nickname "Ruwruw." She was different from Um-Musa in every way. She was very slim, bony, and short. During summer, when she walked in the courtyard without her coat, wearing a dress that exposed her arms and legs, she looked like a dried-up tree or a walking coat-rack for children. She liked having very short hair, cut and styled by the prison barber, who was a prisoner as well. That "stylist" was the one responsible for shaving a big portion of her neck and leaving it to look much longer than normal. The inmates of the other wards liked to joke with her. When she was in a good mood, she tolerated their humor, but at other times she became upset and took her complaints to the office, which was something she preferred to do. She gave orders like a chief and enjoyed commanding us to clean and wash the courtyard after visitations.

Once during the hot summer, I became ill with a skin infection, so I asked for permission to visit a specialist in a clinic at the men's prison. In such situations, a specific day is chosen for the female prisoners. Accompanied by Rafiiaa, I left with other inmates and walked there on a sizzling hot summer day. By pure coincidence, my husband Siddiq was visiting the clinic at the same time! Despite the distance, my husband was able to recognize me (at that time, he had not completely lost his vision). He greeted me, and I responded by nodding my head without words, and each of us went on their way to our respective doctor. Rafiiaa's small and narrow eyes were like mouse's eyes, monitoring like radar every move by the prisoners. She observed the passing greeting between us. I never thought a simple nod would be considered a violation of the prison's rules!

When we returned at noon, before I entered our ward, I heard over the loudspeaker: "Prisoner Anisa must come to the office immediately."

I thought to myself, "May it be good news, God willing." I was still panting from the heat and exhaustion, but I headed toward the office to find out what was going on. I found the prison's chief administrator with other prison employees in an emergency meeting. I greeted them, but the administrator was unhappy (she was the second administrator after we entered prison).

With a tone full of harshness and blame, she asked me, "Did you meet your husband in the men's prison?"

I said, "There was never a meeting but a simple passing silent greeting—a nod, and that was all. He greeted me from afar."

"Did your husband know you were coming?"

"No."

"But you greeted him."

"I only nodded my head!"

"Even so, this is a violation, and doing this is prohibited."

I respectfully said, "Should I have just ignored him and looked the other way? If one of you saw your husband, would you ignore him and look the other way?

She replied, "But you are a prisoner, and the jailer told us that you exchanged greetings."

I assured her that I did not know it was a violation to nod, and that the jailer was not telling the truth, as I had many witnesses.

The interrogation had ended, and I was ordered not to repeat the offense, so I said, "Next time I promise to cover my head so I won't see anyone."

She smiled and said, "That would be a good idea."

Thanks be to God that we were not under the full authority of that rabble-rouser.

Rateebeh

Rateebeh was another jailer with whom we did not have a direct relationship. Her responsibility was the prostitution ward, which was exactly across the courtyard from ours. The two wards were separated by a pool of stagnant water, with stone seats around it, where prostitution inmates sat and chattered all day long. Such a ward needed firmness and regulation.

Rateebeh was completely competent to take that responsibility and exercise full authority. She was firm in reprimanding the prostitution inmates in every way possible, including screaming and swearing, and she did not hesitate to use profanities of their daily low-level vocabulary. At times, she even resorted to kicking and slapping in order to break up a fight if the situation required, then throwing the troublemaker into isolation. And if she was not capable of handling a situation, she called on the police to break off heated quarrels that were abundant in that ward. Even the police would at times grumble and mumble complaints about that ward.

Once, I saw through my cell window a policeman entering that ward after a heated fight. Within seconds, he came out running, cursing, and spitting on the ground. The next morning, we heard why he ran off so quickly. It was because one of the prostitutes had tried to scare him by coming out naked! These types of stories frequently happened in that ward. Some of those inmates were mentally ill, and some found comfort and pleasure in punishments, and others in remaining naked. One of them would sit naked like a statue for hours and would only run inside when a supervisor came.

The prostitution ward was a source of great annoyance to us, especially in the first few weeks of our incarceration, but after a period of revulsion and disgust, we grew to ignore their existence.

One time, Rateebeh escorted us during one of our visits to the men's prison. On the way back, she voiced insults toward us for no obvious reason. One of our Bahá'í girls became defensive of our beliefs and answered her back. I asked her kindly to dismiss what Rateebeh had said because she was trying to lure us into talking about our religion. If we did so, she would go to the office to report the incident. One of the things she said, as I remember, was that we had diverged from Islam and distorted the Al-Qiblah (the direction of the Ka'ba in Mecca where Muslims face during prayers). Thankfully, the incident ended in peace. Thanks be to God, normally we were under no direct supervision from and did not have to take orders from that woman.

Um-Kareem

Um-Kareem was different from the other jailers because of her beauty and smiling face. She was a very pleasant woman who was liked by all, and we had enjoyable experiences with her. She always expressed her sorrow to see us behind bars. She had several children, and at times when childcare was unavailable, she brought some of them with her to work.

After a while, we heard that Um-Kareem was expecting another child, but her pregnancy did not slow her down while she was moving around the wards. We were surprised to hear the news that Um-Kareem had given birth to a baby boy in prison! For her, that day was no different from any other day. She had never complained of being tired while passing through our ward earlier that morning. She gave birth while alone and without any help. She locked the door in one of the prison's rooms and stayed behind the door, holding the door handle in one hand, and covering her mouth with the other until it was time to squat and give birth to a baby. She wrapped the baby with her uniform coat, and only then asked for help from one of the prison employees, who called for the prison's doctor to come and care for the mother and baby. The little boy was healthy and beautiful. She was relieved of her duties that day, took her newborn baby, and left for home! That hardworking lady was poor and strived to make ends meet, and there were times when she collected food leftovers to feed her children.

After our release, we heard that Um-Kareem was murdered by her foolish husband after a simple quarrel regarding some false accusations. Prisons have a bad reputation, and in such a culture, very few families allow their relatives to work in them.

Um-Kareem: I ask God to bestow His mercy upon your soul. You were a hard worker and a striver in your tough life. You hid your pain behind a smile of contentment and left wonderful memories in our souls that cannot be forgotten.

The Prison Office's Policy toward Us

We were extremely cautious not to leave even a tiny gap through which a complaint could be issued by a supervisor. Despite this, there were insignificant, small detrimental violations issued against us, such as one of the young ladies being late leaving the ward on visitation day. It is natural to have certain excuses for being late. For example, sometimes someone would forget to bring seasonal clothing to her family for storage and would have to go back to the ward and look for the clothing. Sometimes someone would want to give the family something knitted in prison and would need extra time to find it. Or sometimes, when family visits were finished, one of us would be unaware of the time or had taken an extra couple of minutes saying good-bye to her family. Other times we forgot to spread the black blanket on our beds.

These kinds of minor infractions received admonitions and scolding. We were in trouble for any little unintentional mistake, and woe to us if they ever found a forbidden item, which would then cause an intensive search to take place. This actually happened when a glass tea cup was found among the belongings of one of us. It had been given as a gift from the prison cook after she watched us drink tea from small plastic milk containers that had a sharp squared edge. Our friend did not want to turn down the gift and insult the cook, whom she previously knew, so she accepted it. When the teacup was found, it was considered a violation worthy of reprimand and warning, as if she had been caught with explosives. We were saddened by her harsh humiliation but forced to apologize as a group for our shortcoming.

Another incident happened one day when we were in need of salt, after we had become self-reliant with cooking. It was a coincidence that there was not a supervisor or a jailer present. When the time for our permitted outdoor walk arrived, two of our young ladies hurried to purchase salt from the prison's little store, which other prisoners visited all day long. The news reached the office, and it was a crime that could not be forgiven. A superintendent came to investigate the occurrence in our ward, interrogate us, and take our testimony!

I explained the situation, and we all had to apologize. It never occurred to us that those few minutes during our permitted time of walking would be considered a violation, while all other inmates were allowed to do it. The superintendent's reply was, "The others are permitted, but not you."

Our apology was not accepted; therefore, the two young ladies were called to the office for a severe reprimand, followed by every one of us being locked up and a prohibition being placed on our daily walk the next day—all for the crime of buying salt!

And this is how we remained—under their watchful eye for any minor mistake—which would then become magnified and exaggerated.

In turn, we multiplied our vigilance. Our nerves were on edge at all times as we tried to eliminate any chance for attack and criticism.

I remember another incident that, without any justification, had upset the office. During winter, we were given fabric for making our uniforms. The fabric was flannel—light yellow, with prints of ducks that were white and tan. According to the common style in Iraq, such fabric was suitable for young children. We joked about it among ourselves without any bad intentions. This was what we usually did to lighten up the situation. The young ladies told us (the older ladies) that we were going to look cute in our kindergarten uniform. That was where the humor had ended.

A short while later, the supervisor came to tell us that the administrator was very angry that we refused to use the fabric! It was of no use to explain to her that we had not refused to use it and that we had only been joking that we would be wearing kindergarten uniforms. The way the news was carried to the office had been exaggerated, with the aim of discrediting us.

I decided, after consulting with my sisters, that it would be a good idea to go to the office myself. At first, the administrator started with reprimanding me for our behavior in refusing the fabric, especially since we were well educated people.

After I explained that it was just an innocent joke distorted by whatever jailer had been listening to our conversations, and that we had full intentions of making very suitable and even stylish uniforms, she began to soften, and we received no punishment.

Heating the Facility in Abu Ghraib

Our first winter at Abu Ghraib was one of the worst winters we had ever experienced. The severe cold froze the blood in our veins and penetrated our bones. From the time of our arrival at prison until the time of our release, there was not a central heating or cooling system, except for fans, in that prison. Our ward was big, with six large open cells—three on each side, with a wide hallway in the middle. The ceiling was high, as was the style in Baghdad's buildings, and the front of the cells was made of iron bars, as was each cell's gate. Attached to the hallway were small cells for individual confinement.

All that space was without any heat during the cold winters, when temperatures drop to freezing or a few degrees below during Christmas time. We had to endure the cold with nothing but the clothes we were wearing and wash our hands, faces, and clothes with ice-cold water. The cold concrete we stood on caused us to lose the sensation of having any toes; instead, they felt like pieces of sponge. Even the thickest socks were not sufficient to keep us warm, so we had to knit additional pairs of wool socks that looked like sacks or tubes into which we inserted our feet. I had to even sleep wearing them because I could not fall asleep until my feet became warm.

We submitted a request to the office to allow us the usage of kerosene heaters. We hoped they might make a small difference in that large space, but our unusual request was denied. Inmates were not accustomed to such luxury. But the following year, after we were allowed to have a tiny television in that large hall, which was open for all the other inmates, only then were we permitted to have one heater for that whole place!

We shared the expense of buying the kerosene, with which we had to fill the heater on a daily basis, and we always carried the heater with us to the hall after sunset. We convinced ourselves that this one ray of heat was penetrating our frozen bodies. At times, we would move closer to the heater and rub our hands together to get the congealed blood to flow again in our stiffened fingers. To see that old and worn-out heater was enough to bring comfort to our souls. Having it was more of an emotional than a material benefit. The sight of it reminded us of our warm homes in winter, and its yellow flame was a symbol of life's warmth, which brought our souls hope and resilience to resist not only the cold but the hard circumstances.

We remained in this situation until the end of that long winter. Usually, winter ends with the arrival of Naw-Rúz (the vernal equinox marking the beginning of spring). The weather remains cool, but not severely cold.

During our third year, we received permission to have a kerosene heater in every cell, but they could be used only as necessary and only after sunset. Then they had to be turned off before sleeping, as was customary in Iraq. We only used our heaters if we did not go to the hall where the small television was. During the day, we were not permitted to use it. We also had to conserve kerosene due to the lack of storage space in the ward and also because we were allowed to buy only a small portion at certain times after standing in line to receive it. The heaters were also allowed on other wards with supervision.

Because of the cold weather, we were vulnerable to catching many cold-related diseases, such as influenza. Hand-knitted wool hats and wool scarves around our necks and shoulders were necessary, even in bed. Prisons are easy environments for spreading germs, and we had to endure illness as well.

When we were extremely sick, we would visit the prison clinic and would be given antibiotics. Only God knows if they were of benefit or harm.

The Heroism and Steadfastness of our Young Ladies— A Chapter of Honor in our Story

Before I finish writing about Abu Ghraib and draw the curtain on a period of time when we were locked behind its bars, I feel a responsibility to share a pride-filled chapter regarding the attitude of our dearest young women: Iqbal, Nida, Kawakib, Warqa, and Fatima. Each was a symbol of steadfastness and an example of bravery and heroism to the highest extent. I can easily say—or rather confess—that we, the older ladies, received courage and steadfastness from the flood of emotions those young ladies had toward the blessed Cause. They led us through their youthful enthusiasm, and they were willing to sacrifice even their lives. I can say with absolute certainty that if the circumstances had been harsher, and malice had blinded our captors' eyes from seeing the light of compassion, and their minds had been wrapped with the cloth of hateful bigotry—as other prisoners unfortunately experienced—our young ladies would have been the first to sacrifice in every way possible. They would have given up life and all its pleasures, given up their future, and given up their dreams of having families of their own. They were ready to face any hardship.

But we, the older ladies, although ready to face any difficult situation, were in a different position. We had no future dreams other than for our families. Each of us had either reached the end of her personal goals or had come close to doing so at that point in our lives. Some of us were retired or near retirement, despite the fact that our retirement wages had been taken away upon our entry into prison.

Without a doubt, thoughts of the future were on the minds of our beloved young ladies. Each one had a dream and a goal for her future, and remembering this goal would often ease their suffering in prison. The dreams for the future were a light that brought hope in the darkness of their cells and planted beautiful trees of hope instead of the depression of being locked behind iron bars. However, as soon as one of them was awakened from her beautiful dream to face the extant reality of imprisonment, she would bravely be in the forefront and ready in the path of sacrifice to uphold the noble cause that had instigated the cruel injustice of our arrest. To each one of you, my beloved girls, I give my love-filled salutation, deep appreciation, and the greeting of Allah'u'Abhá (God is the Most Glorious), wherever you are, forever and always.

If time in our cells seemed to move slowly for us older women—with days that seemed endless and nights that seemed to last forever, with no mornings to bring light—for the young ladies, it seemed to move even more slowly, at a snail's pace. Prior to imprisonment, each of the active ladies had a job, responsibilities, and friends. But time in prison is full of dullness and boredom, similar to a nightmare that cannot be relieved, except during times of prayer.

Dr. Iqbal, for example, had a fine job in the central hospital in Baghdad, where she was highly respected among her fellow doctors and her patients. Nida had a respected job at a government agency, and so did my sisters Warqa and Fatima. All were graduates of higher education. Dear Kawakib was still a student who was happily pursuing a degree in agriculture at the Sulaimaniyyeh University. She had loved her field and dreamed of having her own garden where she could exercise her knowledge and interest, but now she was behind bars with nothing but stillness and stagnation, and she was being forced to hear the same stories from inmates over and over, or insignificant stories about other wards, or stories of pain and bad circumstances that pushed people to choose the path of evil.

There was no way for them to pass the time except by busying themselves with sewing and knitting, into which they put great effort. We all tried to knit to keep busy, despite the harm it did to our eyesight because the lights were very dim. We became competitive in how fast we could produce something and how fine our production was, and we became quite skilled in using artistic designs in knitting, with yarn brought to us by our families during their visits. It was thoroughly inspected at the gate to make sure no forbidden items were smuggled in with it.

In the second year of our imprisonment, the prison office gave our young ladies permission to visit the prison's sewing room once a week. At the beginning, the sewing room was totally empty of prisoners until the Bahá'ís started to use it! Later on, the other inmates were allowed to be in the room while the Bahá'ís were present, but only under supervision by the guards to ensure no exchanges of conversation were made between the Bahá'ís and the others. Later on, when we were given permission to have the old hand-operated sewing machine, we no longer needed to go to the sewing room except every so often.

Since we could now independently prepare our food, our young ladies competed in mastering certain dishes for our meals and even surpassed us older women in their skill. We were very happy, appreciative, and encouraging in our praise toward our younger sisters. Despite the fact that our food ingredients were no different than those of other wards, the taste of our food exceeded theirs, all because of the skill and the care of our young ladies.

Going back to Dr. Iqbal, the highly skilled surgeon busy with a profession that she loved and that included responsibilities with her patients and surgeries—she was now keeping busy knitting, mending a shirt, or chatting with her aunt, who was one of our older ladies and who often reminisced about old family memories while being unsure of her destiny. She was the only one of us who received double the sentencing time in prison (a sentence of twenty years), but despite this, she was as strong as an unshakable mountain. Her love for her Faith and her attachment to its principles were greater than anything else. Therefore she remained proud of her steadfastness, no matter what happened to her.

In our second year, Dr. Iqbal was given permission to practice her profession on a very limited scale by going to the small local clinic and giving assistance to the doctor or nurse by checking on the patients during visiting hours. This had a very positive effect on our souls because a prisoner who was one of us was now being allowed to practice her profession in serving mankind. On very specific light health matters, she was also allowed to help patients after hours, and if she felt that a patient needed further medical assistance, she would let the supervisors know to call for help to take the patient to an outside hospital. The patient would then be transported to the hospital in a special vehicle.

The inmates were comforted by the fact that Dr. Iqbal was with them day and night, and they loved her for her pleasant and kind demeanor. She listened to their complaints, and her ability to listen was the most important part of the treatment they received.

However, this situation did not last more than a few months before an official order arrived prohibiting Dr. Iqbal from practicing her profession in prison. The order had a very disappointing impact on all of us, because it had no justification. She had done an extremely adequate job serving with absolute sincerity and gaining the love of everyone. Dear Iqbal was saddened by the news, but a few days later she returned to her cheerful self and began again to keep busy with a sewing needle and thread instead of her surgical needles and threads, and she wore a smile that never left her face. May God's salutation be upon you, my dearest Iqbal, and may He increase your faith and steadfastness. Your memory will remain in my heart until the end.

And now we have reached the end of the era of our imprisonment in the Abu Ghraib prison, and all the memories that will remain in the depth of our souls always. These memories were combined with pride from cherishing a sacred belief that taught us steadfastness in the face of the adversities of life behind bars. Our imprisonment was neither our choice nor our aim, as it was a cruel and unjustified punishment to each one of us. We had not committed any wrongdoing worthy of such harshness, but our pride and honor was our steadfastness in His Covenant and in a sacred Faith aiming to unite all who dwell on earth and to abolish all differences and prejudices so that the whole earth will become one country under the shadow of love and peace.

My memoir will continue now with events that happened in another prison (Al-Rashaad) to which we were transferred. Al-Rashaad was considered progressive in improving life in prison with less restriction. I will write of more events in the following pages of our honorable account.

Visiting day at Al-Rashaad

8 / Our Transfer to Al-Rashaad Prison

Toward the end of the third year of our incarceration in Abu Ghraib prison, a rumor had spread that the women were going to be moved to an unnamed location and that the buildings in which we were being housed would be converted to be used as part of the men's prison. The men's prison had become overcrowded with new prisoners, and more incoming prisoners were expected. I have previously given a description of the vastness of Abu Ghraib and its varied sections that included the women's prison, which in itself was a very large and spacious group of buildings. The entire complex at Abu Ghraib was one big and dreadful central prison surrounded by very tall walls.

At first, we thought that the transfer story was just a rumor, like many others that frequently circulated around the prison. But in just few days, the rumor became an inescapable reality. We inquired about its validity from the wardens, and it was confirmed. We asked if the next place was going to be much like the current one, and the very enthusiastic reply was: "It is so superior to the current prison that the term *prison cell* will not be found in its dictionary!"

All of us were optimistic about the prospective place, which we thought would undoubtedly improve our living conditions. As to the exact location of this prison, it remained unknown and a secret that the administration kept from us. We wondered if our families were still going to be allowed to see us and whether we would be allowed to continue visiting our relatives among the male prisoners. Those monthly visits were an indispensable change of pace in our lives, despite the difficulties we faced while making the trip back and forth. It was as though we drew strength from watching the men's example of endurance. They were always in high spirits and in a constant state of thankfulness to God, despite their harsh circumstances and being in a crowded space that they shared with other inmates. Their steadfastness was unshakable.

A few days after hearing the news of our move, we were surprised by a night visit from the supervisor, who requested that we do some light packing—only what our hands could carry—and do it as soon as possible, for we were to be moved early in the morning. She said the rest of our belongings would be moved later on by trucks. We began our hurried mission of packing and putting as much as we could into cardboard boxes. We wrote "Bahá'ís" on the sealed boxes to avoid the risk of their getting mixed up with others. As to the iron boxes in which each one of us placed her personal clothing, we wrote our names on each box after locking it. All there was left for each of us to take care of was our handbag, in which we placed our toothbrush and toothpaste, a comb, and other small personal items. Each of us also took her small radio, as we were allowed to listen to the radio as long as it was tuned to the Baghdad Radio Station.

In the very early morning, the jail warden opened the ward's door, telling us that we were about to leave in only a few minutes. She gave us a very limited time to put on our prison uniforms and no time to have anything to eat. It was the wardens' routine to distribute bread each morning, but that day they did not.

We left the ward in a hurry, not having any chance to think about or feel anything toward a place where we had spent three full years. Our memories of it were drowned in sadness and misery. In addition, we left in a state of tension after a night of irregular sleep, overcome by insomnia and turbulent imaginings about our new "home," which we had been eager to learn about. For how can one move to a new home that one has never been allowed to see?

In front of the main prison gate were pickup trucks whose cargo beds had been enclosed with metal wire mesh on each side, with the top left open. After the head count, they loaded us, along with a group of other women prisoners, onto one of them.

We were overtaken by conflicted feelings, some of which moved us to tears. Still, the playful humor of the young ladies among us—Fatmah, Warqaa, Nida, and Kawakib—kept us in good spirits. Their humor stirred in me the desire to laugh—a desire I was usually unable to resist. This nature of mine may not be favorable to some, but I will have to confess it is something I cannot overcome. No matter how hard I try not to, I always give in to whatever makes me laugh, even in awkward situations.

Accompanied by a heavy presence of guards, the procession of these prisoner-transportation trucks began to move. We left the women's prison, then stopped in front of the big gate of the central prison. The vehicles lined up in a row, with the drivers awaiting instructions before continuing on. After some official processing, we left the frightening and dreadful gate—the same gate that welcomed us three years before. But our feelings today were different. When we had first been brought here and had seen this gigantic gate for the first time, it had evoked in us dread and the fear of the unknown—feelings that were intertwined with other feelings of pride and glory, similar to those of a conqueror entering a new city.

When we had entered Abu Ghraib prison, we had left behind, at that gate, our peaceful life and had bidden our beloved children and the simple pleasures of our ordinary lives farewell. Now, we were leaving this gate to go to another, unknown world, and turn a page heaving with memories, sweet and bitter, from an imprisonment that we had accepted with honor for the sake of our precious Faith.

The procession continued speedily on the main road, as though the drivers were carrying a smuggled item and wanted to unload it in a safe place without calling attention to it.

Our vehicle approached the street that led to dear Nida's house, and she longingly said, "This is our street!" I saw the yearning on her lovable face and the sparkle in her eyes while she said quietly, "I wonder what my mom is doing right now. Are my sisters there?"

I was also looking closely at their street, a street with which I was very familiar. Then, and more so as we approached our street, my heart started pounding. As soon as Nida finished her expressions of longing, we crossed over the train tracks, to the north of which was our street, and we saw, a few steps to the right, the street where Dr. Iqbal's house was located. I could see on her calm face signs of yearning and suppressed pain, for she must have been remembering her deceased dad, Muneer Al-Wakeel, and she must have been longing to see her mother.

I knew that our house was empty now and had become only a number. The echoes of the children's laughter in it were no more, and the fragrant flower bushes had ceased to fill the air with their scent. The barking of our dog around the house had also stopped, for she too had been forced to share in the sad fate of our family and had been left homeless, until finally she was hit by a car, and her pain and suffering came to an end. All that was left were the very thirsty trees, which longed for the drops of water that the neighbors or my elderly father might give them whenever he was able to spend a bit of time there. He would sometimes visit our house to relive some old, pleasant memories while contemplating the present painful reality of four of his own children being in prison.

The vehicle moved very fast and passed the stores—which appeared as though they were very fast-moving shots in a film on a screen—where I used to shop. All I could do was to direct my prayers to God, with all my heart, and ask Him to protect my children and family and look after them. I was aware that my children, despite staying with my family, must have been feeling homesick. One's house is one's homeland—the symbol of peace and security. When that is lost, one lives like a foreigner, and all temporary homes seem to blend together.

Our vehicle then approached the streets that led to the neighborhood where my parents lived, and my sisters and I exchanged sad looks, while our thoughts were directed toward our loving and patient mother and our old father. We thought of the difficulties they were enduring in their old age and their need for care that normally would have been provided by their children. But now, all they could rely on was God's care.

An hour passed while we drove rapidly through the streets on the outskirts of the city of Baghdad, traveling from its northwest to its southeast corner. We noticed at a distance the chimneys of brick factories that were puffing thick, black smoke toward the sky. We did not realize at that moment that those chimneys were going to be adjacent to our new home and what they were spewing out was going to be what we were going to be breathing in, every day and every night.

Our transport vehicles came to a stop in front of a gate, which stood at the edge of a tall wall, but this wall was not as tall as the walls of the very frightful Abu Ghraib prison. We got off our truck and were quickly surrounded on all sides by guards, whose job, of course, was to prevent any of us from trying to escape.

Then the administrator of the prison, along with her other staff, began to collect the prisoners. This administrator was rough and ill-mannered to the highest degree. She may have been uptight because it was her last day serving in her post. We learned that she was being replaced by another administrator.

Instead of leaving us with a kind impression to remember her by, however, the outgoing administrator treated us with a rudeness we had never before encountered as she gave her orders for us to line up. Her mean demeanor and screeching voice left me grateful to God for having saved us from her at the right time.

After the head count for each group, we were ordered to enter the prison and were accompanied by the supervisors. They walked us to a big hall where we all gathered, awaiting our belongings. We were overcome by thirst and exhaustion, as the ride had been very rough and jolting. I recall that I headed to the faucet to wash my face, while, for some unknown reason, tears were flowing from my eyes, and I felt a rage that made me forget even to offer my prayers at that hour.

Finally, our exhaustion from standing up overwhelmed us, and we took to the concrete floor with great difficulty. The chatter of the prisoners around us echoed in that large hall, which was followed by a whispering of, "It's the new prison administrator."

The incoming administrator was walking between the rows of prisoners, and I could see that she was a woman of more than forty years old, of moderate build, with hair close to red in color. She was wearing dark glasses, but I was able to see her eyes clearly through them. She was looking very carefully around her, and looking toward us with scrutiny, as though closely and meticulously examining us, while she stood very straight. I remember clearly the examining looks she gave our group in particular from the corner of her eyes as she walked silently many times among us and looked carefully at each and every one of us. As she did so, I in turn looked at her, trying to gain an impression of her. My impression was not negative, as this new administrator—in contrast with the outgoing one we had just seen—appeared to be pleasant and lenient.

We remained in that tiring state for a long time. At times we stood up, and at other times we would go back to sitting on the concrete floor and waiting to finally settle down in our anticipated ward. Many hours passed, late afternoon approached, and hunger overwhelmed us all. We had not carried any food with us, and we had left without breakfast, so some of the prisoners began to complain. The hungry cries of their children began to get louder, and some cried from boredom, so their mothers became agitated. They were screaming at the children in an attempt to quiet them down. This led the supervisor to become coarser and stricter with us in an attempt to establish some peace and calm. This continued for a while. When the prisoners asked for food, they were told that it was coming all the way from, of all places, Abu Ghraib prison, because the kitchens in this prison had not been made functional yet. The prisoners were anticipating a hearty meal worthy of their long and exhausting wait.

At last, the big pots of food arrived. They were being carried on the heads of some other wretched prisoners, who had placed layers of sheets under the pots to try to avoid the heat from them. Cheers and expressions of thanks and happiness were heard throughout the waiting area. Then the portions were served and distributed, with one big aluminum bowl being given to each group. Our bowl was full of some very watery tomato broth (called marga, as you recall), with a few very thin, long slices of eggplant floating in it. Each prisoner received one slice.

This came as a big disappointment for the other prisoners, who had expected kebab, or anything else besides this cursed soup, so they began voicing their complaints and anger. But their complaints were met with reprimands and threats, so they reluctantly quieted down. As for us, our superseding motto at that moment was "contentment is an everlasting treasure," which is an Arabic proverb that encourages one to be grateful to God under all conditions. We learned later that this was going to be our one and only meal for that day.

At precisely the hour of sunset, the trucks carrying our belongings arrived. They piled our things in the main prison hall, and orders were issued for everyone to hurry and carry the heavy iron bed frames. Our supervisor told us that the last section of the prison was designated for us, so we followed her to see our new place.

This prison building was different in its design from the previous one. Perhaps this was because it was being envisioned more as a "correctional facility" than a prison designed for punishment. We heard many opinions that day as to what its original purpose had served. Some said it had served as military barracks, while others said it had been a hospital that served a military base. At any rate, it was clear that it had not been built with the intention of being used as a prison. Instead of cells, the places where the prisoners slept were regular rooms, similar to those in a house. Instead of wards—which were a group of cells—the building was divided into sections, or large groups of rooms. It had many sections, and it had a very spacious common open courtyard.

Afterwards, the rest of the prisoners—each in accordance with her crime— were sent to their places. Some were assigned to the section for serious crimes such as murder, spying, or counterfeiting, and others were sent to the section for less serious crimes such as theft, simple assault, violation of health laws, or violation of trade laws. There was yet another section for prostitutes and for women who had been convicted of marital infidelity.

The section where we, the Bahá'í women prisoners, were kept consisted of a long and narrow corridor on the left side of which were our rooms. Facing our rooms, to the other side of the corridor, was a larger room that later on was made into a store, and right next to it was a small storage room. Next to this storage room was another spacious room that we initially thought was a general hall for our section, as all the other sections in this prison had halls for general use.

But at some point during our three-year stay, the new prison administrator decided to make this room the prison library. Then she changed her mind and made it a room for the study of religion and theology. Then she canceled that idea, and changed the space into a lecture hall where a professor of social studies would come to lecture to the prisoners. The study of Islam was taken to another section of the prison.

We took a quick glance at our place, then hurried with the younger ladies to help with the transfer of the heavy beds from the storage room. We tried to select the less squeaky bed frames. The frames were stacked one on top of the other, and they made a loud noise as we attempted to drag them. Finally, our young ladies, cooperating and assisting each other, managed to carry the beds to our section. We then returned to the big hall to search for mattresses and bedding between the piles of linen and blankets, which had been hurriedly and carelessly placed on the floor. After thoroughly sifting through the pile, we found ours. I carried my mattress over my head, as this was the safest way and the method that every other prisoner used to carry hers. I was utterly exhausted, and so were the other young ladies. As soon as we managed to bring in most of the necessary items, we all collapsed on our beds, after a long, exhausting, and very oppressive—both physically and psychologically—day.

Then the night-shift supervisor came to check on us. The instructions were for there to be two prisoners per room. Dr. Iqbal roomed with her aunt Hajir Al-Wakeel, Nida Sabour with Kawakib Husain, and Bahiyyeh Masjoon with Miss Fakhriyyeh. My sisters, Warqa and Fatima, were placed together in one room, and Badriyyeh Ghulaam Husain roomed with me. Dear Badri-yyeh had informed me of her desire that we be together, and I agreed with her because of the many things we had in common. This general arrangement was decided and agreed upon by all.

Soon after the gate was locked, we all gathered in one room, and we lov-ingly embraced one another and expressed our happiness for being in our new place—as though they had moved us to one of the palaces of a sultan!

It was the first time in three years that we were getting ready to sleep in an actual room—one with four walls and a regular door, instead of one with iron bars for a front wall. The room also had a small window with cement bars in the shape of a cross at its center for reinforcement, with two shutters we could open for fresh air. We were finally freed from the cages of beasts. It was a small room, barely enough for two beds, but it was a regular room like any other in a house. It also did not have a freestanding toilet in the middle of it!

Our young ladies hurried to explore the other parts of our section in that prison. Their laughter and clamor were heard at their discovery of four independently standing toilets and a small, one-by-one square meter shower room. This sight brought us a measure of physical as well as psychological comfort—much more than we had expected.

Thus we found ourselves in a more favorable state of existence, and we commenced our second prison period with a familial, spiritual gathering, and we chanted our prayers at a normal volume and tone, without fear, as now we were far from the other sections of the prison. We supplicated God to provide us with a great deal of patience and endurance so that we might spend our upcoming days with a measure of steadfastness pleasing to Him.

The next day, the young ladies went looking for the rest of our belongings—including kitchen-related items and other possessions—that we had packed in the cardboard boxes. After much searching between the piles of things that were mixed and mingled with the other prisoners' belongings, they were able to gather everything.

Although the life of a prisoner is generally one of monotonous routine, lacking in excitement except on rare occasions, I can say that our imprisonment period in Al-Rashaad prison offered some freedom and a bit of improvement over our previous experience. One such improvement was having normal rooms, as I have already explained. These rooms had wooden doors, which we could close if we felt cold or close for privacy as one does in their own home. We were allowed to hang curtains on our window, so we all chose whatever style curtain fit our tastes. We were also allowed to have blankets and covers brought to us from home, so we replaced the old and worn black prison blankets, which we had been forced to use for the past three years. Just looking at these blankets had always made us feel depressed. The prison administration at Al-Rashaad kept those filthy blankets in a storage room, and one day during our last year in prison, we were surprised to see a repulsive black pile thrown in a corner against a prison wall, across from our section. Flies in unbelievably dense swarms had gathered around it. We looked carefully to try to figure out what was happening, then realized that those were our old blankets from Abu Ghraib—no doubt about it. Our hysterical laughter mixed with our pain at this realization, for we could hardly believe our eyes. Had we really used those loathsome blankets against our own bodies? Yes, those blankets had served as our bedding, the kind that even an animal would reject using for warmth.

Arranging Our Rooms

At this point, our rooms in Al-Rashaad prison had a homey look and feel to them. To add to this "extravagant" feeling, we even dared to persuade the new prison director to allow each of us to have a small rug brought in by our families to be placed in front of our beds. These covered the bare floor, which would get cold to an unbearable degree in winter. I suffered a lot from joint pain in my feet and legs, due to the cold cement floors in all the rooms and corridors. Our feet were constantly in close contact with these floors. I did not enjoy sitting in bed, wrapped in blankets as the older women among us did, so I would at times sit and place my feet on top of empty egg cartons or old newspapers.

To our surprise, the prison administrator accepted our request for rugs, which was presented as part of a list of suggestions to improve the prison conditions. She also consented to having a chair brought in for each of us to sit on, but we also kept our homemade seats that we had made from empty egg cartons covered with fabric. We noticed that other prisoners in the other sections of prison were also beginning to use colorful, non-prison blankets on their beds as we did. Some of them were also using simple seats to sit on instead of sitting directly on the floor. This was not common in the previous prison.

Another advantage was that we were now removed from the constant commotion that came from the section occupied by prostitutes, which, as you recall, had been right across from ours in Abu Ghraib. Their section now was far away from ours. There was an area of dirt behind our section in which wild vegetation grew during the springtime, and this vegetation separated us from the rest of the sections. In front of our section there was an open cement walkway; in front of this walkway was a dirt section that we attempted to farm later on.

Food at Al-Rashaad Prison

Another positive aspect of this prison was that we began to experience a small share of independence in terms of our meals. For example, we were not obligated to wake up early in the morning to have our daily shared breakfast before the usual room search. Each one of us was allowed to make her own tea and choose whatever she wanted to have for breakfast, as we each had our own ration that we kept and used as we wished. These rations were distributed on a regular basis depending on availability. Some items—such as eggs, yogurt, and fruits—were distributed weekly, and others—such as bread, which was what the children in prison snacked on—were distributed daily. We returned to eating the accustomed white bread and said farewell to the heavy black bread, despite its nutritional benefits. It was undesirable due to the way it was prepared.

Eggs were also distributed according to availability. At times, we were given four eggs a week; at other times, they would be unavailable. We tried purchasing them from inmates who sold what they could not use, such as dry milk or yogurt, so they could buy cigarettes with the money. Those kinds of transactions were most of the time ignored by the office.

There was no predictability in food distribution. Full egg cartons would pile up at the prison's storeroom, and on inspection day, the pantry attendant would hurry with the eggs and all other foods not distributed to the inmates as intended, and she would put them on wheelbarrows similar to those used in gardens or for trash. She would then discard the eggs and food outside or give what was still edible to the guards. She did that to avoid being questioned by the office. When the inmates saw the loaded eggs heading to the dump, they became angry and uttered profanities for not being given their shares. Excess rations of suet and tomato paste would be used in abundance in the prison's meals before inspection dates. The same happened with fruit; sometimes fruit would be distributed daily and other times once a week. Other items such as rice, meat, and vegetables were available on a daily basis.

For breakfast or dinner at Abu Ghraib, we often shared a small package of cheese by dividing it into ten equal pieces. We would also do the same with a can of beef. We had no way to refrigerate any leftovers except the Styrofoam icebox that kept them fresh for a couple of days only. In this Styrofoam box, we stored some of the food brought to us by families during our visits.

At Al-Rashaad, we decided to continue sharing our main meal (lunch) together and to individually prepare our personal breakfast and dinner. Additional supplies were brought by our families, and items such as canned meats and cheese were available at the prison's commissary. At times, the ten of us shared a special breakfast brought to us during visits. I remember dear Aala Sabour, who brought us a special Iraqi cream called Gaimar (it is made from whole milk and heavy cream that is cooked until thickened.) It was absolutely delicious, and, at the time, cholesterol was of no concern to us.

We shared our cooking among ourselves as well, especially since our young ladies, who had practiced cooking for three years at Abu Ghraib, had become experts at it. We prepared a weekly schedule for our meals. Our main meal was rice and vegetables with a little meat, which we cooked differently than the other prisoners. Every section had a cook (a designated prisoner), and unsurprisingly, the cook did not put a lot of care into the cooking nor in washing the vegetables while cooking large amounts of food for the entire section. We had become creative in cooking some of the Iraqi dishes; we would use the ingredients that were distributed as part of the rations to all the prisoners (again, they called it "bounty").

We sometimes shared a portion of our cooked meals with the guards and supervisors, and eventually the administrator overheard the guards and supervisors describing our food as superior to that of the best restaurants! The administrator came one day while we were cooking a rice dish that had eggplant and spices.

She complained, "You've been eating better than the rest of the prisoners, and that is unlawful in prison. All must be equal in food."

I replied, "The components are the same ingredients distributed by the prison; the only difference is that we put more care into our cooking."

She became silent, but then she decided that we must have a cook like all the other sections so we could all have the same meals! And thus a cook was assigned to our section. She was a kind woman with a good demeanor, and we helped her in preparing our meals, especially with cleaning the rice, which was always full of small rocks and seeds. We also gave her suggestions on how to improve the taste of the food by using certain spices. She learned how to prepare meals she had never cooked in prison and to reduce the amount of water used in cooking stew. The other sections started to improve their cooking skills as well, after being accustomed to throwing away their bad-tasting food that had the foul smell of meat untreated with herbs and spices.

Our kind cook complained of joint pain in her hands, for which she had to visit the prison's clinic on a daily basis for injections with an antibiotic. With Dr. Iqbal's inquiry about the matter, we came to find out that our cook was suffering from tuberculosis of the bones! By the time we discovered this, she had been cooking for us for a period that exceeded six months. We were in an awkward position to say anything, especially since we had developed a loving relationship with her, and she had become attached to us. But it was hard to conceal our fears while eating food prepared by her. We finally decided to submit a request to the administrator, saying we preferred cooking for ourselves so our cook could get the rest she needed. Permission was received, and we returned to preparing our own meals.

We had to endure the days by keeping busy in every way possible, to try to remain in good health both physically and mentally, and to never give up.

We were allowed to have a gas tank with a small burner attached to the top, but we were not allowed to have a stove or an oven. I suggested an idea of making a simple grill, a method I had tried at home for a quick meal when my children refused to eat a certain dish. How it works is by placing a metal container—such as a large rectangular can—on the top of the gas range, lining up meat skewers on top, and covering the skewers with a lid.

Because I used this method at home, I did not need to use my real oven very often.

Our young ladies liked the idea, and were able to bring a large metal container used for lard, clean it well, and put it on an old metal chair to be placed on top of the gas tank. We put two bricks, facing each other, on the sides of the container, and we asked our families to bring us a few skewers. At times, we asked the food distributer to give us a two-day portion of the meat in advance. That way, we had a sufficient amount to cook in an open area outside our section. We prepared a simple salad—which was never on the prison's menu—composed of tomatoes, onions, and a few leaves of cabbage, with a bit of cooking oil and lemon. If lemon was unavailable, we used a small amount of powdered citric acid (commonly used in cooking). We then planted purslane (a wild edible plant, as you recall) in the small dirt area by our section for cooking and salad.

We thoroughly enjoyed such meals, which were followed by cheerful remarks. This simple joy helped us forget our captivity, even for a short while, and boosted our spirits. It enabled us to ignore what future adversities might come, if God willed for us to stay there much longer. The homemade grill also encouraged us to experiment with cooking other foods. In one of the visits, a family member brought us a fish to cook, so we grilled it in the Iraqi way. I am sure it will stimulate your appetite after reading my next lines, and perhaps you will try this method! After nearly completing the grilling of the fish, we added sautéed onions, tomato paste, sliced tomatoes, and salt and spice on top, then we returned it to our oven until the liquids dried. The meal was delicious, especially in those circumstances. Try it and think of the Bahá'í prisoners of Iraq and their homemade grill!

A Cook Named Um-Hameed (again, *Um* means *Mother,* so her name meant *Mother of Hameed*)

It was apparent that our prison's administrator was determined to assign a cook for our section, as was the case in the other sections. The newly assigned cook was a convict from "hard labor," who was accused of collaborating with her brother in the first-degree, premeditated murder of his friend, who was a rich trader. They murdered him, cut his body into pieces, and bagged them in plastic bags that were later disposed of in a septic tank.

Um-Hameed denied all of these charges and claimed she was innocent. We never addressed this topic with her nor asked any questions, for it was of no concern to us. She always showed us kindness and a good demeanor, and she cared about her appearance and cleanliness and about the cleanliness of our food. Just as all the other inmates apart from us did, she sang the same song of being innocent, and for this reason, we stayed away from mentioning the allegations that had placed us behind bars and deprived us of our social lives. At that point, it was of no use to defend ourselves, as we had accepted our fate in the path of our sacred belief.

Um-Hameed mastered the art of cooking and took what she had learned to other sections of the prison where she cooked. At times, we asked for light meals to take with us on our monthly visits to the men's prison.

We remained on good terms with Um-Hameed until the day of our release. Um-Hameed was constantly anxious about her children, especially her daughter. After our release, I heard that Um-Hameed sought a refuge at a friend's house, which had a bad reputation. She was still "wanted" for revenge (by the family of the victim), and eventually she was discovered by the family and met her certain death. May God have mercy on her soul. She was loving and sincere in the way she treated us.

I apologize for going on at length about our meals and related matters, and perhaps it seems to be unrelated to our situation, but I must say that providing food for sustenance is a vital part of human life, including that of a prisoner. For us, our meals were a distraction from the repetitiveness of the dull days and their long hours; therefore, we found a little bit of pleasure in preparing our simple meals, which we often shared with our families during their visits. This was especially true after our families were allowed to join us in our rooms to eat with us. Having occasional meals and conversation with the family and friends brought joy to our hearts.

After visits, as was customary, we shared some of the wonderful foods we received from our families with the guards. The rest of the time, we sat together after our visits to read prayers and offer thanks to God, especially for His bountiful gift of steadfastness, then together we ate our lunch.

The Prison's Library

While in Abu Ghraib, we had heard that there was a library in the prison, but we had not had the opportunity to visit and explore the books it contained. Nor had we heard of any inmates borrowing any books. However, we did have the opportunity to meet the librarian, a pleasant lady close to forty years of age who taught the Islamic Faith.

In the Al-Rashaad prison, the administrator decided to put the library in our section, in the hall facing our rooms. She ordered metal shelves, and heaps of books and magazines were piled on the floor of that hall. She asked me to be the overseer of the library, and I agreed for the purpose of passing time, despite the fact that it was a hard task. The books were all carelessly jumbled together and covered with dust. I am not exaggerating when I say that I spent hours every day for many days organizing the books by subject and content and creating spaces for each group.

There were lots of magazines—literary and political—and many of President Saddam Hussein's speeches and discourses, which perhaps made up the largest section of the library. I browsed through some of them, but the truth is that I was not into politics and found the political terminologies hard to grasp. Therefore, I discontinued my exploration. Among the books and magazines, there were a number of other political publications and old-style poetry which I had no interest to read. I preferred poetry that was clear in its meaning, and did not like to be bewildered by the hidden meanings and symbolism or obsolete words, despite the fact that I was an Arabic language teacher!

I suggested to the administrator that she supply the library with contemporary publications of various themes and novels that would be easy for the inmates and guards to read. She laughed and told me that there were no requests for any books. In other words, she was trying to tell me that the library was no more than an attractive display.

After all the hard work I put into organization, the administrator came to tell us that the library would be moved to a different section of the prison. The inmates hurried to empty the shelves and pile the books on the floor all over again! I stood looking in disappointment at all the wasted efforts I had invested in cleaning, sorting, climbing chairs to reach the upper shelves, and more. The administrator was an indecisive person who was constantly changing her mind from one day to the next. Her leadership showed weakness, and her relationship with the inmates lacked firmness and consistency. One day she joked with them on a level devoid of formalities; the next day she chose extreme hardness and harsh punishments without valid reasons!

A while later, the same hall was converted into a place for teaching the Islamic Faith to the inmates. The administrator sarcastically told me that I should attend the classes, so I answered her in the same manner and said, "Would you like me to teach there or be there for another reason?" She looked at me with her familiar look, and I continued, "I am serious about that because I taught Islamic religion class in an elementary school at the beginning of my career. I taught there at the request and the insistence of the principal of that school, a girl's school in Egypt for the daughters of dignitaries. That principal was fully aware of the fact that I was a Bahá'í. Besides, I attended religious classes throughout my elementary, secondary, and high school years."

The administrator paused and then said, "We'll see if you (in plural) will be attending the class or not." The word "not" in her sentence sounded more realistic, as she did not truly wish for us to mingle with the other inmates anyway.

The inmates attended the weekly class only a few times before the administrator decided to move the religion class away from our section and to turn that space into a lecture hall for the guards, wardens, supervisors, and other prison staff members for further training. The first lecture was by a lecturer in the field of Sociology. I attended his lecture after receiving permission from the administrator. His talk was mainly about the Baath party, its accomplishments, and the need for attentiveness and firmness. I sensed a feeling of uneasiness by the supervisors due to my presence. Most of the supervisors had only received an elementary-level education, except one who was a high school graduate and another who was in her first year of college. The attendance of a prisoner whose education was higher than theirs appeared to be degrading to them.

The Prison's Commissary

There was a fairly large room at the entrance of the building that had been converted into a small commissary for the prison with an attached small room that became a storage room for the commissary. The woman who managed it was an inmate serving a life sentence without parole for killing her husband with the help of a man who was her husband's assistant at work! It was peculiar how most of the inmates accused of horrific crimes seemed to be extremely pleasant and kind. That inmate—they called her Um-Raad—was a woman in her late thirties or early forties with an attractive face. She was originally from the north of Iraq, the city of Mosul, and had already served several years of her sentence before we arrived at the Al-Rashaad prison.

At times, the prison's commissary carried canned foods such as jam, cheese, sardines, and beef, but at other times it did not. It carried soap, aluminum plates, needles, and thread, and later expanded its inventory to carry knitting yarn, cheap fabrics, and children's biscuits. When rations were scarce, we purchased what we needed from the commissary, and we ten Bahá'í ladies always gathered together for lunch and then the afternoon tea.

Um-Raad welcomed us to the commissary and was always happy to see us.
I constantly thought of her and the tragedy she had brought onto herself, but
I had to hide my feelings while looking at her angelic face and pleasant smile.
I would say to myself: "Is it possible? Is this rational? How is it conceivable
for evil to come out of such a good woman?"

Three years later, a clemency decree resulted in our release and that of many
other prisoners, except for a few new prisoners and others like Um-Raad,
who were excluded from the decree. When we left, I gave Um-Raad my comfortable chair, we said our loving good-byes, and I prayed for a miracle to save
her from the prison's eternal walls.

Having the commissary in our section of the prison was a source of noise
and clatter all day. There were inmates going back and forth to buy cigarettes,
cheap candy for their children, and cheese (the triangular kind), which—just
as at Abu Ghraib—the kids loved and devoured at an astonishing speed!
Quarrels between Um-Raad and a particular inmate, whom we were forced to
have in our section, happened on a frequent basis. I will dedicate some pages
for that inmate later on. The commissary and our rooms were separated by a
pathway one meter wide. We had to endure the annoyance of the noise every
day of the week, with no exception for holidays. When Um-Raad was very ill,
that mischievous inmate I mentioned took over the store and acted as if she
were running a supermarket by shouting and giving orders to all.

The Hall

Every section of Al-Rashaad prison had a small hall with a television
where the inmates gathered at night to watch the programs of one channel
only, which broadcasted from sunset to midnight. After we were moved to
Al-Rashaad, the office provided a large color television that was placed in the
main hall of the prison. Certain inmates were allowed to go there with the
supervision of their wardens, but the Bahá'ís were excluded, of course. The
administrator was kind enough to allow us to have an old black-and-white
TV, which was better than our previous, tiny black-and-white television that

I described in chapter 6. I had then called our old TV "the little orphan" because it was jittery and nervous. It quivered for the simplest reasons and lost reception very easily.

We put our black-and-white TV in a small room about two meters in width at the end of our section, and we considered it our section's "hall." The idea of having the luxury of a larger space never crossed our minds! We took our chairs after dinner (at that time we were allowed to have regular chairs, although we still kept the old egg-carton seats, as well) to watch the TV program and chat. By chance, that small room happened to have a table on which we put the television, and we sat in rows for the lack of space.

At times, we knitted while watching TV and imagined the situation of our imprisonment lasting for a long time. We were trying to accustom ourselves to that life with determined firmness and steadfastness. We prayed that the semi-peacefulness that we had been enjoying would not be ruined by any new complications.

Our Youth Activities

After the assignment of a cook for our section, we had more free time on our hands; therefore, we offered her our help. For our girls, time was plentiful, so they began, with the office's permission and encouragement from the administrator, to occupy themselves with projects that generated a small amount of income. My sister Warqa, for instance, was allowed to cut the hair of other inmates. She was very skilled at providing stylish cuts and using curlers, but unfortunately she did not continue doing it because of the lack of appreciation from the other inmates in that backward environment. Inmates who were happy and satisfied with their cuts at times received criticism from others, due to envy or meanness, and most inmates were villagers accustomed to having long, braided hair, who considered haircuts unnecessary.

For those reasons, Warqa chose to knit instead. She was very patient and meticulous and produced stunning, detailed designs that she sold for very small amounts of money that were unworthy of her fine labor. As for my other sister Fatima, she had pursued knitting for a while but then became proficient at sewing for the supervisors and the inmates—again, all for a very modest fee that was unworthy of her labor.

Our father—God bless his soul—despite the financial struggle in which he found himself due to half his children being abroad and the other half in prison, bought Fatima a sewing machine to lift her spirits. The sewing machine helped keep her busy and took her mind off the monotony of the days. Nida Sabour and Kawakib Husain had reached such a level of expertise in their sewing skills that the administrator and prison staff were making requests from them for all kinds of apparel, including suits. I still keep a two-piece suit made for me by dear Kawakib as a precious keepsake that I will not part with.

Kawakib was given another assignment, which was planting the bare garden beds around the prison's buildings. The office supplied her with a large bag of various seeds and gave other inmates, especially those who were farmers before their incarceration, the task of helping Kawakib with preparing the soil for planting. The open dirt areas were planted with grass, and the beds were planted with vegetables and flowers. The prison's appearance was vastly improved as a result of those efforts.

We asked family members to bring us more types of saplings to plant. Water was brought in tanker trucks, was poured into irrigation canals, and was quickly absorbed by the dry soil. Unfortunately, the good situation did not last, as the water tanks did not always arrive on time and water became scarce, even in the prison's main storage tanks that were used for drinking and bathing. The plants began to wilt and turned yellow. The grass needed mowing and further care and watering, especially before the summer season. As a result of not receiving this care, it became burnt, and thus the hard work of several months went to waste. We had hoped to have a garden to remind us of Baghdad's beautiful gardens, but sadly the fruits of our labor were short-lived.

Kawakib continued to put her efforts into the small patch at the end of our section, however, where we were able to harvest greens such as parsley, chives, mint, and purslane that we used in making salads. A wild tree quickly grew there, and we enjoyed sitting in its shade before sunset, which was the time we were locked inside. That little patch was only three square meters, but it gave our monotonous life some beauty and comfort.

Dear Dr. Iqbal visited the prison's clinic whenever possible, and she developed a wonderful friendship and professional relationship with the lady doctor and nurse at the clinic. She occupied herself with knitting, embroidery, and crocheting. She had replaced her old job using surgical needles with this new job using crocheting needles.

As for myself, I tried to knit for a small fee, one quarter of a dinar (a bit less than a dollar) per every ball of yarn, which took an entire day to knit. That was the going rate in prison, and in reality, it was below the minimum wage, if compared with the labor involved. But in prison, the benefits to one's mental and emotional state multiplies when labor is of help in passing time, which is a prisoner's number one adversary.

The administrator asked me one day to provide a report containing suggestions for improving the status of the prisoners. I wrote a report and did my best to offer constructive and practical recommendations, such as having a cafeteria where the inmates join other inmates for meals—at least the main meal, which is lunch—and I suggested that the prisoners be seated on chairs instead of on the floor, where they discarded their trash everywhere and then swept the floor the next morning. I said that it was important for them to learn cleanliness and the social etiquette of eating with forks and spoons instead of using their hands. I also suggested having physical education classes and recreational games, such as volleyball and other games because, despite the small nutritional value in an inmate's meal, the lack of movement causes her to gain weight and become lethargic. Daily tasks such as cleaning our rooms with a hand sweeper and doing laundry took no more than half an hour, which left us with plenty of idle time. Another suggestion was to replace physical punishments with non-corporal punishments as much as possible. There were other positive proposals, all for the benefit of the inmates and also so that the prison would be worthy of its newly-selected name "Al-Rashaad" (*Rashaad* in Arabic means *Development, Guidance, Correction*, and Al-Rashaad was considered a "correctional facility").

The administrator presented these suggestions to the officials in a meeting related to prisons, and she told me herself that she received admiration and praise from the officials. I remember writing a second report several months later after receiving a request from the same administrator.

Once I was asked by one of the supervisors for help in writing a research paper about the Al-Rashaad prison. She was a student in her first year of college and needed to write the paper for a school assignment. I wrote a report of several pages describing the positive aspects of that prison in comparison with those of earlier times. I remember lauding the administration for the flexibility of its attitude toward the prisoners and the added liberties the inmates had begun to enjoy. For example, the administration had given them extra time to go for walks outside their sections, had permitted them to watch color TV, had improved the inmates' meals, had created a library in prison, had provided prison rooms similar to those in homes, and had given them the freedom to choose to dress in regular clothes after hours and during visitation time with families. Other positive improvements that had been unavailable in the past included having sewing machines in our section and the others; and giving the children better meals, clothes, and toys. I also mentioned any other positive changes the new prison's administration had implemented in favor of the prisoners. The supervisor was very thankful for the report, and she ended up receiving a commendation from her professor.

A National Event Celebration and Other Recreational Activities

I believe it was the first time in the history of the women's prison administration that the officials considered having an entertainment event for the prisoners. In commemoration of a national event, the prison administration arranged to bring one of the renowned entertainers in the country to be the main singer in a concert. The artist asked for a substantial fee instead of volunteering his participation in the celebration.

The program included several musical segments and national hymns, and the administrator asked our young ladies to participate in singing. She asked all of us to prepare a program, but there wasn't enough time to produce it. However, I thought of adding a comedy segment, where I could tell some known jokes in the form of a short play. I prepared the play's script in a humorous fashion that related to members of a family who were all hard of hearing. It was supposed to take place on the first day of Eid (Islamic holiday). The father is talking about a topic, and his wife answers him about another, then the daughter comes in to address a problem, and her little sister contributes to the confusion to put everyone in a humorous conflict. Warqa, Fatima, Nida, and Kawakib all participated in the play with perfect makeup and outfits. My sister Warqa had the main role, which was the mother, and received the highest commendation. The play was a success, and the applause from the attendees, including officials and visitors, was continuous. The play truly was the best part of the program.

Other celebratory occasions followed, mostly for national events, where the programs were limited to speeches regarding the accomplishments of the extolled revolution that cared about the prosperity of its people and the comfort of the prisoners. Other programs emphasized the careful monitoring and high alertness of the governing party toward any violators and those who were ungrateful to the benevolent government.

One of the privileges we were given in Al-Rashaad was the ability to dress in our normal clothes, rather than prison uniforms, during visits with our families. But when we visited the men in the men's prison, we had to abide by the rules of wearing prison uniforms. I used to wear trousers under my uniform because we had to sit on low benches or on a small rug while riding in the truck. I remember the administrator jokingly commenting about our clothes. She said, "Those who see you won't believe you are prisoners during your visits with families."

My answer was, "This is a positive point to your benefit, madam, because our families will be comforted to see evidence of your excellent care reflected in our good health and well-being."

The administrator was very pleased to hear my words and found them to be reasonable. Later on, I heard that the name of the Al-Rashaad prison was changed to "Al-Rashaad Correctional Facility" to reflect the fact that it was designed to reform a person's behavior rather than serve as a punishment for the person. In truth, we cared very much about our appearance during visitation times because we wanted to bring comfort to our families. We tried our best to conceal our troubles from them so they would not observe any signs of despair on our faces or weariness from the long hours spent in confinement to our rooms under strict laws that were very often implemented by uneducated and unpleasant guards. The guards, who had mostly come from backward environments, took advantage of any opportunity to execute their authority, whether justified or not. However, a few were very kind and deserved to be commended.

A Visit from an Educator Working on his Master's Degree

As I have previously mentioned, we had been enjoying some liberties in Al-Rashaad, such as being permitted during the morning hours to take short walks in the walkway adjacent to our rooms, which we no longer called "cells." One day, I was chatting while walking with our girls in the nearby courtyard next to the walkway when a man in his forties introduced himself to us as an educator working on a dissertation for his master's degree. He had chosen "Bahá'ísm" for the topic. He asked if we could offer him help with some information and resources. We apologized for not being able to offer our assistance, due to being prohibited from talking about that subject. I suggested he get his information from his college's library, or the library of the Literary College specifically. (I remember donating some books about the Bahá'í Faith to this college, but I did not mention that to him.)

He said he needed our opinion on a few points and that he had come to the prison for that purpose. We apologized again and told him that we could not share our opinions, as we were complying with a government order. We said the government imprisoned us with the accusation of being active in our Faith and that what he was asking was considered an activity. He told us he had obtained permission from the officials and the prison administration to interview us, but we insisted on maintaining our position and asked that the administrator herself inform us of such permission.

He replied, "As you wish," and then left.

We were happy with our decision, since it could have been a test of obedience for us. A few minutes later, he returned with one of the supervisors, who confirmed that the office had given permission for him to freely ask his questions and for us to freely answer them without fear of any reprimands.

He began to ask his general questions about the Bahá'í Faith, and each of us answered a suitable answer. At times, we collaborated in giving our answers. He recorded everything on paper.

Since I am documenting my personal experience, I clearly remember one question he asked me in particular. He asked me, "What is the Bahá'í position on Arab nationalism?" He then continued, "I believe you are opposed to Arab nationalism, and there aren't any among you known for his/her patriotism. No Bahá'í has called for it or become enthusiastic about it!"

I said, "I beg your pardon, sir, but this is incorrect, as we pride ourselves on being Arabs. One of the aspects of patriotism is being proud of exceptional aspects, such as our rich, ancient civilization and admirable traits of pride, generosity, hospitality, and protection of one's guest that Arabs are famous for. Who wouldn't be proud of all that? The Bahá'í Faith, however, calls for an expanded and inclusive approach, a concept of looking at humanity as a whole. That approach includes all nationalities, all their civilizations, and all their unique qualities. Including something in a larger whole does not, in any form, make it lose its individuality." I then briefly went on to explain to him about the progressive development of a society—how it begins with the family unit that then expands to become a tribe and then a community—as we had previously learned in school.

The visitor said, "This isn't satisfactory. We call for holding on to our pure Arabic nationalism that is contingent on the teachings of Islam, not any other teaching differing from them." He then asked me another question with a reprimanding tone, "What was lacking in Islam that caused you to abandon it? What have you found in the Bahá'í Faith that is new?"

I calmly answered him, "Bahá'ís have never, God forbid, said that Islam was inadequate, but as you know, sir, with the progress of time and the advancement of societies, new human requirements develop to suit that progress." I gave him analogies from the Bahá'í writings regarding a baby, and how milk is at one time the perfect nourishment, but as he develops further, his body begins to require other nutrients. This development does not by any means indicate faultiness in the milk but rather the need for other elements. As the body continues to grow, the need for clothes accommodating the changing size arises. Another analogy is that of a teacher in an elementary school teaching at the level of his/her students, which is not a measure of his/her competency or that of the curriculum. The teacher might have the same proficiency or even higher than another teaching high school.

The guest was listening without interrupting; therefore, I was encouraged to continue. Our girls contributed their share of answers as well, but his patience had run out before I gave the example of the desertion of black-and-white televisions and the switch to color, despite having the same broadcast! He then quickly left, discontented with our answers and unsuccessful in convincing us of his point of view. Exasperation was visible on his face, while we had an opposite feeling of joy.

One of the supervisors informed us later on that as he was leaving, he angrily stopped by the prison's office and said, "It is true that Bahá'ís are known for their scheming and deception!" We chuckled at his comment, as we knew that our answers were truthful and logical, calm and respectful, unlike his lame discussion, contentious style, and false accusations that portrayed a lack of resourcefulness and a weakness in proofs.

The Kerosene Heater

The prison office gave permission for us to have one kerosene heater per room. We were not allowed to have an electric heater—even a small one—and the excuse given was that the electricity would cost too much and that all of the other inmates would also demand one as well.

As I previously mentioned, we occupied five rooms, and during winter's strong winds and bitter cold, we closed the doors of our rooms for a while and kept the heater on for a few hours after sunset, while exchanging conversation or knitting. My roommate was Ms. Bedriyyeh Husain.

On a very cold day, Bedriyyeh had taken the heater out to be filled with kerosene. The level of the fuel had to be at a specific measure—lower than the upper area of the heater's base. Also, cleaning the base and wiping the exterior of the heater free from any droplets of kerosene was a significantly important matter.

Despite the fact that such details never escaped Bedriyyeh's mind, she must have been distracted that evening, and she filled the fuel higher than the required measure. Some of it leaked onto the base. As soon as she lit the heater and positioned the top half in place, the fire spread to the base, and flames shot up in the middle of our room.

If an incident like this is dangerous and alarming enough in any house, it is disastrous and can have serious repercussions in prison. For instance, Al-Amn could call for an investigation and an indictment for the people responsible, and some prisoners might even receive severe punishments that could be physical, as we had seen in other sections.

At that moment, I was in the outside passageway, and when I entered the room, the flames were rising to a startling height. I suffocated my scream out of fear of creating a commotion. Thank God, we were alone in the building with no strangers. It was evening, and fortunately we had been given permission to lock our own main door (to the outside of the building) at a specific time, in case the guard on duty was absent. Bedriyyeh hurried to carry the flaming heater to the outside passageway, but I had to yell at her to stop immediately and step away from danger. I ran to bring a heavy pillow (stuffed with wool) that I used to put on my chair, and I placed it over the flames. Then I hurried outside with an empty container to bring some sand from the edges of the yard, ran back in a minute, and scattered a heavy layer of sand onto the heater. Our girls noticed the commotion, and each ran to bring more sand until the flames were finally put out. The whole shocking incident only took minutes, but we remained trembling with fear of anyone finding out and our having to face serious complications with the Al-Amn.

We took the heater outside to empty it of fuel and clean it very well. Then we began cleaning the room from the sand and removing any evidence of the incident. I took off the burnt pillow case and the burnt portion of the wool and discarded them in the trash barrel outside our building, took the remaining portion of the wool and stuffed it into another pillowcase, then hurried to lock the outside door and open all the windows and the back door for ventilation. We bore the bitter cold that night with peaceful hearts. None of the other inmates had noticed, for they had all been asleep. God had helped and saved us with His grace from inevitable troubles. Again, we were extremely lucky; otherwise, the other inmates' screaming would have reached the heavens, as it normally would for the slightest of causes.

The Gas Tank

Despite our attempts to be extra vigilant during every step of the way of our imprisonment, it was still impossible to avoid some minor incidents beyond our control.

We were very thankful to receive permission to have a gas tank, on top of which we attached a burner. The lunch we had cooked in Abu Ghraib on the top of the small kerosene heater had always taken two hours to be ready, but with the aid of the burner in Al-Rashaad, our meal was now done in less than an hour. We took turns bringing a full tank of gas from the distribution center, which was located across from the main prison gate, or from the kitchen of the heavy labor building. Two of us, sometimes more, would carry the tank to our section. Later on, it was the cook's responsibility to do this.

One day, we brought the heavy tank but were unable to start a fire in the burner because, at times, the tanks were filled beyond capacity. As a result, the gas inside the tank was exerting pressure on the small check valve, which prevented the gas from reaching the ignitor. This had previously happened several times at our home before we entered prison. We had learned to move the check valve with a narrow piece of wood, such as a toothpick or a matchstick, and then the gas would leak out to the burning area and ignite.

It was my turn to cook that day, so very carefully, I tried the same method here. Since it had worked before, I was confident that it would work now. But the second I moved the valve, the gas gushed out into the kitchen. Thankfully, there were no inmates smoking, and fortunately my friend Bedriyyeh Husain, whom I call "a lady of action," was with me at the time.

We picked up the gas tank together and hurried to the outside of the building. Trembling with fear, we carried it and prayed that no adverse consequences would ensue. The gas was gushing out as highly dense, white smoke. Panting with exhaustion, we took it to the outside gate and were noticed by some of the inmates, who hurried and called the warden, who ran to investigate. Our girls came to help.

As the warden opened the gate, the guards took the tank and quickly discarded it, far away in the outside area, beyond the walls. It started to roll while the gas was still gushing out with such force that I had never seen before!

The guards returned to their stations and sat on their chairs unfazed and undisturbed by the incident, as if it were just an ordinary, trivial occurrence. But for us, a potential disaster had been averted, and God and His mercy had protected us from being held responsible for any damage or injury that might have resulted. No procedures for following up with the incident were issued by the office, and the episode slid by as if insignificant.

I remained distraught the whole day and felt as if I had committed a harmful and dangerous act. I took advantage of the absence of the supervisor and kept checking through the lock hole of the outside gate to see if the smoke had stopped, but it continued to gush out in full force until the tank was completely emptied by the afternoon.

By that time, my patience had completely run out! Only then could I relax. It was as if a heavy load had been lifted off my chest. I thanked God again for His mercy and also for saving us once again from the responsibility of being investigated by the Al-Amn.

Seventeen out of the nineteen Bahá'í men imprisoned in Abu Ghraib.

9 / Al-Rashaad Prison,
Visits from Officials, and Our
Exclusion from the Pardoning Decree

The Prison's Transportation Truck and Visiting the Men's Prison

After our settlement in the Al-Rashaad prison, my sisters Warqa and Fatima and I sent the prison office a request to visit our brother Munis and my husband Siddiq and our uncle Kamil, who were still being held in the men's prison at Abu Ghraib. Dear Nida also sent a request to visit her father Nimaat Sabour, and dear Bahiyyeh Masjoon requested to see her cousins Nimaat 'Abdu'l-Wahid and Ihsaan 'Abdu'l-Wahid. Our requests were approved, and we were given permission to visit them once a month.

Those visits were considered very important events for all of us, despite the difficulties we faced in riding in the prison's truck. It was high off the ground with only one door next to the driver, and it had a ladder that only had one rung that we climbed with great difficulty. The sides and top of the truck bed were made of wire mesh, and it had no seats except two narrow boards, supported by metal legs, that were each no more than one span (the distance measured by a human hand, from the tip of the thumb to the tip of the little finger), on each side of the bed of the truck. Those boards were exasperatingly difficult for me to sit on, because they were so close to the wire mesh. To keep the mesh from poking my skin, I was always forced to teeter on the edge of the board, with nothing to hold on to. I had to put my thumb through one of the gaps in the wire mesh to hold on, and this caused pain and stiffness in my thumbs that lasted for days after each visit. Moreover, the truck sped exceedingly fast over bumps that caused us a lot of pain because our bodies would be violently bouncing up and down on the board.

The ride usually took an hour and fifteen minutes until we reached the men's prison in Abu Ghraib, but there were times when our trip took much longer, despite the high speed of the truck, because the driver wanted to avoid the heavy city traffic and the streets that were crowded with pedestrians. Also, the officials wanted to avoid the curiosity and reactions of civilians seeing us; therefore, they often chose alternate routes that would take longer than the normal route. Very often, the route around the city would take us on the remains of Nathum Pasha's dirt dam, which was constructed during the reign of the Ottoman Empire to protect Baghdad from the floods of the Tigris River. The flooding from the Tigris used to drown a large portion of the city before the construction of the dam.

During our trips, as the truck sped over the bumpy road, I often felt as if my vertebrae were separating from each other, especially since my lower back had suffered an injury in the past when a vertebra broke due to a fall. I felt as if it were breaking all over again every time my body slammed into that board I was sitting on, and even the organs in my gut felt as if they were violently colliding with each other. We often had to hold on to each other's shoulders for support.

In winter, it was exceptionally difficult to deal with the bitter cold wind that made us shiver despite the very heavy wool clothing we put on. I had to wear trousers under my uniform, even though it was not customary attire for older women in Iraq. But I was forced to do it. During rainy days, we took covers to protect ourselves from the water dripping from the roof. The other inmates, who had committed crimes with their husbands or other family members, joined us on the trip and preferred sitting on the floor of the truck close to each other. At times, they would bring their children along to see their fathers, and having the children ride along was a means of entertainment. The children would always stand up and look at the streets through the mesh with such astonishment. They were observing a strange world that was unfamiliar to them.

During the summer, the heat would be overwhelming. At times it exceeded 53 degrees Celsius (around 127 Fahrenheit). To shield myself, I took a scarf dipped in water and covered my head, forehead, and part of my face (a cooling method I had learned from my dad, may God rest his soul). But the sizzling-hot air coming from every direction would soon dry the scarf, which I had to wet again with water from a plastic bottle I carried with me. I usually took it to have a little drink until we arrived at Abu Ghraib, where my husband would have cold water in a thermos waiting for us.

Most of the time, we arrived in a state close to unconsciousness caused by the extreme heat and by thirst, and then, of course, we had to undergo a thorough search. If the female guards were people we knew, the search would be ordinary, but if they were strangers, the examination could be difficult and embarrassing.

After meeting our men and drinking some cool water in a shady area, our strength would return. We could not carry our own thermoses because of their weight, since we took some canned goods and other food with us to share a meal with the men. Our visits with the men were always too short, and before we knew it, we would have to get back on the truck again to return to Al-Rashaad.

I had to carry a covered seat made of egg cartons so I could step on it to reach the prison's truck and then get off again once we had reached our destination. I left it in the truck during the visits, and the guard would hand it back to me before my getting on again. I tried to take a thermos with me once, and as soon as the other inmates spotted it, everyone asked for a sip either for themselves or for their children. It was empty moments after, and my mouth remained as dry as firewood for the rest of the trip.

After this episode, I did not take a thermos with me again. It was not because I did not want to be generous and do a good deed, but every other mother could have thought for herself and brought water for her child and herself just as I did. Most of the inmates, however, were negligent. Perhaps their troubles and woes had disturbed their thinking ability, destroyed their emotions, and left them in that state of carelessness.

During these journeys to and from Al-Rashaad, Baghdad's streets and parks, which my Bahá'í sisters and I had dreamed to see and walk through again, and which made our hearts flutter in longing every time they appeared on TV, seemed to me to be crowded, depressing, and totally unfamiliar. Baghdad no longer felt like the same beloved city where I had been born, that I adored and had burned with desire to see again while I was away in Egypt during my university years. At that time, I had found no happiness and comfort away from it. But now, as I viewed its people walking those streets through the wires of the truck, they seemed to be moving images, similar to an animated movie that was playing at the speed of our vehicle. There were no sentiments of humanity or familiarity tying me to them. I felt as if they were creatures from another world.

During the first few times the vehicle approached the street where my sisters' and my home was located—the home that had embraced us as a family before injustice befell us—and at the sight of the railroad track close to our street, I found myself prey to a sudden attack of emotions that poured out beyond my control. Images from the past flashed through my heart, and tears streamed from my eyes. I saw my daughters in their uniforms while I accompanied them back and forth to school, my son Abir returning from college during school break and our immense happiness to see him, and my husband tending the flowers in his garden. I pictured myself preparing their meals or all of us spending time together sitting on the large lawn swing in our garden.

But even these emotions of longing started to diminish gradually with the tedious repetition of these tiring rides and the long days and nights spent in prison. The suffering of prison life slowly replaced my yearning for a normal life with other sentiments with which only people in captivity are familiar. I would not describe these feelings as losing hope in God's mercy, but rather I would define them, in my personal opinion and own experience, as as a state of utter submissiveness to His will. It was as if the boundaries that separated happiness and misery, hope and despair, had been lifted, and all that was left was to be resigned to the will of God.

After the departure of my children abroad during our last year of imprisonment, while on the prison's truck and while passing by my old street, I felt no flaring emotions inside me any longer. It made no difference any more. Our old street was just like any other street with which I had no association, nor any right to walk on. Everything had become strange to me. I no longer had a home that was shaded by the colorful bougainvillea trees on that street. It was no longer the house where my children's laughter echoed inside its walls or where we enjoyed family times around the dinner table or watched a TV show together. There was no longer a living room where we gathered with relatives and friends while enjoying the fragrance of the jasmine, carnations, and jasminum sambac (a species of jasmine native to that region). There were no longer trays of food placed on the green grass where we would joyfully come together at times, as if on a picnic.

Everything had become different. My daydreams of bygone memories began to blur together and appear as mysterious pictures from a faraway past. Happier memories of my family began to blend together with the sad reality that my children were gone. If God willed and we were freed, would I be able to resume my life after prison had filled my heart with despair? And where were my children now? What would my life be when it had been turned upside down?

This is how my thoughts began to gradually collapse and how the lights of these pleasant daydreams began to dim little by little until they lost effect. My mind started to shut down, resulting in a total silence inside my brain, a drainage of emotion, and a halting of any imagination except for one thought—a thought that ran over and over through my mind: I am a prisoner.

My home now is half a room in Al-Rashaad prison, and no other home is left for me besides that. My name? There is no longer a meaning for my name, as it has become a number in the prison's records. My children? They have their own lives now. My husband? He is a number in the prison records as well.

Then, I would think to myself, let whatever happens to me happen. Let the circumstances grind me more and more until my number is reduced to zero. Who knows, perhaps there would be another beginning. Do not all beginnings start from zero?

After our visits with the men, we often wished to return to Al-Rashaad as soon as possible to change into lighter clothes and pour some cool water on

Anisa and family enjoying an afternoon at their garden.

our heads and bodies, which always felt roasted by the hot wire mesh of the truck. If it were not for the difficult seating on that cursed narrow board and the violent bouncing of our bodies on it, we would have wished for the driver to double his speed, because the sizzling hot wind felt as if it had come from a volcano, and it burned our skin like hot needles.

Every time the vehicle approached our prison, we felt a sense relief, as if we were approaching our true home, where there was security, shelter, and cold water to quench our thirst. We were happy to see our friends, as if we were returning from a voyage or festivity. As soon as we saw the smoke stacks of the brick factories surrounding the prison area and their heavy black smoke decorating the tops of the prison's barbed wire, we were delighted to know it was almost the end of the agonizing journey. As soon as we reached the prison, the wardens hurried to receive us, as if receiving cargo they needed to inspect to make sure it was whole and complete. Our names would be called, and our number would be counted to make sure we were all there; then we were all inspected for a second time.

Those were the sentiments associated with riding the prison's transportation truck, which at first brought us great embarrassment because we were always accompanied by heavily-armed guards with machine guns. In the beginning, we tried to conceal our faces and our indignity, so no one we knew could see us transported in that "suspicious" truck. But that embarrassment gradually turned to feelings of pride and honor. For despite the fact that we rode with a group of offenders of different crimes, deep inside, we knew that our situation was different from the other prisoners. Our imprisonment was not a punishment for a wrongdoing we had committed but was rather due to injustice and persecution. It was an attack on our human rights to freedom of thought and conscience.

Can you imagine our happiness later on when the gate of the prison was opened and we saw the prison truck waiting for us? Trust me when I say that our happiness to ride in it, despite all the associated difficulties, was far greater than a regular person's happiness of riding in a limousine or any other fancy car. The other inmates, who were not lucky enough to accompany us, would stand and look at us from afar with great envy. Other inmates were only able to ride in that truck if they had to be transported to a police station for further questioning or to be taken to the border for deportation.

Occasionally, we would be greatly disappointed to hear that our visit had been canceled. Sometimes we received word of a visit's cancellation after we had been preparing for it as early as dawn, cooking some fast meals, and waiting for hours in anticipation. At times, a visit would be canceled because of an official's visit, disturbances at the men's prison, reprimands or punishments given to us (or to the men), or executions. We would miss the prison truck to a great extent and would long for its squealing wheels, rattling wire mesh, and roaring engine. We would also miss the sendoff and welcoming back reception by guards holding rifles and closely watching every prisoner as she climbed up the truck before departure and came down again after arrival. Sometimes the presence of these guards made it seem as though we were ambassadors of renowned countries or high-ranking and influential visitors on a mission and that we needed to be protected according to required rules and etiquette.

Upon our arrival at our section, our friends would surround us to make sure we were OK and to hear news of the friends we had visited at the men's prison. We would always relate to them the details of our visit with our male colleagues, but we would often conceal the troubling stories the men had related to us, such as the health problems or some of the harsh treatment they were facing. We brought back positive news first, and other news relating to their strength and steadfastness. Some were facing beatings, humiliation, or solitary confinement as punishment for the most insignificant reasons. These punishments were designed mainly to pressure them to renounce their belief in the Bahá'í Faith.

My husband, who was legally blind, was continuing to lose what remained of his eyesight, despite a report from the visiting eye doctor, who had written that my husband urgently needed to seek immediate treatment from an outside hospital because he had suffered detachment of the retina in both eyes in the past. He had avoided complete blindness through treatments he received abroad, in Europe, but a very severe case of influenza in prison had traumatized his body and caused another detachment of his retinas. Despite the urgent report, the prison's administration denied him medical treatment. As a result, he suffered a complete loss of vision.

Our colleague in prison, Dr. Jameel Ihsan, who used to be the director of the Kirkuk Hospital and who was allowed by the prison's administration to practice his profession inside prison, was utterly humiliated by having his hair shaved extremely short (a buzz-cut called "number zero" in Iraq) as a punishment for listening to a foreign radio station. He had fallen asleep, and one of the guards had spied on him and reported him to the office, as if he had committed an unforgivable crime.

Other male friends of ours suffered illnesses that led to their deaths—either while in prison or shortly after their release—mainly due to the harsh treatment and pressure they endured.

Perhaps we were in better conditions at the women's prison, or perhaps a woman's endurance, resilience, and fortitude in the face of adversities are stronger than a man's, and that is why God has chosen her to bear the pain of childbirth—which men could never bear or even imagine—and why He has chosen her to be the symbol of sacrifice and selflessness for the sake of her children until they are able to face life on their own.

Some of the Events at the Al-Rashaad Prison

Just like any other prison, there were plenty of annoyances and aggravations at the Al-Rashaad prison, although they where comparatively fewer than those at Abu Ghraib. Every moment of peace was always being interrupted by something that exacerbated the nerves. One might say in response, "Yes, that's how life is for everyone everywhere. Problems are always a part of life." But enduring hardships inside prison is different than enduring them outside. While outside, we are able to find relief from our problems by seeking solutions or asking the help of friends and family. Even in the absence of these types of relief, we are able to leave home and change our mood, perhaps by taking a walk through the streets and parks, watching television, or reading a book. In the worst-case scenario, we might go to bed and seek seclusion.

None of these solutions are available in prison. A problem can persist and suffocate a person's emotions, and the simplest of things can become amplified until it feels like a weighty and inescapable nightmare pressing on the chest.

Once, right at midnight, we heard a knock on the ward's door. I hurried to ask who it was, with Badriyyeh following me. An answer came from the night warden, who whispered for me to let her inside. By that time, both Hajir and Bahiyyeh had come as well. The younger ladies had gone to bed.

We opened the door, and she entered. Visibly disturbed, she said, "Tonight Al-Amn men knocked on the outside prison gate, but I did not let them in. I was troubled by their arrival so late at night, and asked what they wanted. They said, 'Bring the Bahá'í girls to us immediately.' When I apologized for not having the power to hand them the girls without an official authorization from the prison office, they responded with objections and threats, but then left. I remained terrified and shivering until I was certain that they had left, when I heard their cars leave. I am here to let you know."

We were in a state of gratitude listening to her, though our hearts were shivering with terror at hearing the name of Al-Amn. We thanked and hugged her while saying, "May God create more like you" (which is an Arabic proverb), and we also said, "May God bless you for your good deed, and be assured of God's recompense." Those phrases were meant to both comfort her and ourselves that nothing bad would befall us, but she expressed deep concern that they might be coming back, for they had threatened to do so!

After the supervisor left and we locked the door, we gathered in a room dimly lit by the hallway light and softly discussed the surprising news. We wondered what reason had prompted the Al-Amn's midnight visit and their request to take our girls? Would we be facing interrogation all over again, even though we had been sentenced and had been serving our sentence for the past four years? And what was the urgency to come at such a late hour?

Each one of us had concealed her darkest worries from the others and pretended to be calm and composed while inwardly quivering with anxiety and wondering what would happen if those men came back again to take the girls.

Those questions remained without an answer. At the same time, we were worried about the warden. Was she going to receive a reprimand for disobeying the Al-Amn men and not giving them what they had come for?

Luckily, our girls were in deep sleep. When one of them had heard the door being locked and had asked what was happening, we had told her that the guard had come to check if the door had been locked.

In that critical hour, there was nothing left for us to do except beseech God with humble and suppliant hearts and ask Him to protect our girls from every mischief, and to block the path of those men from ever returning again, no matter what the reason was. With soft voices we prayed so we would not wake up the girls or cause them to worry. We prayed for an hour or more; then each one of us went to her bed and continued her prayers for protection.

I went to my bed while utterly awake. I tried to dismiss any thoughts of worry and comforted my mind that, truth be told, we had not received any severely abusive treatment—many thanks be to God—despite the difficult time at the Al-Amn General Directorate of Security and despite the harshness of those days during which we had feared the unthinkable, such as the desecration of our honor, as in the numerous stories told about that place.

But then I would return to thinking about why the Al-Amn would come at such a late hour and what they had wanted from our girls. Was this a new set of tactics to pressure them into submission and renouncing their belief in the Baháʼí Faith? Sleep had abandoned me that night as my thoughts continued to wander east and west while listening to the door. Was I going to hear another knock tonight? As I prayed to God to shield and protect our girls, I also prayed for the warden to escape reprimand for her disobedience, which by itself could have been God's will.

Hours passed, and the men did not return. My soul began to calm somewhat, and I finally was able to close my eyes. The next morning, we told our girls about what had occurred, and hearing about it left them shaken, but they were thankful that nothing had happened. They had a conversation about what would have happened if they had been forced to accompany those men.

Later, the warden came to let us know that the prison's office had praised her conduct and told her she had done the right thing.

Visits from Officials

The Al-Rashaad years were full of surprises, and among them were unannounced visits from the officials, especially to our section. One of the visits was during the time we had our last administrator (Fatima) whom we had had since the beginning of our imprisonment. Despite the fact that all the prison administrators—from the beginning of our imprisonment in Abu Ghraib until now—had differed in character, they had shared a common disposition in the way they treated us, in particular. They had to obey the direct orders coming from Al-Amn and the Ministry of Internal Affairs. No matter the efforts we put forth to project the most exemplary behavior in obedience to the laws, in accordance with the writings of our Faith, we still received a callous and apathetic attitude from them for no reason. This happened despite their frequent admission that we were model prisoners. They wanted to avoid being portrayed as sympathizers of the Bahá'ís or as giving them special treatment.

As I mentioned previously, the last administrator (Fatima) we had before our release was a kindhearted lady, who was close to forty years of age. Despite being inwardly supportive of us, she used to introduce us as "the Bahá'í group belonging to a Faith they claim to be new, who were caught in their den (as in a den for thieves and criminals) practicing their activities, and who were brought to jail"! She did this because she still had to obey orders from the government, and in order to not show obvious favoritism to the Bahá'ís, she had to maintain this image of disapproval of us in front of others.

I was alone with Fatima one time outside our section, so I said to her, "If I may get your permission to correct your opinion, Madam, the den accusation is new, as we do not have a den, but rather a large building called a Ḥaẓíratu'l-Quds, where we gathered for prayers. It was confiscated by the government back in 1965. Each one of us was arrested at her home at separate times and in different circumstances."

She said, "You did have a den in the town of Baqooba."

I answered, "You are referring to another Ḥaẓíratu'l-Quds, Madam, a place of worship in the village of Aawaashiq, which was confiscated as well."

She replied, "That is what we heard."

Then we ended our conversation. Deep inside, I felt her satisfaction with what she had heard from me. Her attitude towards us remained humane and noble, though in concealment because of her responsiveness and compliance to the officials, which she was obligated to maintain.

Another time, Fatima, accompanied by three guests—among whom, as we were told, was a high-ranking official from the Ministry of Social Affairs—came to our ward. Fatima introduced us with an ample share of praise for being exemplary prisoners because we always obeyed all rules and maintained good conduct.

At the time, we were standing in a row inside our narrow hallway to meet with them.

The high-ranking official's response to the administrator's words of commendation was that of sarcasm. He kept on repeating the words, "It's all a show, nothing but a show."

After hearing these comments, we felt a resentment that we could not express, but as he continued with them, I was bound to politely respond. I said, "Sir, can a person maintain projecting a false goodly character for the length of his life?"

He replied with sarcasm, "Yes, until you would be called 'good people.'"

I said, "Sir, if you ask about the Bahá'ís, you will hear that they are indeed good people."

He repeated his mocking words, and I had to choose silence.

At that time, there were plenty of rooms available; therefore, I had my own small room at the front of the section. I had neatly organized my room with nice bedding brought from home after we were allowed to discard the dreadful black prison blankets. We were also permitted to have one chair in each room, which we carried outside to the courtyard during designated times, and each one of us used a nylon stocking as rope to hang some of the clothes we did not wish to wrinkle. Then we used a sheet as a curtain to cover the invented closet; therefore, our rooms were neatly arranged and did not reflect the depressing feel of a prison. Many prisoners followed our lead, as they were also allowed to bring suitable covers for their beds.

On his visit, that visiting official thought that to have such neat-looking rooms was beyond what we deserved because a prisoner deserves nothing but degradation and humiliation. He went inside my room, then came out enraged and said to the others, "Is this prison or an inn? Look at their rooms resembling those of a hotel!"

I said to myself, "It seems that this man has never seen a decent hotel." I was not even thinking of a five-star hotel! I had coincidently just asked the storage overseer for some egg cartons to make a seat, just like we did in Abu Ghraib, so I could use it to climb into the prison's truck. The cartons were sitting in my cell.

The official pointed at the cartons and said, "Look at the piled egg cartons they have, while the free people outside have to stand in long lines to receive a carton of eggs!"

I laughed inside at that man's animosity and gathered some courage to correct his assumption. While we were as prisoners a trust from the government, no visitor had the right to address us with criticism for any reason. I said, "Sir, these empty cartons were going to be discarded and thrown into the trash. We collect them to make seats." I hurried and uncovered a seat in my room to show him what it looked like inside, then went on to say that we had not been receiving any special treatment or treated differently from the other inmates. I mentioned that at times, we received only two eggs a week and other times no eggs.

Fatima chimed in and agreed that all prisoners were treated equally and received the same food. Her intention in bringing the visitors to our section was pride in our order and cleanliness as well-educated and law-abiding prisoners, but unfortunately, the visitor's negative remarks had spoiled her mood.

If that official could have only investigated the teachings of our Faith, he would have found them to be a great institute for learning. He would have discovered that those who attempt to implement its teachings, even to the smallest degree, become exhibitors of human exaltation and true lovers of humankind, and have no need for false appearances.

My Stroll around the Prison

At 10:00 a.m., we had permission to walk in the walkway parallel to our section, which was about twenty meters long. The permission to walk was in effect only if the circumstances allowed, meaning the absence of visiting officials and other visitors. At times, we placed our chairs near our section's door so we could breathe the fresh air and enjoy looking at the sky. There were no other views worthy to look at because the tall prison walls completely obscured the outside world. No street utility poles, no trees, nor even one bird were to be seen. All we could see was the sky with its sun, wintry clouds, starry nights, and moon in summer, when we were allowed to sleep out-doors. Besides that, there was nothing but the depressing walls. Later on, we were granted permission to walk later in the afternoon in the courtyard that encompassed the walkway. The courtyard was the separating space between the prison's outside gate and the other sections, and the other inmates were allowed to walk there as well.

One day, I went for a walk while occupied in my thoughts, and I was unaware of the time, which was near midday when the sections were locked. I crossed the courtyard in a hurry and saw a warden taking inmates to the hard labor section. I saw her looking at me very carefully, but she uttered no words or remark. I noticed a trail to a back path and said to myself, "This must lead to the back of our section, where the door remains open during the day. Perhaps it is a shortcut that I should take to return to our section more quickly." The trail was narrow and adjacent to the tall outside wall. I walked hurriedly, and at the time I could walk fast easily. I thought to myself, "If walking on this trail was a violation, the warden would certainly have said something to me." I arrived at our section in minutes and avoided having to pass through the courtyard. I did not think that my quick stroll would be considered a violation, and I sat on my bed waiting for lunch to arrive.

Soon I heard that same warden shouting how all prisoners are equal, and no one should think there are preferences being given to anyone! I did not pay much attention to her shouting, as we had gotten used to hearing such instructions and orders from the guards—especially those given to inmates in other sections.

A short while later, one of the inmates came to inform me that I had been asked to go and see the administrator in her office. I greeted the administrator—Fatima—and she asked if I had taken the back path to my section.

I replied affirmatively, and I continued, "I was in a hurry to return, and it seems of a certainty you heard about that from the warden."

She was surprised and said, "How did you know that?"

I replied, "Because she took a long glance at me as if she was giving me permission to go on, and she never told me that it was a violation." I apologized to the administrator and said it was a first-time mistake, a spontaneous and undeliberate decision I had made that would not happen again. I was just trying to return in a hurry, and if the warden had warned me, I would have been obedient indeed. The administrator was pleasant and understanding.

I remember other similar incidents of slander and unjustified allegations directed at us by that same warden. Perhaps they were due to her ignorance, prejudice, and rancor. She had once come to our section close to sunset and kept on blathering with the girls until it was dark. It was winter, and we had been instructed to lock our door exactly at 6:00 p.m. We locked the door after she left, but the next day, the administrator called for one of our girls and placed harsh blame on us for not locking the door on time, despite her trust in us in following all the rules. When our young lady told her that the warden was in our section, the administrator replied that the door should have been locked despite that fact. Therefore, from then on, we lost the privilege to lock and unlock the door from the inside of our building and were treated like the other sections by having it locked from the outside by the guards.

The same warden had worked in the Abu Ghraib prison during our time there, and she had often disparaged us with the administrator there as well. Once, she had gone to the office at Abu Ghraib to report our girls for being late in leaving the ward on visitation day, even though she had been with us the entire time. Interestingly enough, the same warden later on received severe punishments for being irresponsible in her duties in the prostitution ward due to her incompetence and low character.

Other guards and wardens often made similar allegations, unjustifiably accusing us of violating rules, despite our efforts in maintaining a relationship of respect and pleasantness with all. We often witnessed a sudden change in attitude by wardens—who outwardly would seem friendly and pleasant—whenever they reported us to the office. Therefore, we had to be extra cautious and vigilant.

My Trip to the Hospital

In the sixth year of our imprisonment, I started to show rapidly developing symptoms of exhaustion, constant thirst, and lethargy. Although those signs were ordinary for those in our condition of minimal mobility, various stresses, and the poor living conditions of unhealthy food and exposure to cold or severe heat, the doctor at the prison's clinic suspected that I had diabetes. Therefore, she referred me for a follow-up at an outside hospital, and I was placed on a waiting list. I had to refrain from eating and drinking starting the evening before the day of my appointment.

That morning, I was waiting with other inmates for the vehicle to arrive. We waited until noon, but it did not come. Therefore, my appointment had to be canceled. A week later, I and other inmates waited for hours again until the designated vehicle finally arrived at 11:00 a.m. It was a small pickup truck that was open in the back with narrow seating on the sides and nothing to hold on to. After being searched and counted, the waiting inmates pushed and shoved to get into the truck. My turn arrived, and I put down my carton seat, which enabled me to step in and be seated at the end of the vehicle.

The truck instantly took off, as fast as lightning. One of the guards took my carton seat and threw it out. I pleaded with him to ask the driver to stop for a second, as I was in need of that seat to climb in and get off the truck. But I was totally ignored. The vehicle sped along, and anger was consuming me while I was trying to hold onto the edge of the truck's side. Everyone sensed the danger of that speed, and preferred to sit on the hot metal floor, since falling out was inevitable. I wished to sit with them, but I was unable to because of the calcification in my knee. So I held onto the edge of the seat with one hand, and with the other I held onto the shoulder of one of the passengers. Because of the mad speed, we were all shouting, "God have mercy!"

We finally arrived at the hospital's parking lot, and the inmates, accompanied by the guards, hurried out of the truck. I was the last one left on the truck. I yelled for help to get me down, but no one came to my assistance, as if they were certain of my inability to escape. I missed my carton seat and, deep inside, cursed the guard who threw it away. I continued to call for help, but no one seemed to care. With great difficulty, I sat on the burning hot edge of the truck and tried several times to work up the courage to jump, carrying my shoes in my hands, but I could not seem to muster the will to do so. There was nothing left to try, except the method all of us have used to climb down during our toddler years. I turned onto my stomach and tried to slide down gradually, and I was able to climb down until my feet touched the burning hot pavement. Furiously, I put my shoes on and followed everyone into the hospital.

After all the prisoners had been counted, I saw the specialist, explained my symptoms, and handed him the report from the prison doctor. He told me he would send me for a blood test, despite the fact that it was too late. I then asked him why it would be too late for a blood test.

He said, "Because you have been fasting for so many hours and your blood sugars must be at a very low level."

A blood test was done, as it was an official procedure that had been ordered. A week later, the result came back and, as the specialist had predicted, showed a severe drop in my blood sugar level.

As for getting back inside the truck that day after my appointment with the specialist, it was a tad easier. I was able to pull a rock on the curb over to step on, and I begged the driver to come close enough for me to climb in. Many thanks to God, the driver reluctantly agreed, and the other inmates helped to pull me in. I swore I would never go again, even if my blood sugar rose a ton, since it was a hideous experience I would never forget. I was fearful of falling off that speeding truck and facing inevitable death.

Simone

When I visualize my memories of that matchless period of my life through rapidly moving images that, once again, leave their effect in the depths of my emotions, I see among them a photo of a big-boned, very tall, fair-skinned woman in her thirties. She had an assertive voice, was very opinionated (regardless of whether she was right or wrong), and was determined to force her ideas on everyone around her. Woe to those who disobeyed her, as they would certainly hear her obscenities and become susceptible to any of her slander that could cause them to end up in the prison's office. If I were to write about each one of our days in prison, then there would be at least a line about her in every page of the hardships that we endured. Stories about her presence with us could alone fill a large book, equivalent to her size and loud voice. I have changed her name and given her the name "Simone" to preserve her privacy.

One afternoon while in the Al-Zafaraniyyeh detention center, where families of the detainees were allowed to visit at the outside entrance to the hall, this woman came in, and suddenly there was a big excitement and welcoming of her by the leader of the prostitutes, whom—as you may recall—was known as "Fifi." Fifi's club of women greeted her with hugs and kisses, and the young among them hurried to kiss her hand.

We asked about the identity of the visitor who deserved such a warm reception, and one of the girls replied, "She's our mother."

I foolishly and sadly asked, "Are you sisters?"

She replied, "Yes. Myself, and her and her . . ." She pointed to many other girls and said their names.

I asked, with the innocent mind of someone unfamiliar with that environment, "Is Fifi your aunt?"

The young woman said, "Yes."

I said to myself, "There seems to be no resemblance between these girls," and I kept wondering what possible family problems could have happened to those young women that brought them to this polluted pit. Since dear Bahiyyeh had been a nurse in a women's prison in the past, she had more knowledge about such women. She took me aside and explained that there were no real family ties between those girls and that the term "Mother" meant the "Madam" who had operated the prostitution house. It was just a slang term describing their business relationships!

Upon hearing Bahiyyeh's explanation, I remained in a state of gloom, especially when I witnessed that chief visitor raising her hand and slapping one of the girls with such force that, without any exaggeration, it left red impressions of her fingers on the girl's face. With pouring tears, the girl's

response was to fall on the visitor's hand—the hand that had slapped her—
and kiss it and beg for forgiveness while receiving filthy profanities from that
woman, who was trying to hit her again and would have done so were it not
for her "sister" Fifi, who came to intervene. That visitor, "the Mother," was
Simone.

Simone's visits to the detention center continued, and we had no knowledge what fate had in store for us. We had no way of knowing that we would
have to endure the company of this domineering "Mother" during our later
years in prison. I never imagined officials allowing such a woman to share
captivity under the same roof as young ladies from honorable families. Tra-
ditionally, in Arab society, a line is drawn between the decent and acceptable
segments of society, and the segments that are highly condemned and considered abhorrent. This line is to be honored and respected at all times. While
it is true that all are equal in prison and must abide by the same rules, the
prostitution ward was a separate entity. "Decent" women—no matter what
their crime had been—should not have had to mix with the inmates of that
ward. But it was God's will that we be tested and learn to endure all trials and
difficulties.

I would like to give you a general idea about the Iraqi culture and its customs so you can understand the point of the focus I put on her presence with
us. In Iraq, prostitutes belong to a stratum of society that must be avoided.
Even the word "prostitution" is inappropriate to utter.

I remember when I was a child living in the heart of the city, there were
branched alleys with police guarding their entrances. We walked in a hurry as
we passed close to that area on our way to school. If by accident we saw in one
of those alleys a woman dressed in revealing clothes and heavy makeup, we
ran in horror as if we had seen a monster. For an obvious reason, we did not
dare to tell our parents what we had accidently seen. Cultural customs in Iraq
prohibited prostitutes from walking in alleys in neighborhoods where honorable people lived, and if someone suspected a neighbor of such a disgraceful
act, they hurried to tell the others and inform the neighborhood's foremost

man (an elected man similar to a mayor), who would investigate the matter. If proven right, the suspect would be asked to vacate and leave, because that home had become a source of shame and embarrassment for all. There is a term in Arabic that translates into English as "lacking decency," meaning something vulgar, usually used in reference to those in the despised business of prostitution, and also used for great insults or swears, which usually are worthy of indictment at court.

I had once read a short story about a rich American father who had filed a complaint against his town's police department. An officer from that department had arrested his daughter for a traffic violation, then the department's administration had jailed her for one night with some prostitutes. The father was suing the department for an amount beyond reason, all for one night of incarceration with street girls!

Yet, what could people like ourselves say while being incarcerated for two whole months in one hall with such people? We were forced to hear their foul language day and night, while twelve of our Bahá'í girls were as young as fifteen and sixteen years of age. How could we defend our rights while confined with the madam of the most famous house of prostitution in Baghdad, who was trafficking young women in a house that was open day and night, and remained in operation even while she was in jail? We could not do anything but leave our affairs to God, the Omnipotent and the Supreme Ruler.

We might have been able to tolerate such a horrible situation, but what about when our girls were separated from us in a different section while that woman was their jailmate and was trying to be close to them with her scheming ways and become the sole controller of the section without opposition? The officials attested later on that we had treated that woman and those like her in accordance with the admirable teachings of our Faith.

Our tests with Simone started back at Abu Ghraib. As I mentioned previously, on the second day after we entered Abu Ghraib prison, an isolated ward was selected for our accommodation. We were hoping that our situation would remain as it was, with ourselves separated from the other inmates, but this hope did not last long. The isolation ward became filled with inmates of varying charges. Worse than that, Simone was brought in with other prostitutes.

We attempted to avoid these inmates by trying to indirectly create a boundary between us. We used the excuse of being prohibited from intermingling with other inmates. But Simone did not accept such boundaries, and with her persuasive and clever talking style took advantage of every situation to start a conversation with any of us. She asked questions and commented on anything that happened and collected information that she interpreted as she liked before taking it to the prison's office. I saw her myself, every day, going to and from the office. Therefore, we had to remain vigilant, despite the fact that we had nothing to hide. There was no way to avoid interacting with her. She took every opportunity to offer her precious advice to withdraw from our position regarding our belief and to do what was asked of us so we would be freed. She expressed her sympathy and regret at seeing us confined with criminals, and she repeated over and over that it was irrational to hold on to our position and that we must ask for clemency and not challenge the authorities.

No one dared to argue with her, nor were we able to avoid her. All we could do was be cordial and say, "We are hopeful that the officials will understand our situation and see that we are innocent of committing any wrongdoing against the government."

This prison "colleague" never missed an opportunity to stop and advise me, in particular, to think about my daughters and about my husband's and my long sentences, especially since my daughters were "beautiful teenagers prone to much trouble"! The effect of her words felt like a poisonous sword through my being, despite the fact that logically I did not give any weight to her words. But somehow, they exacerbated the motherly emotions in my heart and the anxiety I had about the polluted prison environment and what could happen to the daughters of some of the prisoners. But my answer to Simone was always, "I have left my daughters in God's trust and in His protection," and her answer would always be, "If I were you and I was asked to convert to Judaism, I would have done it for my daughters, so why wouldn't you step down from your position and accept Islam?" (Simone was of a Christian background, but since she was being held with Muslims, she pretended to be one of them.)

Once she brought me a book that she said she liked, and she claimed it was based on a true story. She told me it was about a girl who suffered for her political view. She insisted that I read it, and I had to agree because I had been placed in an awkward position. I reluctantly took the book, randomly flipped through a few pages, and began reading it. I found trivial topics, foul language, with no morals to be found. Therefore, I returned the book to her with my apology!

Our kind behavior had a positive impact on her, however, and she began to compliment us in front of everyone. One time she spread the news that she saw in a dream a saint, a female, praying by the fence surrounding the courtyard of the Bahá'í ward. The saint had a halo that illuminated the whole ward and beyond it to the rest of prison. Her dream had an effect on the prisoners, and everyone hoped that we would be released soon because we were virtuous people.

Simone had an authoritative control on the prostitution ward. Her bed would be prepared outdoors in their courtyard every night during the summer, and when she arrived, she was surrounded by companions and slowly accompanied outside, as if she were a princess. We sensed her presence even in our own courtyard, as the scent of her perfume filled the air. She told us she owned a closet filled with expensive perfumes. She came to our ward one day carrying a fine-looking iron box, about a square foot in size, and she called for me! I came out of my cell, and we exchanged our greetings. Then I asked, "What is it?"

She told me she wanted to leave that box in my trust.

I had a good idea of what would be inside it, and I asked, "Why me and not the prison's office?"

She said, "The box contains most of my fine jewelry. It was brought to me during the visit. The office does not want to take responsibility, and I am not comfortable leaving it with them."

I politely said, "You are putting me on the spot, but I am really sorry. I cannot take the box because we don't have a safe place for it, and as you know, we must obey all the rules."

She went on insisting and pleading in God's name, over and over, that I take the box.

I finally agreed to take it on the conditions that I inform the office and that I would not be responsible if it got lost.

She agreed and said, "If anything happens to the box, it will be OK and a sacrifice for you honorable people."

I reluctantly stopped arguing and asked her to open the box so I could see what was in it.

She opened her treasure box, which had neatly organized jewelry of all kinds that were astonishing to look at. She then locked the box and kept the key with her, swearing that she would take the box back on the next visitation day and hand it to someone else. And thus I had to bear the load of another burden in prison.

There was a guard with whom we had a very good relationship. I told her about the box, and she told me that the office had seen the box's contents and had estimated the value of the jewelry to be around 35,000 dinars (old dinars were worth about $3.3 dollar each, so the total value of the jewelry in dollars was around $115,500)! She said the office did not wish to take responsibility for keeping the box, especially since the office was closed after hours and they feared that the box would be stolen.

I had to guard that box day and night for two weeks, and I was unable to leave the ward. I was reprimanding myself for taking it and cursing the day when that woman became our partner in prison and brought us so much trouble. I remained anxious even at night because I was aware of the shady ways in which professional thieves operate.

Visitation day finally arrived, and Simone, with much appreciation, came to take her trusted box. I was thankful, as well, to rid myself of that heavy load and responsibility I was forced to take.

Months later, we received a visit from the general administrator of all prisons in Iraq. The time was close to sunset, and I was talking to a female guard near the door of the ward. The administrator did not enter our ward but came to ask the guard who the occupants of the ward were. The guard listed everyone's name, including Simone's.

The administrator immediately became visibly agitated, and I heard him say, "How did that happen? How did you put a prostitute with the Bahá'ís?"

The guard replied, "They were orders from the office."

He said, "This is unacceptable! Ask her (Simone) to take her belongings to the prostitution ward." (As I mentioned previously, the prostitution ward was to the front of ours, so that their windows and ours faced the courtyard that separated us.)

The guard respectfully requested to have until the next morning to complete the general administrator's request, so that she could arrange the proper procedures for the transfer with the administrator of the women's prison, but upon hearing her, the general administrator grew even angrier. He said, "You must do this now and at this second!"

I could hear every word he said, as I was standing next to the door. I was consoled and comforted by his words, as if someone had given my dignity back to me. I gained respect and appreciation for this general administrator.

I went right away to inform my colleagues, who were thankful as well. Sure enough, and within minutes, Simone was taken to the prostitution ward, where she could take a place of leadership and command, and where she was feared and obeyed by all the inmates there. We took a sigh of relief at her absence and from the continuous chatter about her adventures in luring high-profile people and foreigners into the hands of the Bureau of Security, and her other relationships with prominent members of the government, which were conversations we had continually tried to cleverly avoid.

Simone in the Al-Rashaad Prison

As fate would have it, Simone accompanied us during our transfer to the Al-Rashaad prison. She had other charges that had been added to her sentence, such as having a relationship with a government official who had rebelled against the government. We had been occupying a section of the prison and had it all to ourselves, and we had a library and a small store run by a very kind inmate. Since Simone was a habitual shopper and gift-giver, she was at the commissary from morning until evening, as if it were her job. At times, verbal disagreements between Simone and the inmate managing the shop occurred and often ended with the submissiveness of that poor inmate to the mighty domineer.

The hallway that separated the commissary from our section was very narrow—about one meter in width—therefore, Simone's commotions, quarrels with other inmates, and loud laughs easily penetrated our ears all day long and caused us unceasing annoyance. I wish that tedious situation had been the only problem we had to deal with, but on one miserable morning, with her voice preceding her, Simone arrived in the company of a guard and with a convoy of inmates surrounding her. Every inmate was carrying objects such as suitcases and pots. The ground rumbled beneath their feet, the procession entered our section, and simply and unsurprisingly, Simone was given a room, as if fate had destined that her path remain intertwined with ours.

At that point, it was obvious that voicing our opinion would be a futile gesture and that we were expected not to say anything. Thus, that mischief-maker became our ward-mate yet again, and she continued to interfere in our business day and night with never-ending remarks. She made every effort to make us like her through small gifts, which put us on the spot because gifts in prison have a different meaning from gifts outside of prison. In prison, when a gift is given to someone, the unspoken understanding is that the recipient of the gift then owes a favor to the giver of the gift. The prison's administrator was later convicted of felony for receiving gifts from prisoners. That colleague, Simone, behaved—especially toward our young ladies—as if we were her own personal assignment.

I remember once on a sizzling summer day, when the hot air from the fan was sweltering on our faces, we decided to take an afternoon nap (a siesta, a customary tradition in Iraq) in the hallway that separated us from the commissary store that had been provided that summer with a small water air-cooler (commonly used in Iraq). Since Simone spent most her days at the small commissary, she loudly chattered, cursed, and yelled at the shoppers. The store manager had to submit to her orders and her constant interference with the sales; otherwise, she would receive shouts and profanities.

We had just lain down on the mats, and we were trying to enjoy the cool breeze, when Simone started her arguments with a loud and bothersome voice. I quietly pulled back to my room, followed by the other Bahá'í ladies. Simone noticed what happened and became enraged! To the shop's manager she loudly said, "Who do those spies think they are? Do they think they are better than me? Why don't they want to hear my voice?" Her words were as bullets penetrating our ears, but we were unable to respond. I heard her raging voice while shaking with anger, but we had to silently bear her insults because she had the capability and expertise to mount any accusation against us and take it to the office, the Bureau of Security, and more. It was a miserable and upsetting day that shook our nerves indeed, but she returned the next day and shamelessly talked to us as if nothing had happened.

One day, while coming back to our section, I was stunned to witness a quarrel between Simone and the inmate who managed the shop and who was fearfully trying to defend herself. I had to back away because Simone had a broken brick in her hand, which she threw at the woman. If not for the good fortune of that woman, who moved her head just a bit, a disaster would have happened. The brick flew parallel to her head. The woman ran inside the building in terror, followed by Simone, who was swearing at her with profanities.

I went to my room angry at the circumstances that brought us to face such miseries and more. The worst thing of all was being forced to tolerate and appease such an ungodly woman, no matter the situation. She forced the inmate who had become the cook for our section to make her special meals and desserts—some of which, at times, she offered us. It was woe to us if we accepted them and woe to us if we refused them, for, as I mentioned, gifts in prison have a different meaning among prisoners and by the office than outside. Once, she asked the cook not to cook anything for us, as she was going to invite us for a barbeque! We were put in the same awkward position again, fearing both to accept or refuse her invitation. That afternoon, we reluctantly had to accept the sandwiches she served us. The news spread like lightning—better than any news agency—among the other inmates.

She was in control of everything inside our section from bathing to cleaning schedules, and she took advantage of my sister Fatima, getting her to sew many new dresses for her, which she put on every afternoon. She brought Fatima, who was a very peaceful and kind person, loads of fabrics and insisted that Fatima make her dresses, each equivalent to two or three dresses because of Simone's large body size. Fatima could not refuse the chore, because doing so would have meant refusing to sew for everyone else. That she could not do, because sewing had become her outlet for passing time in prison and earning a few dinars.

You might be wondering why I am dedicating so many pages to this woman (Simone) and writing about what must seem to be ordinary events. I can tell you that if you are outside of prison and faced with irritants and stressors, you might be able to avoid the annoyances. But our situation was different. We were locked inside from evening to the next morning, and that inmate was with us at night and most of the daytime. Every time I saw her, I was reminded of this portion of a poem that reads, "And among life's miseries is for an honorable man to find no recourse but to befriend an enemy."

Truth be told, no one thought of her as an enemy but rather someone whose mischief we wished to remain safe from in those cruel circumstances of imprisonment. I thought of her as a unique character whose company we were singled out to endure for years while in the same isolated ward!

As mentioned earlier, Simone continued to run her prostitution business even while in prison! She received visits from the woman she hired to run the business, and together they went over the accounts. One day, the woman brought with her a beautiful little girl of four, originally from India. Simone claimed she, Simone, had officially adopted the little girl because her mother was poor and had approved the adoption in exchange for a sum of money! I was astonished to hear of a mother pushed by circumstances to sell her own daughter to this type of new mother, and what would become of that little girl? And how did an official government agency approve of such an adoption? Those questions upset my soul to the limit. The little girl seemed to be afraid of Simone and tried to avoid her by clinging to the other woman, but Simone, her new so-called "mother," shouted profanities and pulled her little skinny arm, which looked in her hand like one of the small branches of a tree in the grip of a mighty giant. The little girl's face turned pale and remained motionless, then was lost in her alleged mother's lap, who was seated on the floor.

A short while later, I saw the little girl's face, and it had been transformed into that of a comic doll! On that thin face, they had put heavy makeup: wide black eyeliner, penciled eyebrows, and a black dot (a bindi) in the middle of her forehead. That unfortunate little girl had to endure makeup sessions portraying Simone's artistry while being forced to sit on her lap, hearing her profanities, and being exposed to disgraceful behavior that ruined her purity and innocence. I was tempted to write to child protection agencies asking about adoption procedures and how it was even possible for people like this woman to adopt a child in need of proper upbringing and care, but my circumstances were difficult, and raising such issues would most likely bring the kind of trouble from which we wished to be spared.

During one of the visits, Simone decided to keep the little girl with her. Prison laws allowed mothers to care for their young children; therefore, it was within her rights. The little girl was being forced to stay while crying and holding on to the hem of the dress of the woman who brought her, but Simone screamed at the child and pulled her by the arm. Simone tried to tempt her with sweets and brought her a bed from the daycare. Fearfully, the little girl resigned herself to remaining quiet, as she knew very well that any sign of rebellion would be met with curses and punishment.

On the following day while I passed the hallway, I saw the little girl confined to her bed. The day was over, and the same thing happened on the next day. I wanted to inquire if the little child was sick, despite the fact that she looked normal and was still wearing makeup, so I asked Simone why she was in bed. Her answer was, "It's best if she always stays on her bed so she won't misbehave."

At that moment, I felt as if a heavy nightmare were sitting on my chest while seeing that innocent child lying as a prisoner in her bed, which had iron bars. The little girl looked like a beautiful confined animal that had lost its ability to move and had become resigned to its inability to express its pain and suffering. What had the little girl done to deserve spending a miserable childhood with that tyrant? If she had had a choice, no doubt she would have preferred poverty and deprivation to this cruelty. If her biological mother had kept her, she would have been loved and would have been able to enjoy freedom. The poor soul remained in that state of confinement and of constantly being scolded by Simone until it was time for the next visit.

Fate destined for Simone to accompany us until the last seconds of our confinement. In fact, later on, when we received clemency and were about to leave the prison's gate in an open police truck that was barely big enough to fit the ten of us, I was shoved aside at that last second by her large body, as she was determined to accompany us until the end!

At the time, I could not be irritated, since we were at the start of a new and unknown epoch, and the days of prison seemed like a movie that had ended with us leaving the theater where it was being presented. The country music was blasting on that truck with a repetitive, rhythmic tune that evoked laughter and various other emotions. The joy of being liberated from confinement had been fused with the bitterness of persecution and the worry of the unknown. Simone remained on the truck until we arrived at a rotary in the heart of the city, where we said our good-byes and rode away, each of us in the car of a relative. Thus we ended a chapter that was filled with good and bad memories of the Al-Rashaad prison.

The Murderer

One day, a young woman dressed in black was brought in. She was crying and bemoaning her bad luck that had brought her to prison and had forced her to leave her children with her family. She claimed that her verdict for murdering her husband was based on suspicion only. She said her husband at the time was taking a nap in the afternoon when a bullet, entering through the window, penetrated his heart. Since there was no one else at home except her and the children, she had become the main suspect. During questioning and examination, the police discovered the smell of gunpowder and traces of gunpowder residue in her hair. I kept on wondering, how did the gunpowder and its smell get in her hair, which became the evidence of her guilt?

But we had to receive any convict in our section with acceptance. I was asked to empty my small room for her and return to being with my friend Bedriyyeh. As usual, the newcomer was distressed on her first day. She kept on repeating and swearing to God that she was innocent, but after a while, she no longer mentioned any of her husband's positive traits that would have caused her to mourn his loss. During her stay with us, she hired a skillful lawyer to find a way out of her sentence.

It became an opportunity for Simone to befriend the new resident through her clever means and by offering her help. Soon after, they had become very close friends. Through that friendship, the newcomer found an outlet for her distress. She had high hopes, reinforced by her lawyer, of being acquitted of the charge that had been brought against her. Simone suggested that this woman pledge an offering to God. (This offering is called *nithr* in Arabic. It is a common practice that consists of a promise made to God as an exchange for answering a specific request.) The nithr, she suggested, must involve a sacrifice on her part so that God would answer her plea in gaining her innocence. The nithr was of a peculiar nature, but the woman agreed to do it, especially since Simone had sworn it would work. She was told it had been proven to work for all those who agreed to try it!

The newcomer was pleasant with us; therefore, we treated her with the utmost kindness and expressed our good wishes for her release, in spite of the evidence indicating her guilt. One day, laughingly, she said, "To God, I will pledge to do anything I'm able to do, especially what Simone suggested!"

I was alone with her one day and had a deep curiosity to know what Simone's suggestion was, as I was ever suspicious of her intentions. I jokingly asked about it, and her answer was, "It's something between me and God."

I said, "God wants us to do that which is good and righteous, and I am not going to put any pressure on you to tell me anything."

She then took me aside and whispered in my ear, "I was told that if I broke my promise, I would be severely rebuked by God; therefore, I must implement it."

She told me about the nithr, and I was shocked and repulsed to know the dishonorable nature of it, which involved sexually intimate behavior with three strange men!

With great astonishment, I asked, "And did you agree?"

"It's a nithr and not my choice to commit what's disgraceful, but I have sworn to God to fulfill my promise if He would help me," she replied.

I said, "How can you expect to receive a reward from God when you are planning to commit that which does not please Him? Aren't you afraid of an even more severe reprimand from Him? You are trying to escape one trouble just to fall into another!" I could not help but caution her not to choose a thoughtless act she would regret or to be dragged into a greater evil than being a prisoner.

It was as if she was shaken out of her heedlessness and woken from her sleep, so that she began to tell me how she was too naive to believe that nonsense.

After remaining with us for a period of two months or more, she had a final trial and was found innocent. She said her good-byes to everyone, while Simone and her loud voice was following her and reminding her of her promise to God and warning her not to dismiss it!

The newly-released woman and I exchanged a long glance, then she smiled at me in a way that portrayed assurance that she would remain on the path of dignity and honor. As she was moving farther away, I was wondering if she had truly understood that if a human loses his integrity and self-respect, the most excellent of lawyers can never defend him against his own conscience. That conscience will confront and agonize him before God, who is the Great Judge.

10 / The Winds of Change and the Opening of the Cage Door

A Visit from the Chief Administrator of All Prisons

In our second year of imprisonment at the Al-Rashaad prison, we received an informal visit from the chief administrator of all prisons in Iraq. The visit was being taken without any administrative preparations, and he entered our section unaccompanied. He went to the room of the prisoner I previously mentioned (the one who was accused of murdering her husband), and I heard her loudly discuss with him aspects of her case, as if perhaps he could be of help.

When he came to examine our room, I asked him whether there was any hope of our release by including us in clemencies offered to other prisoners.

His reply was, "Yes. In our thorough investigation, it's been confirmed that you are citizens with 'no destructive intent.'"

I was shocked by the word *destructive*, so I replied to him with astonishment, "Destructive! Your honor, as you see, we are honorable citizens who loyally and faithfully served our jobs and professions. While you've been serving as an administrator, have you ever heard of a Bahá'í entering prison on charges of any crime, never mind destruction?"

He said, "You (Bahá'ís) are a minority; therefore, of course, nothing like that has happened." Then he continued, "But your communication with your Universal House of Justice in Israel is clear."

I said, "The Universal House of Justice is a supreme spiritual institution that is international. As individuals, we have no business to communicate with it."

He said, "That's what Christians say as well, but the Pope in Rome directs them as he wishes. Look what happened to the Muslims in Lebanon at the hands of Christians!" (At that time, a civil war was taking place.)

At this point, I preferred to terminate our chat and remain silent. We ended the conversation with a request for his kind assistance, and in return, he promised to write a positive report about our good conduct in prison as confirmed by the prison's administration. We thanked him and hoped for a good outcome in the near future.

More Visits from Officials

After that, visits from officials became plenteous. At times, groups of three persons would arrive, and at other times, more would come. The purpose behind all those visits was to persuade, or even pressure, us to formally renounce our belief in the Bahá'í Faith, or as they called it, "the Bahá'í ideology." I clearly remember telling one of the officials, "We look at the respected government as a father figure who equally cares about all of his children. As a minority, we await equal treatment with all the other religious minorities."

He said, "But yours is not a divine religion."

I said, "As you wish. Consider it a belief."

He said, "Not even that. It's nothing but a notion of a tiny minority."

I said, "Whatever it may be, we are still part of this society, a part that is honest and obedient to its government."

The main focus of their persistent pressure was on our young ladies. Wide-ranging approaches were used to persuade them to retract their firm position. The authorities had the impression that our young ladies were under the influence and direction of the older women; therefore, a decision was made to separate them from us.

In one of the visits by some officials, their questioning and comments turned provocative and condemnatory to our position of persevering in our belief. Addressing his speech toward me personally, the chairman of the committee said, "What do you think about your Universal House of Justice receiving its instructions from the White House (in America)?"

I calmly replied, "That is impossible. We have absolutely no association with any political entity, as partisan politics are prohibited in the Bahá'í Faith. Therefore, it is intuitive that the Universal House of Justice would be the first to implement that law."

He said, "I have a photograph of them at the White House."

I replied, "Perhaps it is of other people."

He then said, "What if I showed you the photo? Would you then renounce your belief?"

Because I was so certain about the absurdity of his claim, I hurried to accept his challenge.

At that moment, the women's prison administrator became agitated and turned to me, saying, "Is your information regarding such matters better than that of the officials?"

I then chose to remain silent.

The chairman of the committee then said, "Tomorrow I will send the photograph to the administrator so you can see for yourself."

The administrator affirmed this by saying, "Do you need a better proof than that? I will send for you to come to the office to look at the photo yourself."

I said, "Very well, madam."

The next day came and others followed, and, until the day of our release more than a year later, I was never asked to go to the office nor did I have any doubt in my heart that such a photograph never existed!

Separating Our Younger Women

Distress and pressure began to mount after a decision to separate us from our younger women took effect. The office placed Simone with them and took us to a new section with two designated rooms for us to occupy. The prison's clinic was in a room adjacent to ours at that same section. My roommate was dear Bedriyyeh Husain, and in the other room they put dear sisters Hajir Al-Wakeel, Bahiyyeh Husain, and another Bahá'í lady.

It was a very difficult day when we had to separate from our girls after being imprisoned together for several years. Perhaps it was not as difficult for them, because having a youthful, cheerful, and enthusiastic spirit meant more adaptability and resilience. Each of them had been busy perfecting skills. Nida, Fatima, and Warqa had all become proficient in sewing, just like dear Kawakib, who was already excellent at sewing before entering prison. All of them had also perfected the art of knitting. Dr. Iqbal had at the time been given permission to visit the clinic and work with the doctor or the health agency administering the prison's clinic.

As for the rest of us, it was more difficult to be separated from the younger women, for the exchange of stories had been depleted, and there was not anything new to talk about. The small one-channel television remained in the section where our girls were. They had lost interest in watching it, as Simone had imposed her presence on them and her continuous babbling and chatter did not stop.

Daily visits by the prisoners to the clinic were continuous, and the smell of meds and antiseptic filled our rooms, since the clinic was right next to them. In addition, there was the constant noise of crying children and chatty inmates, most of whom would pretend to be sick just so they could leave their sections or receive sympathy and attention. I have seen with my own eyes and heard about those who threw their medication in the trash, and others who stored different meds for difficult times, in case they needed to end their lives.

Our days were long and dull, especially after being excluded from the clemency law, for which I will dedicate a portion in this book. Because we were prohibited from meeting and talking to our young women, we were careful not to have any contact with them, except an occasional passing greeting from across the courtyard. With time, the pressure subsided a little, and we could meet with them a bit during the common visitation with our families, when we could eat together what was brought to us. But during regular days, we remained separated, and each group had to prepare meals in their separate sections.

The Release of Our Young Ladies for a Period of One Week

Because of the focused attention on our girls by the government officials, the prison administration began a campaign aimed at pressuring the young Bahá'í women to abandon their heroic and unyielding determination and to recant their belief in the Bahá'í Faith. This campaign was the implementation of an order by the Ministry of Internal Affairs. A committee was sent to meet with our girls to persuade them to disavow their faith, and they were threatened with severe punishment, such as life sentences, if they refused to do so.

When our ladies remained steadfast and refused to give in to the pressure, the committee made a decision to release them on the condition of their never mentioning their faith to anyone and their discontinuing all Bahá'í activities. The request was reasonable for all; hence, it was accepted, especially since the older ladies had given up on being released. We told the girls that they did not have to worry about anything, since they had not performed any activities in the past anyway and did not need to mention their faith to anyone.

The decision was implemented, and our five young ladies, who with their excellent conduct had gained the love and respect of all, were released. We were utterly delighted by their liberation from that corrupt environment and their return to the outside world, where they could live a normal life. Ululations and good wishes accompanied them until they left the outside gate.

On an evening barely a week later, we were shocked by the return of our girls! They were in a state of utter exhaustion. I remember being outside the section when I saw my sister Fatima, weeping bitterly, heading toward our building. I ran toward her to investigate what had happened and embraced her until she became calm enough to tell me that there had been a reversal in the decision of the release and that they had been sent back to prison.

The Directorate of General Security agency (Al-Amn), prior to the girls' return to the prison, had sent a private and secretive report to the prison administrators. The report was not opened that night, and this caused great anxiety to all of us. But the next morning, we came to know that the report had reinstated each of the girls' original prison sentences. This news was actually a relief since our girls were brought back to the same prison and not taken somewhere else.

We gathered the night of their return and asked about what happened and if they were transferring their beds and bedding from the storage room back to their cells. They told us that the Minster of Internal Affairs himself had wished to be certain about the girls' position regarding their belief in the Bahá'í Faith; therefore, he had requested that they come to his office at the ministry for questioning. After calmly and pleasantly presenting an introduction regarding the duty of civilians toward their government and the governing party, and their expected loyalty and collaboration, he turned to one of the young ladies and surprised her with this question, "What's your religion?"

Her immediate reply was, "Bahá'í."

That answer created an instant awkwardness in the meeting. The minister became extremely angry and turned that day into an utterly difficult one. His callousness added to the ever-present terror of being at the ministry and being surrounded by the Al-Amn men. Memories of the horrible interrogation period came rushing back into the heads of the girls with great intensity, especially when the minister gave the Al-Amn men his order to arrest the girls and send them back again to prison (although at the time our girls had no idea where they were being taken and feared the worst).

The news instantly spread throughout the ministry that arrests had been made inside the ministry, and the building was locked down. It was as if dangerous criminals had been arrested! After completing the arrest procedures, a special agency truck was called, and the girls left on it. They did not know their fate until they found themselves inside the gates of Al-Rashaad.

The situation was difficult on all of us that night, especially since our girls had enjoyed their freedom in the outside world, even for a short while. Each of them had hoped to get back to a normal life of socializing and work. At that moment, we came to realize that the most important objective for us was to return to our love and unity through prayers and supplication to God. As time went by, our young ladies came to accept the reality of their circumstances. Through our sincere prayers, God bestowed upon us patience, endurance, and steadfastness in the face of adversity. Hence, life continued with the same repetitiveness, until God permitted at a later date that we leave the prison, with each one of us holding on to the memories—whether bitter or sweet—of Al-Rashaad prison.

Our Exclusion from a Pardon Decree and the Departure of My Children

Before the end of our fifth year of imprisonment, rumors spread that a decree of pardon from President Ahmed Hassan Al-Bakr was to be enacted, and would include all prisoners in Iraq except those with serious offenses. We felt a renewed sense of hope and optimism that we would be included in this decree. This news elicited a joyful response throughout the sections, and ululations rose from every side. As the days went by, our hope began to build, and we began to dream of leaving that dreary environment forever, of rejoining our loved ones at home, and of resuming our normal lives.

We dismissed any negative thoughts of being excluded from the decree; therefore, the news spread to our families, and they began to joyfully prepare for our return after five long years of separation. When the rumor became a reality, all the inmates were eagerly waiting to hear the official news announcement on television that evening, as told by the prison's office. It was a hot summer season, and we had placed our metal beds outside our section, inside the courtyard. We gathered around our small TV, which we had brought outside after connecting it with an extension cord. We were in a hurry for the programs to end so we could watch the news at 10:00 p.m. Our pulses began increasing as time passed, and we heard repeated alerts from the news anchor to anticipate the announcement of very important news regarding what was called the "Clemency Act."

When ten o'clock finally arrived, everyone became silent, and we turned up the volume of the television all the way, in great anticipation of the critical moment!

'Abdul-Sahib, the well-known news anchor, appeared with his usual cold smile and customary enthusiasm during such occasions. Practically shouting, he announced, "Presidential decree number such and such—The Leadership Council of the Revolution, headed by the President of the Republic of Iraq, Mr. Ahmed Hassan Al-Bakr, decrees clemency and orders that all prisoners be released, with the exception of the Bahá'ís, murderers, and those charged with espionage!" There was an arrogant and malicious smile on the hate-filled face of that anchor at the end of his announcement, which I remember very well. If I were an artist, I would have painted it to depict and immortalize the attributes of spite and joyful satisfaction in someone's pain—a trait of arrogance that is repulsive to watch.

A spirit of disappointment swept over us as we received the unexpected news, especially in that magnitude. Loud commotion and ululations from all sections furthered our anguish as the other inmates went out to celebrate and dance in joy, while the lights in the courtyard were all turned on. Such celebrations were expected, and I would not be exaggerating if I said that our joy for them was not any less because of our exclusion. As human beings, they had the right to be free, especially after suffering incarceration. However, in those critical moments, we were in need of quiet to reclaim our spirits and be capable of overcoming our human weakness and the pain that was instigated by the injustice of such a cruel decree, a ruling preventing us from being equal to the other inmates in the right of freedom. We did not cry, nor did we allow the circumstances to conquer our spirits, nor did any of us allow herself to surrender to an emotional breakdown. We chose to be in control and prepare for even tougher challenges ahead.

As soon as the jubilation and noise finally quieted down and the other inmates all went back to their places to prepare for their release the following day, the superintendent came to investigate the effect of the news on us. We were in a state of absolute peacefulness and total submission to the will of God. She must have been astonished to witness no sign of the distress or sobbing that most of the other inmates excluded from the pardon were demonstrating.

That night, we gathered for consultation and shared our thoughts and views on what had happened. One horrifying question occupied all of our minds, yet none dared to openly discuss it: Would our end truly be here? Is the government serious in its threats of never allowing us to leave prison, even after completing our sentences?

The answer to those questions remained a mystery trapped within our chests. When and how God's tender mercy would encompass us was a question that kept us restless that night. The next morning, we were awoken by the noise and commotion of the departing inmates and the office clerks finishing the procedures for releasing them.

The effect of our exclusion from the decree fell harder on our families, although they never gave up their hope of God's mercy. On the visit following the event, I heard from my daughters about how they had gone to our home, after it had been neglected for a long period, to return some items and tidy the place in preparation for our return. They told me how they received the news of our exclusion from the pardon. Despite their kind and comforting words of encouragement, which ignited a spark of hope in my heart, I read on their faces the lines of hopelessness that their lips could not utter.

To reassure them, I presented an image of strength and fortitude in an attempt to fill their hearts with new hope. I used words such as "perhaps," "who knows," and "we must resort to patience more than ever," but each one of my daughters now had a different view of my imprisonment in the core of her thinking and the depths of her heart. Their lives were moving in a different direction than in the past, and they now had different objectives they were striving to achieve. The situation became clear after only a short period of time, when separation appeared to be the ideal solution after the hope of our release was lost, and the constant pressure and threats made by the officials confirmed one fact: that we would die and be buried in prison.

On the following visits, my daughters and I exchanged thoughts about their travel abroad and what direction it would take. I could sense the tremendous mental anguish my children were experiencing and could almost feel their overpowering anxiety. Neither one of them openly told me about the difficult circumstances and the daily increasing tension while living in my family's home. My elderly parents were in poor health, and my brother's house where they all lived had become overcrowded. My younger brother had married a young lady who was completing her education and who now had a baby; and my older brother, the owner of the residence, had decided to get married as well. His house was not designed to host four families.

Life had become complicated in such a crowded space, and understandably, the new wife wanted to reduce the number of occupants in her home, and the raffle was not in my daughters' favor! When I sensed my brother's hint of discontent, I suggested to my daughters to quietly pull out and move to my other brother's home until God willed what would benefit them. For me, their dignity was more important than anything else.

They eventually did move to my other brother's house, but it was not logical for them to stay there indefinitely, and going back home was not possible because my son Abir had completed his education, graduated from university, and was now enrolled in the army (a compulsory enrollment). After a couple of years, he finished his service and started to work in Basra City (in the southern part of Iraq), which was very far from his sisters.

So what was left for my daughters to do? The only remaining option for them was to find a future that was away from the problems and the possibility of even more serious complications if they decided to stay, such as imprisonment (the threat of their imprisonment was brought up during efforts to pressure us while in prison).

As I have mentioned, my daughters were experiencing plenty of difficulties during their parents' and aunts' absence. Additionally, my beloved son Abir was subjected to torture and severe pressure to recant his faith by the Iraqi Intelligence Service (Al-Amn) in very harsh circumstances, of which I was not aware until our release from prison. He had hidden those details to protect me from potentially having an emotional breakdown.

In the two visits that followed our exclusion from the pardon, we lightly spoke about the idea of my daughters leaving. Perhaps, and without intending to, I had given them the green light to pursue that notion. My husband had refused the idea initially, simply because he was not fully aware of their hard circumstances. When I told my little beloved Ruwa that her father did not favor the idea and that it was best for her to stay and wait, she became reluctantly silent. She had been seriously considering the idea of leaving Iraq, and she had become convinced that it was the right thing to do.

In the following visit, I was surprised by a friend visiting us who told me that Ruwa had indeed left to go to Turkey. The news shook my whole being like an earthquake. I had not expected that our reflections on travel were going to become a factual reality. I felt that my heart was being forcefully ripped out of my chest. I went inside my room unconscious and not knowing what to do. I repeated to myself, "No, no, this is not true, you can't leave, my beloved, you can't leave me alone. Will I remain long enough in this life to see you again?"

I was speaking with a loud voice like a fool. My dear friend Bedriyyeh hurried to calm my bewilderment and comfort me with words of encouragement to seek fortitude. God rescued me with a flood of tears that allowed me to feel and express my grief until I woke up from the effect of the shock. I was able to hold myself together and placed my affairs in God the Almighty's hands to do with as He pleased. At that moment, I asked Him to take my daughter by the hand and guide her to what was best for her. With suppliant hands, I asked Him to join her with her siblings to be together under His loving care.

When I met with my beloved daughter Alhan and my beloved son Abir afterward, they told me how Ruwa had been determined to leave and had given up her admittance to the Engineering University. There had been nothing else on her mind except accomplishing her plan to leave Baghdad, the beloved home on whose precious soil she had been born and had grown up. After our imprisonment, she had gone through difficulties with the loss of her home. Home is the minuscule symbol of homeland. Without a home, a person becomes lost in God's vast land.

During this same visit, my son Abir told me that the company he worked for had selected him to serve (after his service in the army had finished) as a representative who would travel to Tunisia.

The news hit me with conflicting emotions. I was comforted by the fact that he would be away from the highly charged circumstances we were all experiencing and that there would be a chance for him to ensure the safety of his sister, if they were able to meet. I could sense, with my motherly intuition, his discomfort and unrest. He seemed to be in a state of anticipation for God's mercy to save him from the whirlpool of the grinding events from which we were all suffering—especially him, though he had concealed his experiences of being tortured from me.

My beloved son asked me to pray for him, so God would aid him with his wish to leave. When I told him that I prayed for all of them all the time, he said with a cherished smile: Increase your prayers, Mama. I could feel the anxiety he was undergoing in case things did not go as he wished.

Alhan, my other fragrant flower and my older daughter, was employed by then. Her sister's departure had compounded the stress of having her parents in prison and had made her situation even more difficult. She came to visit and told me that Ruwa had arrived safely at my sister Semera's home in Istanbul, Turkey. I started to look at the possibility of her leaving as inevitable. Concealing the part of my emotions that wanted desperately to hold all my children close to my heart, I asked her, "What do you plan to do? Don't you wish to be with your sister?"

She said with a compassionate voice, "What about you, Mama? What do you wish me to do?"

I suffocated my motherly cry inside my chest and embraced her, saying, "Do what is best for your future, my loved one, and may you be in God's protection. Leave your father and I to our destiny, as we will be in God's protection as well. Hearing good and comforting news of your happiness is our highest aim and desire."

If I had had a camera with me that day, I would have taken a picture of the most beautiful and pure recollection I have stored of Alhan in my memory until this day, as she was in her most magnificent appearance! She continued to turn around and wave to me as she walked away in the hallway, saying good-bye with me smiling in encouragement and saying to her over and over, "Go in God's protection, go in God's protection."

I could not leave the room, neither did she allow me to take her to the main gate of the prison. We were forced to be satisfied with this memorable farewell, while I was barely keeping myself from collapsing on the threshold of the door. Where would the currents of life take them? Where would their home be, and would they be able to overcome life's difficulties away from home? What if our separation became too long, and I could not see them? I could not continue my thoughts any further. Those questions, though taking seconds, seemed to linger for ages.

Alhan left Iraq, and thus I remained lost without my children. The fetters no longer mattered to me. The pressure could not crush me any longer. But the separation from my children had left me as a hollow tree filled with cavities and holes. Its leaves had fallen, and it could no longer give shade to anyone. The beautiful birds had abandoned it after losing the security of their nests.

Weeks after Alhan's departure, God's will—and a series of His miracles we will forever be grateful for—eventually led Abir to reunite with his beloved sisters. It was a blessed beginning for him and his sisters since they had left Iraqi soil. They remained at my sister Semera's home in Turkey for several long months, until they were able to reach the United States, the land of freedom and peace. My son Abir has documented a narrative about his historic journey.

Hearing this news put me at some level of ease when realizing that Alhan must have been comforted to see her sister, who was in my dear sister Semera's home in Istanbul. My mother delivered to me a small folded paper, a written note from my beloved Alhan before her departure. I saved it and treasured it as I would a piece of my heart. In it were phrases of immense love and regret for the circumstances that had forced her to move away from me. She prayed to God to fill my heart with faith and fortitude.

We continued to exchange letters, but that small letter had left a profound impression on my soul. I left that letter in Baghdad before traveling many years later to come to the United States. I did not want anyone else to read it, especially the inspectors at the airport who would crudely and carelessly search personal pocketbooks without any respect or consideration.

Letters remained a source of warmth and comfort to all of our souls, despite the fact that our family tried to conceal our distress from each other. My mother carefully carried my children's letters in her purse or inserted them in the folds of clothes she gave us—not because there was anything illicit in them to fear but because in prison everything is open to misinterpretation and misunderstanding. I always carried the letters on my chest (under my blouse) and remained eager and anxious until nighttime, when the other inmates and the superintendent had retired to sleep and everything was calm and quiet. Only then could I take out the letter, kiss it several times, and read and reread it multiple times until I had memorized all the news and events, with my imagination wandering far away until it met with my children.

Whenever I received a letter, I always brought a pencil and paper into my room and copied down the tender phrases addressed to my husband and me—phrases that reflected kindheartedness and deep faith. I summarized the rest of the letter and saved it in my secret safe in our room! Afterward, I would take the original letter, tear it into small pieces, go to the sink, wet it and mold it into a ball, squeeze the water out, and crumble it before throwing it into the trash barrel. At night, I memorized the beautiful phrases and recalled the events until it was time to visit my husband. I would then relay to him the news. His spirit would lift, and his prayers would be raised. Then I would go back to my notes to reply to every letter, tuck it between the items I handed to my mother, and beg her to mail my reply as soon as possible.

This process is how the last year of imprisonment went by, with our exchanged letters traveling and reaching their destinations safely. I had enough written notes in my safe to make up a notebook, and after our release from prison, our children continued to send my husband and me letters, and we continued to reply through the postal service.

My son Abir stayed with his sisters in Istanbul for a short while, then traveled to Italy, where he started preparing to immigrate to the United States. His sisters were eventually able to follow him after spending nearly a year in Turkey under the loving care of my sister and brother-in-law and my two nieces. With God's loving assistance, my daughters Ruwa and Alhan were able to obtain permission to travel to the United States.

As fate would have it, my daughters arrived in Italy shortly before our release from prison. They were able to call us immediately after we had left the prison, as they had received the news before we could even send it! Hearing their voices again that day was a historic event for me, and God enabled us to talk on the phone every now and then in the following years. Perhaps they will write about their own experiences and God's endless bounties that surrounded them during that period.

Writing a Petition

I will summarize some of the situations I experienced prior to the departure of my children, when dreariness and boredom had begun to penetrate our souls. Since we were now alone in our section and away from our young ladies, our long days seemed to have no end, and the darkness of our nights now seemed to stretch on and on, as if they would not be followed by morning.

Our young ladies, as well, had begun to grow tired of the constant monotony of their lives, especially after being forced to return to prison in a tyrannical manner that was far removed from reason and forbearance. Because of prison's dull and cruel repetitiveness, life was effectively standing still for them, while youth outside prison enjoyed the quick passing of life's events, which filled their time in productive ways and kept them busy. Despite our high spirits and readiness for sacrifice, we were still human beings and longed for the normalcy of life, such as being able to be close to our loved ones and to share with them what had happened during the day.

I tried to distract myself from the loneliness that often flooded my chest, but at times I was left powerless, and the nights tore me apart mercilessly with constant insomnia. There was nothing left to do but go, in the darkness of the night, to the hallway next to our room and prostrate my face on the ground to beg God for His deliverance. I tearfully beseeched and begged the Greatest Holy Leaf (daughter of Bahá'u'lláh)—may my soul be a sacrifice to her lofty rank—to accept the plea of a helpless mother and protect my children, and from her high station, to be their surrogate mother, as I was no longer able to support them. I said, "God, I am unworthy of wearing the crown of sacrifice when my endurance is nearly depleted. You are my helper, and on You I have put my reliance."

With a mother's intuition, I also knew very well that my parents, at their advancing age, could not be parents to my children. They already had four of their children behind bars and four others abroad. They were in poor health and in financial hardship, because the government had confiscated their children's salaries. Thus, life's hardships had befallen us, perhaps more than other families.

While roaming in my own thoughts, an idea came to my mind to write a petition to Mr. Saddam Hussein. At the time, he was vice president to President Ahmed Hassan al-Bakr, and held in his hand the entire ruling power of the country, as everyone knew. I wrote a touching petition that briefly explained my service in the field of education and how I had taught several generations of children with the upmost sincerity. I had not only served as their teacher but also as their surrogate mother, guiding her daughters to the best and loftiest of conduct and to all that opened and liberated their minds from conformity and rigidity. I had not committed any wrongdoing deserving of this harsh sentence, and my daughters were at an age that required my care and proximity.

I kindly requested that he look into my case, and I submitted my petition through the prison's office, which encouraged me and supported my claims, but I received no reply. That is when I realized that God's will was beyond what I had wished. The time of my release had not yet come, as if God had ordained that this medal of honor remain on our chests without interruption under any circumstances. At that time, some of the other ladies made similar attempts, but they failed as well. We had no regrets in trying, as we wished to be certain about the government's position toward our case. Moreover, we tried so no one could say we had not made the effort or that we considered ourselves superior to everyone else, who put many efforts into obtaining clemency. God had willed that we would all leave at the precise hour He had chosen for us, despite all the obstacles that were laid before us and the hindrances that confronted us with attempts to destroy our hopes and shake our faith.

Safiyyeh

A few months before our release, a new Bahá'í prisoner was added to our unit, and her name was Safiyyeh Yaqoob. One day, during the late afternoon,

299

right before sunset, I was sitting in front of our section when I heard a commotion caused by some inmates. One of the superintendents was trying to separate them from a new prisoner, who was a youth and who was standing in bewilderment in the courtyard next to the prison's main gate. It was customary for the inmates to surround any newcomer to inquire about her story and ask her all kinds of questions, just as all skillful TV news reporters do. The story then goes through all types of changes and alterations, far away from the truth. As I was looking out onto the courtyard, I saw some inmates running toward our section to tell us that the newcomer was a Bahá'í!

I ran toward the newcomer and gave her a tight embrace, with tears pouring down, but she bravely comforted me while being very calm and resolute, despite the utter exhaustion that was visible on her face. She had had a long day of difficult procedures. She had been transferred from the detention center to court, then to a police station, and finally to Al-Rashaad prison.

I asked, with great astonishment, "What happened? This is an unforeseen surprise."

She replied, "It is an unexpected situation for me as well."

At that moment, the other Bahá'í friends had come to welcome her with hugs and kisses. Then the superintendent came to escort Safiyyeh to our section of the prison. Thus, Safiyyeh became a prisoner in our group—which used to be comprised of ten ladies before an elderly ill colleague left us— and she said her farewell to the world of freedom from behind the walls of Al-Rashaad.

Safiyyeh, who was lovely in appearance and pleasant in her manners, was tremendously brave and proud of her sentence. She acted as if she had been on a vacation and had just returned home. A smile never left her face, and she always repeated that she was very happy to be with us. Because of her contented attitude, I felt uplifted and welcomed her in sharing our uncertain destiny with us.

Her arrest and imprisonment was a source of concern to us. We feared the arrests of other youth on fabricated charges that they had broken a law that prohibited Bahá'í activities. We Bahá'í ladies were supposedly being punished for breaking this broad law, even though we had been unaware that our activities had violated it. As I mentioned, such violations had included the possession of a small piece of paper with a prayer written on it, the purchase of a tiny house not larger than fifty square meters that was near the house of Bahá'u'lláh, and other similar accusations that had resulted in our being sentenced to anywhere from ten years to life imprisonment.

Safiyyeh's arrest was also an indication that the officials, by their continual harassment of the Bahá'í community, had remained firm in their attitude toward our case, and it was also a serious confirmation of their threats of keeping us inside these prison walls indefinitely. However, Safiyyeh's courageous attitude inspired us to share her positive outlook. The superintendent allowed us to stay with her for a while that evening and listen to her story of arrest and other news about the Bahá'í friends outside the prison. We said our good-byes, then headed to our designated buildings. The next morning, we saw Safiyyeh walking with our other young ladies on the side path in a natural way, as if she had been with them since the beginning of our time together. She shared a room with Dr. Iqbal, and in a few days, she received the prison uniform, which she was very happy to wear. She sent a request to the office to visit her father, who was one of our Bahá'í brothers in prison. On visiting day, she accompanied us and was happy to ride the prison's truck with the wire mesh sides all the way to Abu Ghraib.

It was destined for Safiyyeh to remain with us in prison for several months until our release, and together, we left Al-Rashaad to continue a new and different part of our lives. Safiyyeh married a Bahá'í young man, and later on was blessed with children. May God's blessing be upon you, my beloved Safiyyeh.

Another Trip to the Hospital

Every now and then, certain gifts donated by kind people made their way to the prison. I am not clear why some think of offering such gifts to prisoners. Perhaps they themselves were prisoners at some point or had relatives who were in prison. Before entering prison, I do not remember thinking of anyone behind bars as needing our loving care, because people's general opinion of prisoners was that they were criminals deserving of punishment.

Sometimes, there were gifts such as children's clothing or a large quantity of a certain kind of fruit. When the amount of food exceeded our usual share, and we asked about the reason behind it, we were told that a generous person had donated it. I remember once someone sent a truckful of fine Turkish apples. The prison employees took their share and then distributed the rest in generous amounts to the prisoners. They were the best type of apples.

On a day I will never forget, a gift arrived at our unit. It was a large tray of rice and an Iraqi dish called *qeemeh*. The occasion was Ashura (the day Imám Husayn, the grandson of the Prophet Muhammad, was martyred. It is a day of mourning). It had fallen on a very hot summer day, and we had just finished our lunch, which meant I was not able to have any more food. But the prisoner who brought the food told us about the special holy occasion and waited to make sure we accepted the gift. My colleague Bedriyyeh, God rest her soul, out of courtesy, went to take a few bites and whispered in my ear to do the same, so no one would say Bahá'ís had refused food cooked in respect for Imám Husayn.

I remember taking not more than two spoonfuls in tribute to Imám Husayn—may God bless His mention. But that food almost ended my life, as shortly afterward, I began to feel the symptoms of food poisoning. Perhaps the food had been cooked at dawn that day and had been sitting out in the extreme heat. After hours of more symptoms of severe poisoning, I collapsed, and an ambulance had to be called. It was night, and one of the guards accompanied me while I was dragging my legs.

As soon as the ambulance reached the hospital and I was placed in a bed, the doctor hurried to administer an IV and some other injections, and I was then asked to explain to him what had happened. At the time, I did not care if restraints had to be placed on me—since I had heard from other inmates that this was standard practice when a prisoner was transported to the hospital—but in my case, no restraints or restrictions were ordered.

After a couple of hours, when I started to recover, the doctor told me that I could leave the hospital. I returned to prison, still in a state of extreme weakness, and almost collapsed on the ground next to the prison gate. The female guard took a long time to open the gate, but she helped me to reach our unit. I was still experiencing extreme drowsiness and fatigue. When the medication finally took effect, the night went by smoothly. I lost my appetite for days after that incident, and I swore never to force myself to eat anything out of politeness or for any other reason.

The Sentencing of the Administrator of the Women's Prison

Every time we were consoled by the fair and humane treatment of an administrator, we would witness how that same administrator, after a time, would change and become overly harsh toward us for no tangible reason, despite our total compliance with the regulations. This change in behavior occurred because of orders that came from the Al-Amn and other officials. After receiving these orders, the administrator would place us under certain restrictions that the superintendents and guards would implement as well. Their pleasant treatment would turn to callousness as we lost some of our privileges and would have to accept the new restrictions, such as a reduction in the time of our outdoor walks or their cancellation entirely. At other times, the door of our section would remain locked for the entire day, or our meals would be delayed for hours for insignificant reasons, or our girls would be prevented from going to the sewing room.

When we arrived at the Al-Rashaad prison, we were optimistic about the new administrator because of the the flexibility she presented and her desire to make positive changes. She made frequent visits to our unit, joked with everyone, and made friendly conversation. As time went by, we began to notice inconsistent behavior from this administrator, who would interfere in the affairs of inmates who were of no concern to her. She did not conform to the required wisdom of someone in her position, and since the Al-Amn had informants inside the prison, they kept a firm and close eye on the office so that no important information would slip by them. The administrator, therefore, was always being carefully watched, and any negative information would be unfavorable for her.

One time, this administrator spread a rumor that impending pardons were going to be given to all the prisoners. She had confirmed the news and asked everyone to tune in to the evening broadcast to hear it. I had personally heard this information from her subordinate, who announced it in the commissary, which was in our unit. But the hopes of the inmates were crushed after the end of the evening broadcast because there was no mention of any clemency. Clearly, the administrator—for whatever reason—had spread false information.

The next morning, the administrator came in as I coincidentally was coming out of my room, so I greeted her and simply said, "The anticipated news did not happen last night. We had stayed up eagerly waiting for it."

She instantly became extremely annoyed, as if my words were the last straw that had broken the camel's back! She had earlier heard that and received denunciations from inmates of another section, and she was starting to fear the consequences of her diffusing false news. Before she had left that section, one of the inmates had given her a stinging comment that raised her concern even more. It was only a short while before everyone was called to the office for a very "important reason."

It had not occurred to me that the call was for the purpose of assigning blame and deflecting attention away from the prison administration. As soon as we met, the administrator and her assistant who had helped spread the rumor both accused me of criticizing and accusing the administration. It was a hard shock I had not expected. I defended myself by saying, "I heard the news in the same way as all the other inmates, and I never criticized or made any comments prior to that one simple sentence I uttered in front of you." She insisted that my words amounted to criticism, which is prohibited. The intent was to frighten me so the office would be exempt from being accused of spreading rumors among the inmates.

The entire matter angered me to a great extent, as I felt beset by baseless accusations all over again. I did not want to utter another word; instead, I left them to their consciences. I went back to my section simmering with anger and distressed by their tyranny.

By then, it was noon. Still shivering with fury, I sat on my bed and declined my lunch meal. I begged God with all the sincerity in my heart and said, "Lord, Thou hast pledged Thyself not to forgive any man's injustice. This administrator has wronged me. May this bed be hers so she can taste the suffering of the oppressed." I prayed in agony and with tears, as if the doors of heaven were opening. I recited a phrase from the Holy Qur'án about the Prophet Noah invoking God and saying, "I am vanquished; make me victorious."

In a few days—not even a week—there was a huge uproar in the prison! The administrator was brought in as a prisoner! Where to? To our section! Where in the section? To my room! And what bed to sleep on? The bed that I had occupied! Praised be God, praised be God.

As God is my witness, when I saw her completely broken, pale in face and having lost a significant amount of weight because of the hardships she had faced during that week, I had absolutely no ill feelings of malice toward her. In fact, I felt compassion toward her, and I went close and consoled her with the utmost love and sincerity. We all surrounded her with loving care and comfort. She had been charged on several indictments, with each one requiring a certain period of imprisonment. Some of the violations were poor management and disrespect of her position.

She only remained in prison for a few months, but she left us a changed human being—calm, collected, and unhurried in her movement and activity. Perhaps she had learned in those few months what she had not learned in years, or perhaps the taste of the fetters and captivity had changed her.

Meeting with an Elected Committee from the Republican Palace

A few months before our release, we received notification from the prison office to be ready for a meeting with an important committee from the Presidential Palace; the committee was to arrive that same week. We remained wondering about the reason behind this meeting and what type of questions they had prepared to ask us.

During the evening of the appointed day, we were accompanied by a superintendent to the large meeting hall, where chairs were prepared for us to sit. The new administrator was present, along with all the other superintendents and staff. There was a podium and a microphone where Minister 'Abdu'l-Husain stood. We sat on one side of the hall, while the Minister of Labor and Social Affairs, Mr. Ba Bekr (who was a Kurd) and several Al-Amn members sat on the opposite side. Our young ladies were seated on the same side as Minister Ba Bekr, who welcomed us with a smile and gave us permission to sit down. His facial expression portrayed manifestations of humanity and kindness that put me, and perhaps everyone else, at ease in that worrisome meeting with the Al-Amn members yet again.

The meeting began with an introduction given by Minister 'Abdu'l-Husain, which was mainly about the government's mindfulness of all violators and its willingness to be forbearing with those who recant their opposing ideas to the governing party, and to pardon them from severe punishments. After his introduction, he began to heavily criticize our position and persistence in holding on to our Bahá'í belief. He continued to say, "You are a group that have strayed from Islam; in fact, you have turned against it!"

In response, each one of us, in her own way, gave her defense against that blunt accusation. When my turn arrived, I said, "How can we be deniers of Islam, while we consecrate the Qur'án, which is God's holy book, and sanctify His beloved Prophet Muhammad?"

Mr. Husain then replied, "Would you say the Shahada?" (The Shahada is a creed and one of the five pillars of Islam, declaring the oneness of God and the acceptance of Muhammad as God's Prophet. It is used as a declaration of Islam.)

I loudly answered with the Shahada: "There is none other God but God, and Muhammad is His Messenger."

That is when Ba Bekr added, "His Prophet and Servant," and I repeated it again with all the other ladies.

Mr. Husain said, "You are truly confusing all of us! How can you say the Shahada, then say you are Bahá'ís?"

I replied, "The Shahada is a declaration of the oneness of God, that Islam is true, and Muhammad is His true Messenger. We have accepted the message of Bahá'u'lláh, the Messenger of our time, while accepting all the previous divine religions."

Mr. Ba Bekr gently commented, "No, there is no Messenger after Muhammad, nor any divine religion after Islam. Muhammad is the Seal of the Prophets, and Islam is the Seal of the divine message."

At that point, I did not wish to become further involved with his comments, as it was untimely and futile to do so, and perhaps would have had an adverse effect. Therefore, I returned to silence.

Then Mr. Husain, who was conducting the meeting, asked if we were continuing to practice Bahá'í activities.

Our answer was, "What activities could we perform while incarcerated and under your supervision? Besides, we never had any specific activity before entering prison, other than some religious sacraments such as praying, fasting, and reciting supplications that glorify God's essence and others to ask for healing, aid, and protection."

He then asked, "Are you sure you haven't been performing any activity?"

We asked, "Like what, sir?"

He said, "If we searched you and your rooms now, would we find paper clippings?"

Nida, one of our young ladies, answered, "What kind of clippings do you mean, sir?"

He said, "Correspondence between you and the older ladies."

We found such accusations to be astonishing and absurd, as we had been kept separated in two different buildings. Nida's answer was, "Here are the keys to our unit and rooms inside, where you can find our private boxes. Please feel free to thoroughly examine them as you wish. We do not have any clippings. You can confirm this with our older sisters on visitation day."

(Note: Ironically, we later learned that a few months after this interview, while we were still in prison, this man faced his execution, along with many others who were accused of plotting against the government. We were told that the cause was a tiny scrap of paper (a clipping) that contained a suspicious phrase that was considered a proof sufficient for his indictment. That scrap of paper was caught by a hidden camera while being transferred from his hand to the man next to him. It was a camera that targeted with absolute precision every move of the audience.)

The minister stopped his comments and diverted the conversation to another antagonizing subject. It was their style of interrogation to commingle leniency and sternness in order to create an atmosphere of uneasiness and terror. Every time the interrogated person felt a level of comfort, a charge would be thrown at him to leave him in terror. It was an interrogation tactic that aimed to lead the defendant to gradually accept what he was being asked and to become submissive to their command.

After this, he threw yet another allegation by saying, "None of you possesses any patriotism or any love for her country! Which one of you went out to the streets to hail and acclaim her country?"

In response, each one of us took a turn to say, "Iraq is our only country and home." When my turn arrived, I said, "How can I not love my country Iraq, when I was born and raised in it, received my education in it, and served it for twenty-four years as an educator?" I also added how I had lived in Egypt while receiving my academic education at Alexandria University, and despite it being an Arab country that is dear to my heart and where I received the love and generosity of its people, I still longed for my home country and cried during my separation from it.

Mr. Husain then moved to another topic and criticized the writings of His Holiness Bahá'u'lláh. He said, "I have read some of the writings of the Bahá. There is no doubt He was a clever man when He took Qur'ánic verses, rearranged them, then took another portion from the Qur'án, stitched them all together and attributed them to be His own!"

His comment offended me; therefore, I said, "Sir, what you appear to be saying is that He quotes the Qur'án sometimes. If the words of God are reiterated through the tongues of His Messengers, it is for the purpose of educating humanity. Even if the words repeat themeslves, the source (God) is the same."

The minister simply went back to restating, "Yes, the Bahá is clever indeed!"

Next, he referred to Simone, who had been forced on us from the prostitution ward by the prison's office itself. As I previously mentioned, she had been running a prostitution house, even while still in prison. The minister said, "How did you permit yourselves to get close to her, with her being an unworthy person who is able outside prison to pull any girl off the street and drag her by her hair to the house that she managed?"

Our girls replied, "She was in our section and occupied a room amid ours. Day and night, we saw her, and the exterior door was locked for all of us alike. How, then, was it possible to avoid talking to her on some level?"

He said, "There is no doubt that you liked her and tried to charm her! As an example, one of you aided her in writing a request for clemency. We could tell from the writing style that the person who helped her was one of you!"

At that moment, I knew that his remarks meant me personally. That inmate had insisted in an unbearable manner that I write for her a request for clemency, just as I had previously written similar applications for other inmates. Most of the time, such applications were brief, uncomplicated, and contained a few respectful sentences and a plea for forgiveness. Some of them generated positive results, and the inmates were released from captivity. My answer to the minister's comment was: "Upon the request of that inmate, I wrote that appeal, just as I had done for others. It was done with the office's permission. At times, I wrote similar pleas at the office's request. My reason was not to charm her or win her over." I had to add, "Who is she, that we would try to charm her?"

When signs of resentment were apparent on my face, Mr. Ba Bekr, nodding his head, gently signaled to me to let it go.

Mr. Husain sarcastically continued, "Yes, of course, you have proven that you are immune to those types of people!" He said that because he knew very well that prostitutes such as this woman could destroy the reputations of honorable people and drag honorable girls into their profession.

(That night, I could not sleep, and one of the reasons for my insomnia was thinking of this absolute injustice. They had forcibly imposed that miserable human being on us, then put her alone with our girls with all the annoyances she caused, yet they accused us of trying to win her over? What injustice! Her rightful place should have been the prostitution ward, but we could not complain about it or even make a hint of our displeasure).

The minister moved on to a different topic and asked, "How about the Jews among your community (he meant Bahá'ís from a Jewish background)?"

We replied, "What Jews do you mean?" Then we explained to him that the people to whom he was referring were Bahá'ís of a Jewish origin and that they had all left Iraq before we entered prison.

He said, "I will read a list of names to you, and you must tell me about them." He then started to read names of long-deceased believers that no one recalled.

We all answered with one voice, "We don't know them." He went on reading names, and with each name, he received the same reply: "We don't know them."

Mr. Ba Bekr, the Al-Amn, and the prison staff all began to laugh, but Minister Mr. Husain said, "You are all pretending to be naive. It is impossible that you don't know them. How about Hizkiel (Ezekiel)? Don't you know him?"

This is a very common Jewish name in Iraq and is frequently used to refer to Jewish people, and there have been many derivations of it in the vernacular, some of which are contemptuous but more commonly used as humorous. Mr. Ba Bekr burst out laughing, and so did everyone in that hall.

After the long exchanges of conversation that alternated between their attempts to persuade us and our repeated steadfastness, it was past midnight, and some of us were given permission to leave the hall. Signs of displeasure were visible on the faces of those officials. Despite the late hour, they asked our younger ladies to remain in the hall for some time as a last attempt to sway them into submission into recanting their belief! Among what Mr. Husain told our girls was that our case was baffling him and that he had paced the streets of Baghdad the night before until it was almost dawn. He said his thoughts of us were ones of pity. He could not understand our position and insistence on adhering to our beliefs, while we could be freed with just a small word! That man, who had reached the highest of positions and eventually lost his life because of one small word on a scrap of paper, did not realize that the word he was asking for—a recantation of our belief in the Bahá'í Faith—was impossible for us to consider and unthinkable for us to utter, as it was a word worth our entire lives.

A meeting infused with everything that could provoke us and stir our emotions had finally ended. We thanked God that it had concluded in peace. As God is my witness, I could not sleep the whole night. I went outside the section at dawn and beseeched God to increase our fortitude so we would remain steadfast in His path, just like firmly-established trees that strong winds can shake but never uproot.

The Period Prior to Our Release

Before the general amnesty—which occurred a year after the Clemency Act—that resulted in our release on August 20, 1979, a team from the Presidential Palace repeatedly visited with us to increase the pressure on us to submit a petition for clemency—meaning a plea for forgiveness—so that our case would be taken into consideration. The pressure came in various ways, and the team was clearly implying that any reluctance on our part to submit the plea would not be to our benefit. They warned us that our firm stand might be taken as a sign of disrespecting authority or feeling superior to all other inmates who had sought clemency.

As previously mentioned, I had assumed the role of a petition writer for many prisoners in the past. Finally, after many consultations and exchanges of ideas, we decided there was no harm in giving our respect to our government and asking to be included in their compassion toward the rest of the prisoners. We decided that the petition would be written using the same commonly used template written in similar requests, which are brief and simple.

But after reading our petition, the officials hinted that our request must be comprised of all mandates, meaning it must include their previous demands that we recant our faith! This subtle pressure by the officials caused us to waver once again. Perhaps, we reasoned, we should not submit our request after all if this would be demanded of us.

Right before Saddam Hussein officially announced his presidency, the head of the committee came to visit the Al-Rashaad prison. As he walked into the area of our unit, I gathered the courage to go up and meet with him, and asked, "If we may request from your honor in simplicity, what exactly is expected from us?"

He then took out from his pocket a piece of paper and an ink pen, placed the paper on a column by the walkway, quickly wrote a very short note, then handed it to me.

What he had written was, "Her recognition of Islam, her obedience to the governing laws, her loyalty to the Revolutionary Command Council, her promise to fulfill its progressive agenda, and her desertion of her Bahá'í belief." He then said, "This is what is asked from each one in your group."

I saved that piece of paper until we were about to leave Iraq years later. I chose to dispose of it, as I feared being questioned at the airport.

After I read the paper from that official, I was shaking at his last request—"her desertion of her Bahá'í belief." The request was impossible, and I knew none of us would waver, even if it meant that the government would implement their threats of keeping us behind bars indefinitely. I went to the administrator, who was still outside talking to some superintendents, and I informed her of that official's statement. I said, "As far as the first requests, they are all reasonable; in fact, they are indispensable, for we believe in Islam and its message, obey all the laws, and appreciate all the accomplishments of the Revolution. Our teachings instruct obedience to the government. But the last request is impossible to fulfill, for it is our faith and belief. It is not contrary to progress. We encourage progressive thoughts that benefit the public."

The administrator replied, "Those were the committee's demands. You should obey them, and follow the lead of the two men who recanted their Bahá'í belief." She was referring to two of our Bahá'í brothers who had been placed in isolation away from the others. Each was subjected to all kind of mental pressures and stresses, and they were released a very short time prior to our release. After informing my Bahá'í sisters about the content of the paper, we came to a decision to give the committee our apologies and to dismiss the idea of writing any further requests. We remained steadfast in our position.

Following our decision, the officials' visits continued, and they began to insinuate once more that we should write the plea, signed by all of us, in which we would ask the authorities to be included in their clemency for other prisoners. We decided again to try writing a brief request to be included in the pardon, used only the general template for those circumstances, and submitted the request to the office. It said something such as, "We, prisoners so and so, who have signed below: it is our privilege to submit an appeal to your honors to be included in the upcoming general amnesty, with our sincere gratitude." Obviously, it was written with the help of the prison's office and sent to the Presidential Palace; therefore, it included phrases of reverence and good wishes.

After our submitting the request, the superiors began to offer their assurance of our inclusion in the amnesty. Also, Fatima, the kind administrator whom we all liked, did not conceal her strong optimism about our inclusion. Only a few days later, she brought the good news that we were to be released, and she asked us to prepare for leaving prison!

And thus hope returned to our spirits once more after a period of hopelessness, psychological warfare, uncertainty of whether we were going to spend the rest of our lives behind bars, and reflection of whether God would ever ordain for us to leave that isolated and tightly enclosed world with all its hardships and problems. It was as if life started to return to our extremities as each one of us began to prepare her suitcase and donate unneeded items to other inmates. Hope filled the hearts of each one of us of returning to our lives once again, continuing to live as we used to do in the past, and being with our loved ones.

My heart's wish—that circumstances would enable me to be with my children again in some way and in some destined hour—had begun to revisit my mind. With that hope, I left my affairs in the hands of divine providence.

Our families had heard the news that the general amnesty included the Bahá'ís; therefore, they were awaiting our return. The anticipation of that memorable day stirred a variety of emotions and activities from the prisoners. The prison was like a ship steered by the events. Every hour, news came of this or that prisoner who would be meeting with her children after a ten-year separation; or of another who had been rejected by her family; or of another who had gone to live with her parents because her husband had remarried, and who preferred living with her mother and father to living with a second wife. Because prison is the highest shame and disgrace in a closed and conservative society, many young prisoners, as I have mentioned, dreaded punishment from their families and relatives.

On that memorable day, and from all sides, ululations were heard with sounds that reached the sky, and dances of Dabke filled the courtyard. We went to see what was going on and to share the joy from a distance without joining the Dabke circles, but our reluctance caught the attention of the supervisors. They asked us to show our true joy and gratitude through actual participation; therefore, we had to offer a polite expression of praise by clapping and singing phrases of appreciation to the authorities.

While we were there, we received an order from the prison office to come to the large main hall to meet with a committee from the Presidential Palace! As usual, terror and suspicion enveloped us, and we began to ask ourselves, "What brought them here now, when only a few steps separate us from the prison's gate? Have they come with a demand we are unable to fulfill? Have they changed their minds about our release? Are they going to use force to make us sign something we are unwilling to sign?" And hence their visit became the last leg of the series in their psychological warfare.

We met with the committee once more, with the loud celebratory commotion going on outside, and we could barely hear the committee members above the din. At the meeting, we were accompanied by members of the Daa'wa party (an Islamist group) inmates. After we exchanged greetings and were seated, we learned that the committee's visit was solely to advise and instruct us about our duties after leaving prison. The instruction from each member of the committee contained some type of warning against any exercise of Bahá'í activities, despite the fact that for years before our imprisonment, the Bahá'ís of Iraq had suspended any activities relating to the practice of their Faith.

After this, the head of the committee added a comment with a threatening tone. He said, "We know you are firm in your belief and have not given it up, and the fact that you will practice your ceremonies behind the curtains!" What he meant was a reference to a rumor widely spread by the uneducated and deceitful that Bahá'ís meet in groups, pull their curtains, turn off the lights, and commit, God forbid, what is abhorrent to God, meaning "sexual activities."

We had all heard this rumor during our childhood; in fact, those people had given the repugnant activity a name. Sadly, some of the educated strata of society had been influenced by the rumors and had started to believe that our religion encouraged promiscuity. After our release from prison, a magazine published the same falsehood, using a renowned author as a reference. Sadly, that author, who had in the past written about "Bábísm and Bahá'ism," and had been well-informed about the Bahá'í Faith after attending many of our dignified, honorable, and lofty gatherings, had supported the magazine and had not denounced its false claims. Perhaps fear and cowardice drive such souls to accuse the innocent with such falsehoods. There was another man, a college professor, who also came on television and radio stations with several fabricated lies about the Bahá'ís.

The head of the committee ended his speech with another threat, saying, "Beware of publicly announcing your belief, or we will break your backs, and your sentences will double."

All that we could do was to assure him of our obedience to all the laws ordained by the government and that we would do what was asked of us.

We stood for the committee members as they were leaving the hall, but Fatima asked us to stay. She asked each of us to sign an affidavit. This occurred minutes before our departure from prison, while we were still hearing the ululations and the loud drums and folk music outside. I asked the administrator to please read aloud the wording of the affidavit, which she agreed to do. We did not find any mention of renunciation or denial of our Faith. They were all pledges to obey the laws of the Republic, to suspend all Bahá'í activities, and to never conceal any information from the government.

Each one of us had her turn in signing the affidavit, and in return, we received an official form of non-discrimination that allowed us to leave the darkness of prison and enter the world of the living, without harassment from anyone! Then they surprised us with another courtesy of fifty dinars (about $160) for each one of us!

The loud traditional folk music band (usually consisting of drums and trumpets) was awaiting us outside with the open pickup trucks. We rode the vehicles with other prison mates. As I mentioned earlier, I remember our former colleague Simone was my neighbor in the back seat and that she had applied heavy makeup with bright colors. I don't know how to describe the emotions that overcame me in that moment. I was both happy and annoyed, and I had tears pouring down my cheeks without hindrance. The loud, foolish music was causing every nerve in my body to vibrate, and all this stimuli caused me to burst into uncontrollable laughter that was hard to repress and that caused my body to shake.

Before riding the pickup truck, we had one final inspection by the guards, who took away our newest prison uniform for that season. I saved the old uniform, which I brought to the United States and which is still with me in my closet to this day. It will be my garment of honor when I leave this world, as I have instructed my daughters that I wish to be buried wearing it.

That night, my emotions were a combination of happiness, pride, and pain for the oppression that had been inflicted upon us for nearly six years. All of my emotions were expressed through my heavy tears while looking at the streetlights on the way to my brother Suhail's home, which was over an hour away. The streets of Baghdad were filled with people and families of the prisoners celebrating the big event with loud ululations. Many felt that releasing the prisoners was a huge accomplishment by President Saddam Hussein, who had just assumed the power of presidency. The families of the prisoners had hired folk music bands, which were following the cars that carried the prisoners to their homes.

When we reached the home of my brother Suhail, who hosted us for a while, many relatives and friends were awaiting our arrival to offer their congratulations and share the joy. I was missing my children in an unbearable measure and feeling an emptiness that no one could fill. My children had left nearly a year earlier.

I was in the utmost state of exhaustion that evening, similar to a patient who has just left a hospital after being quarantined and is still in a state of recovery. In the period prior to our release, we had become accustomed to quietness and stillness, but now we had to return to a normal life and start

Anisa's prison uniform

over. We had ended a chapter of selfless perseverance in His path, and we would cherish its beloved memory despite the lengthy days and nights of hardship. We would remember that period with pride and honor, similar to a soldier who has won a battle but whose body is still decorated with scars. Every mark and scar is a trophy reminding him of his steadfastness in the path of righteousness, the path of our Best Beloved!

As for the period that followed our release, it extended beyond eleven years, during which we were deprived of seeing our beloved children. However, God had bestowed upon them His blessings and miracles. They were able to rely on God and themselves to have a good life under the shade of His beloved Faith.

With God's ordinance and the benevolence of many, we finally met our children in the United States. Our days of separation had not been easy, especially for my husband and me. Without our children, our home was no less gloomy and lonely than the prison we had left. I would constantly catch myself reliving memories and saying to myself, "This is their place; these are their rooms." The sounds of their voices, their laughter, and their comments were still in my ears. I would look in the pages of their old photo albums to see their pictures, and I would count the days until I received their letters. I did this continually until God had ordained for us to meet again. To Him, our gratitude is given at all times, and under all conditions.

Dear Reader,

As I come to the conclusion of this memoir, I feel a sense of relief, as though years of burden have been lifted from my heart. Surely by now you must also be feeling sympathy, appreciation, and a sense of pride and glory for the fortitude and steadfastness offered in the path of a sacred Faith, which was sent down for the unity of the world, for its well-being, and for love.

Anisa Abbas

Anisa by the Mediterranean Sea in the late 1940s

Abir, Alhan, and Ruwa before leaving Iraq

Afterword

Dear reader, I am Anisa's older daughter Alhan, and I am the person who translated this memoir. The original copy was handwritten by my mother in our native Arabic language in a very eloquent and poetic style. Though my humble translation could in no way do the original text justice, nevertheless, I hope that her touching story was able to move and inspire you.

Life After Prison and the Continued Assault on the Bahá'ís

To begin this Afterword, I would like to emphasize the fact that the government of Iraq had no real interest in keeping the Bahá'ís in prison all those years. The goal was to break their will and force them to comply with the government's demand to abandon their belief. Although the Baathi government publicly embraced Islam, too many of its decisions seemed governed by a secular outlook. With that said, the Bahá'í prisoners had a choice from the beginning of their imprisonment. They could either recant their Faith and gain their freedom, or they could spend the rest of their lives in prison. This tradeoff was eminently clear, and various government officials continually presented this offer. "One word is all you need" was the message the prisoners received over and over. The prisoners bravely made their choice to remain steadfast in the path of their precious belief until they obtained their freedom.

Two months after their release from prison in August of 1979, the previous 1970 law (Decree #105 prohibiting Bahá'í activities) was revised to include stern and brutal changes. It stated that a punishment of fifteen years to life in prison would be handed down to first-time offenders, and the possibility of execution would be meted out to previously imprisoned lawbreakers. The law was unforgivably broad in its scope and terrifying in its vagueness because any normal event could be interpreted as a Bahá'í activity by the government. Bahá'ís were also sternly instructed never to make any mention of their Faith, even if they were asked, for this would be considered a serious offense. Those released from imprisonment were required to appear at Al-Amn centers near their residences on a regular basis for questioning or simply to be intimidated and reminded that they were under close watch. Some were asked to cooperate with the government by eavesdropping on other Bahá'ís and passing on implicating reports. Bahá'ís often got around these requests with excuses such as poor health, advanced age, and family responsibilities. Nonetheless, the mental strain of such a life was considerable.

One of the former Bahá'í prisoners told me that in some aspects, life in prison was easier and more dignified than life outside of it. In prison, at least, they were free to identify themselves as Bahá'ís and to practice their Faith, such as by praying and fasting. After their release, they could not utter a word about their belief—in essence, they were required to deny their identity—this time with the stakes being execution rather than incarceration. She said that once Bahá'í prisoners were released, it was as if they had been imprisoned all over again, but this outside prison was even larger and more treacherous. A cloud of terror hovered above their heads at all times, and this tense situation remained in place for many years. Slowly, the remaining bits of their Bahá'í identity were chipped away. An earlier law in 1974 had removed the word "Bahá'í" from all personal identification cards. Marriage certificates had to be changed, and the word "Bahá'í" was forcefully replaced by "Muslim." The same was true of birth certificates and other such documents.

Being Left without Their Children

As one might expect, many aspects of my parents' imprisonment was deeply traumatic for myself and for my siblings. Our earlier life had been one of ease and comfort. We were pampered and exceptionally cared for by our parents. Their sudden imprisonment meant more than losing our comfort and security because my sister Ruwa and I had to deal with life's many struggles on our own. Even money became scarce. Prior to their imprisonment, our parents received a very comfortable retirement. Once they were imprisoned, however, the government confiscated our mother's salary and took a large portion of our father's pension to feed him and our mother in prison. The remaining portion was not adequate to feed or to clothe us, and this made living truly hard. As time went by, an additional threat to our welfare became hard to bear, and this was the increased surveillance and open stalking by Baathi informants who often followed us back and forth during our daily activities as a way of trying to intimidate us. One of our biggest challenges was making the agonizing decision to leave Iraq while our parents were still behind bars. Even forty years later, recalling that decision still floods my heart with sadness and guilt, even as I can recall clearly the circumstances that drove us from our homeland. At the time, my older brother Abir was facing renewed harassment by the government. He was dragged back to the Al-Amn again and received severe foot whippings, called the "bastinado," so he would collaborate with the Baath party in spying on the Bahá'ís, which he refused to do. As for myself, I was pressured at school—although I never gave in to the pressure—to join the students' union (in association with the Baath party), and I was placed under the surveillance of the Al-Amn. Meanwhile, the transfer of our mother and the other Bahá'í ladies to Al-Rashaad prison, which was more than an hour's drive from Abu Ghraib, often required us to have to make the heart-wrenching choice between visiting her or our father during visitation days. (We were the only family with both parents in prison.) We could no longer divide the two-hour visitation between the two as we did in Abu Ghraib. Dividing the visitation time between my parents was difficult, especially for our mother, but she realized there was no other choice.

During those days, life at our uncle's house was extremely chaotic and difficult. It had no stability, no security, and no hope for normality to return, especially after the multiple exclusions of Bahá'ís from privileges such as the clemency decree, permission to visit one's home and family, and pardons that other prisoners received after submitting petitions. Because of all those hardships, my sister Ruwa, who was only eighteen years old at the time, eventually made the agonizing decision to leave. She headed to Istanbul, where our aunt and her family were living at the time. I had no choice but to follow her, since I had been given the role of being a mother figure to her. By the grace of God and only a few weeks later, our brother Abir was miraculously able to leave danger, as he was in a team his company sent abroad for training. He was eventually able to join us in Turkey and once again become the loving elder brother who looked after us, as he always had.

The Long Separation

One of the heartbreaking agonies our parents had to face was the inability to reunite with their children for nearly eleven additional years after their release. That was especially hard on our mother, who had an extraordinary love and attachment to her children. The names of all former prisoners had been added to the government's black list, which made it effectively impossible for them to obtain passports and travel abroad. As for my siblings and myself, now living in the United States, we did not trust the Iraqi government enough to visit our parents because of the torment and danger we had witnessed in the past. Both Abir and I had also abandoned our government jobs upon leaving Iraq, and we knew that this decision could be seen as an unfavorable act worthy of retribution. The only option we had was to await God's mercy in reuniting us all.

Our Correspondence

After my siblings and I had settled in the United States, we continued to correspond with my parents through letters. It was a terribly slow method of communication that took weeks and lacked privacy. Our letters were opened and read by Iraqi censorship, then carelessly glued shut before any of us received them. At times, the glue leaked inside, causing the papers and photos to stick together. Later on, when my siblings and I married and had our own children, all we could do was to send photographs of our new families to our parents. It took weeks for these photos to arrive, and of course our dear father had become totally blind while in prison, as my mother describes in her memoir. We longed for our family back home to be able to see our beautiful children in person and to enjoy watching them grow, but for years we were deprived of that bounty. Those photographs and letters at least helped us maintain some semblance of connection until the day we could be reunited.

Phone Calls

Another added strain on our parents was that they were unable to have a home phone for a long while after leaving prison. Because of surveillance, my parents, to gain a simple necessity such as a phone, had to make requests and obtain various approvals in a process that took months or even years. Somehow, our mother and father managed. Once per month, they took a taxi for a nearly hourlong ride to the central post office in the heart of Baghdad in order to make a five-minute telephone call, which they arranged with us in advance, to the United States. We could hear the breathing of the surveillance operator listening to our conversation. On those calls, we did not dare share anything private or personal, and we spent most of the brief time exchanging simple pleasantries. A year or so later, our parents were able to get a telephone at home, which was a tremendous bounty. Still, our costly conversations had to be very discreet, for the censorship continued.

Weddings of their Children

In 1982, my brother Abir and sister Ruwa were both married. A year later, I was married. Our parents were deprived of joining us on those happy occasions. Such occasions mean so much for parents, especially those from the Middle East, where weddings are often the high points of family life and a tremendous source of joy to the extended family. My husband and I obtained written consent from my parents prior to the wedding (in the Bahá'í Faith, two individuals must not only consent to be married, but they must also obtain the consent of each parent. This is to ensure unity and accord within the family).

Our mother was deprived of the joy of participating in all the typical preparations for our weddings, such as choosing a wedding dress. My sister and I missed her presence very much, and that time of joy in our lives was somewhat soured by her absence. She could eventually see some humble pictures of the events, but my poor father, being totally blind, had to rely on her to describe every detail.

Birth of Grandchildren

When I was expecting my first child, it had been six long years since our departure from Iraq. My mother was very eager to be with me for the birth of her first grandchild, as she had missed us so very much. Since they were not allowed to leave the country, our mother wrote a very moving letter to President Saddam Hussein to ask for special permission to attend the birth of the baby. Her application was ignored, as she received no reply. She was heartbroken but acquiescent to the will of God. Their deprivation of such joy continued with the births of their other grandchildren. Mom could only see them in photographs.

Arriving in the United States

In 1990, right before the invasion of Kuwait, the government of Iraq, confident and proud of its achievements, had decided to be more lenient with its citizens and open to the world. Citizens were allowed to apply for passports and travel abroad for vacation. Our parents were finally allowed to obtain new passports, but their request to receive a visa to visit the United States was denied by the American Embassy. With my sister Ruwa's persistent efforts and the extreme kindness of people at the Iraqi Desk (the office representing Iraq's interest in Washington), and God's help, a miracle at last occurred, and a visa was granted to my mother and father! It was absolutely remarkable because shortly after my parents' arrival, Iraq's doors to the outside world were closed once again with the onset of the war with Kuwait. Our parents would have not been able to leave once the war began.

Our reunion in New York, nearly eleven years after leaving Iraq, was truly memorable. Tears and extended embraces were exchanged for a long time. The event felt surreal, as if it were only a dream from which we were afraid to wake. Our parents were finally with us, and they were finally able to embrace their four grandchildren and to be present for the birth of their fifth grandchild later on. My dear mother was finally able to sleep through the night, and my dear father was able to touch our faces and imagine how we all looked.

Upon their arrival in the United States, it was evident that my parents were not in a state of health to be able to return to Iraq and be on their own. Mom, in her late sixties, suffered severe pain in her joints, and Dad, who was in his late seventies, was feeble and totally blind. My sister and brother-in-law helped them apply for refugee status, and—by the grace of God and thanks to the American government—the application was approved. They remained in the United States until their passing.

Our parents gladly accepted a very humble living arrangement close to their children. They resided near my family in Nashua, New Hampshire, and we enjoyed frequent visits with them. Mom was a very good cook, and though she was in her seventies, she still enjoyed preparing nice traditional Iraqi meals (such as dolma, okra merga, kebab, and kubbah) for us every now and then. Even though they lived a simple life in those days, they were finally free—free to think, free to move without being watched, and free to practice their belief as Bahá'ís.

Some of the Challenges they Faced While Living in America

Even though my parents were able to breathe a sigh of relief after settling in the United States, they experienced new challenges. They faced a different climate, a different culture, and a different way of life. The Iraqi culture is very warm—family members, friends, and neighbors continually socialize and visit one another, and phoning a loved one for no reason at all other than to chat is common. By contrast, New England culture can often be cool and reserved. Our dad's English was quite good, with a rich vocabulary, but our mom often struggled to express herself, and this was a source of frustration for a woman of her eloquence and knowledge.

Despite her lack of English, she was well-loved by her neighbors and our small Bahá'í community. She was always grateful for her life in this country. Being free and close to her children and grandchildren made her happy and content. The weather in New Hampshire was certainly a challenge, with long frigid winters and heavy snow that forced my parents to remain indoors most of the time, and they missed the almost continual sunny days of Iraq. But there were new joys. Mom enjoyed the cooler summers in New England, and she loved the seasonal loveliness of the region. She found the flowering trees in spring breathtakingly beautiful and the foliage in fall absolutely amazing! Dad also found joy in listening to her description. My father was himself a lover of nature, especially flowers.

Our parents proudly received their American citizenship a few years later. Our mother frequently pointed out the positive aspects of the United States, such as its beauty and the generosity of its people. She would often say that the United States had welcomed and honored them with its grace and nobility, while the country of their birth had abused and mistreated them, even after they had served it with every ounce of their being. She wrote a poem in Arabic in praise of her new homeland, and she titled it simply "America." My brother Abir translated it into English, and it is included below. The poem won a literary contest in New Hampshire.

The Passing of our Dear Parents

Our beloved father passed away in February, 2008 at the age of ninety-four. His unshakable faith and courage will always be the most preeminent among his attributes.

A couple of years later, Mom experienced some health issues and severe back pain. These were followed by a series of unfortunate complications, several weeks of hospitalization, and finally her passing two months later.

Her Prison Uniform and Her Wish

Our mother's old prison uniform was a treasured symbol of what she often called the proudest years of her life. She brought it with her to the United States, as she mentions in her book, and I have included a photo of it here. She had instructed her children of her desire to be wearing it when she departed this earthly plane. By the grace of God, we were able to grant her wish, and she was buried in that cherished garment. Our beloved mother passed on July 13, 2011 at the age of eighty-six.

Another thing Mom told us was how hot Abu Ghraib could become during summer. (As you recall, she talked about it in this book and how the concrete walls and floor absorbed the 120+ degree summer heat and radiated it back onto the prisoners.) She said that one extremely hot day, she prayed to God that she be buried in the cold snow. She was that desperate. I think about her request to God every time I visit her snow-covered grave in Milford, NH. God has granted her yet another wish.

Beloved Mama, thank you for your extraordinary love. Thank you for your cherished prayers, both in this world and now in His heavenly realm. And most treasured of all, thank you and our beloved father (Baba) for being shining examples of dedication, fortitude, sacrifice, and steadfastness in the path of service to the Almighty for your daughters, your son, your grandchildren, and hopefully many generations to come. May God bless your pure souls in His glorious paradise. Many thanks be to Thee, dear God, for everything with which you have blessed us.

"Bestow upon Thy heavenly handmaiden, O God, the holy fragrances born of the spirit of Thy forgiveness. Cause her to dwell in a blissful abode, heal her griefs with the balm of Thy reunion, and, in accordance with Thy will, grant her admission to Thy holy Paradise. Let the angels of Thy loving-kindness descend successively upon her, and shelter her beneath Thy blessed Tree. Thou art, verily, the Ever-Forgiving, the Most Generous, the All-Bountiful." ('Abdu'l-Bahá, in *Bahá'í Prayers,* pp. 43–44)

Mother's poem titled "America" was originally written in Arabic in a rhyming style:

America

Oh America, garden of Paradise for the righteous!
America, for the tyrant and the wicked, a dark and thorny jungle.
Carnival of flowers, festival of birds,
Prairies of velvet, farther than the eyes can see,
Towering pines standing guard. Dignified.
America, still a child, yet excelling thy neighbors.
Progress, creation, invention, innovation, in all fields.
Haven for the Captive, home for the Free
Lighthouse guiding the Perplexed and Lost, at night, and in day.
Meeting place of nations, like rivers joining the sea

AFTERWORD

Each of your peoples openly serenading its own beloved Juliet,
Oh melting pot of civilizations coming together.
Your young beauties strolling by, like bright moons and stars
No veils hiding the sentiments on their faces
And your Old, always challenging the passage of time.
America, you whisper to me your call
A mysterious melody on the strings of a sweet harp.
Your new dweller is chanting your praise.
Roots standing strong in the face of the currents, you remain
Dream and desire for the desperate, but also for those who can choose.

—Anisa Abdul-Razzaq Abbas

Anisa and her husband Siddiq in later years